# The Words to Say It

## Books by Marie Cardinal

ÉCOUTEZ LA MER, 1962
LA MULE DE CORBILLARD, 1964
LA SOURICIÈRE, 1966
CET-ÉTÉ-LÀ, 1967
LA CLÉ SUR LA PORTE, 1972
THE WORDS TO SAY IT, 1975
AUTREMENT DIT, 1979
UNE VIE POUR DEUX, 1979
AU PAYS DE MES RACINES, 1980
LE PASSÉ EMPIÉTÉ, 1983

# THE WORDS TO SAY IT

An Autobiographical Novel by
## Marie Cardinal

Translated by Pat Goodheart

Preface and Afterword by
Bruno Bettelheim

VanVactor & Goodheart
Cambridge, Massachusetts

*First printing*, 1983

Published in 1983 by
Van Vactor & Goodheart, Inc.
24 Lee Street
Cambridge, Massachusetts 02139

First paperback edition published in 1984 by Van Vactor and Goodheart

Originally published in French as
*Les Mots Pour Le Dire*

Copyright© 1975 by Éditions Grasset & Fasquelle

Translation Copyright© 1983 by Van Vactor & Goodheart, Inc.

English translation rights by arrangement with
Editions Bernard Grasset

Preface and Afterword Copyright© 1983 by Bruno Bettleheim

Library of Congress Cataloging in Publication Data

Cardinal, Marie.
  The Words to Say It.

  I. Title.
  PQ 2663.A7M613 1983
  616.89'0092'4 .B 83-10330
  ISBN 0-941314-09-5

Printed in the United States of America
Designed by Leslie Evans

*To the doctor who helped me be born*

"What one truly understands clearly articulates itself, and the words to say it come easily"

Boileau, *L'Art Poétique*

# Preface

Tolstoy begins *Anna Karenina* by saying that "... every unhappy family is unhappy in its own way." This is also true of individuals: no two life histories are alike, and the more desperate someone's history is, as is the one told in this book, the more unique are the sufferings, their causes, and the way to free oneself of them. Hence no one process of psychoanalysis is exactly like another; no two people probe the same path into their unconscious in the effort to become able to cope with what they discover hidden there. Still, since we are all human, there are also important similarities in our experiences and in our responses to them.

In this autobiographical novel, there is much with which we can empathize from our own experiences, together with many features unique to this particularly harrowing voyage of self-discovery. The book is deeply moving because of the way this story is told, and because of the unique interest due to the person who completed this journey.

Like Dante's voyage of self-discovery, and those of many others before and since, this one also begins "in the middle of the journey of life," when the author found herself "in a dark, impenetrable place where the straight way was lost." Like Dante, to find her way out of utter confusion and darkness, she needed a compassionate guide who possessed the requisite wisdom to steer her along the right course of self-discovery, to help her uncover the most carefully hidden, the least accessible recesses of her mind; and who had the particular skill of the psychoanalyst which would make it possible for her to work out her very own way to inner clarity. To permit this her analyst had to be mainly a silent guide, and so he was.

Marie Cardinal worked with him for seven years at the horrendous task of freeing herself of her insanity, of coming to understand what had projected her into it, and also of creating a new life for herself, so different from the old that she felt as if reborn. And she indeed became a new person, a successful writer who created this novel which permits us to understand what is involved in truly discovering all about oneself, in finding one's way to great inner clarity—not with Dante in the thirteenth century, but with Marie Cardinal today.

Reading this novel permits us to comprehend what is involved in a psychoanalysis as seen from the perspective of the patient, as experienced by her. There are many accounts of psychoanalyses written by psychoanalysts, the most important and famous of all being the very first: Freud's self-analysis, in which he was analyst and patient at the same time. But Freud wrote mainly from the analyst's point of view, telling about his discoveries and how he made them. His account is largely an intellectual story, conveying little about his inner feelings when he made these discoveries about himself. Nor does he tell what it did to him personally to find this out. Although it changed his life, Freud did not let us know what this analysis achieved for him. However, all his later achievements were based on it; from these only can we attempt to discern what he might have experienced in his analysis.

Since Freud's day, practically all accounts of psychoanalysis have been written by analysts, from a professional point of view. There are only a few stories of analyses written by patients, and even fewer which are any good. One of the best is H. D.'s *Tribute to Freud*, but in it she speaks mostly about her analyst, as the title of her book indicates. Of all accounts of psychoanalysis as experienced by the patient, none can compare with this novel, so superior is it in all pertinent repects. Marie Cardinal's great art permits us to relive her experience as we become acquainted with the essential content of what transpired in her psychoanalysis, and we experience vicariously what she experienced.

I am writing this preface, and the afterword at the end of this book, because in my opinion *The Words to Say It* is the best account of psychoanalysis as seen and experienced by the patient. I do not know of any other that would render such a true picture of what the patient's experience of his analysis is like. The author's struggle with herself was truly heroic. It is also a report of returning to the world of the living by one who for years had vegetated in the darkness of insanity, haunted by per-

# The Words to Say It

# Chapter I

The little cul-de-sac was badly paved, full of bumps and holes, bordered by narrow, partly ruined sidewalks. It worked its way like a finger between private houses of one or two stories, pressing one against the other. The little street stopped at iron gates overgrown with scraggly vines.

The windows revealed no sign of life within. It might have been the country; nevertheless it was the heart of Paris, in the XIVth arrondissement. There were not the extremes of poverty or wealth here, only the petite bourgeoisie, hiding their valuables, their woolen socks even, in chinks, behind toothless shutters, rusted gutters, decrepit walls, the plaster flaking off in scales. Yet the windows were barred and the doors were solid.

This quiet corner of the city must have dated back fifty years, for there was a modernistic feeling in the mismatched architecture of the dwellings. Who lived here? Seeing these particular glass doors, door frames, these vestiges of decorative finish work, it could be said that some retired artists ended their careers behind these facades, hack painters, old opera singers, ancient virtuosos of the stage.

For seven years, three times a week, I traveled this little street on foot to the end, as far as the gate on the left. I know how the rain falls here, how the inhabitants protect themselves from the cold. I know how, in summer, a life which is almost rustic establishes itself with geraniums in pots and cats sleeping in the sun. I know how the days go in this cul-de-sac, and the nights, too. I know that it is always empty. It is empty even when a pedestrian hurries toward one of the entrances or a driver is pulling his car out of a garage.

I can no longer remember what time of day it was when I first entered the gate. Did I see only the abandoned state of the small gardens? Did I feel the gravel on the narrow path? Did I count the seven narrow steps to his door? Did I take in the fieldstone wall while waiting for the door to open?

I don't think so.

On the other hand, I saw the little dark-skinned man who gave me his hand. I saw that he was very slight, very formally dressed and very distant. I saw his black eyes, which were smooth as nail heads. I obeyed him when he asked me to wait in a room which he revealed by opening a curtain. It was a dining room done in the manner of Henri II in which the furniture—the table, chairs, buffet, and sideboard—invaded almost the entire space, impressing the newcomer, which I was, with its carved wood, sculpted with little gnomes and ivy, its contorted columns, its copper trays and Chinese pots. This ugliness was not important. What was important to me was the silence. I waited, on the watch, tense, until I heard the sound of the double doors opening to the right of the curtain — a space for two people — then the opening of the door in the vestibule, a voice murmuring: "Au revoir, Docteur," no answer, and the door closing. Again, muffled movement in the direction of the front door; seconds later, the parquet creaking under the rug, the cold air coming in — a sign that the door remained ajar — then some incomprehensible noises. Finally, the curtain was lifted and the little man had me enter the office.

Here I am seated in a chair in front of his desk. He is leaning back in a black leather armchair to the side of the desk, so that I am forced to sit sideways to look at him. Against the wall facing me are shelves full of books, into which is fitted a brown sofa with a bolster and a little cushion. The doctor is waiting for me to speak.

"Doctor, I have been ill for a long time. I ran away from a private sanatorium to come to see you. I can't go on living this way."

He showed me with his eyes that he listened attentively, that I could continue.

Prostrate as I was, withdrawn into my own universe, how to find the words which would flow between us? How to construct the bridge which would join the intense to the calm, the clear to the obscure, which could span this sewer, this river filled with decomposing matter, this treacherous current of fear, that separated the doctor and me, the others and me?

I was ashamed of what was going on inside of me, of this uproar, of this disorder, of this agitation; no one should look, no one should know, not even the doctor. I was ashamed of the madness. It seemed to me that any other form of life was preferable. I was sailing endlessly in

3

extremely dangerous waters full of rapids, falls, wreckage, turbulence, while having to pretend that I was effortlessly gliding on a lake like a swan. The better to hide myself, I closed off all the orifices: my nose, my ears, my mouth, my vagina, my anus, the pores of my skin, my bladder. The better to block these openings, my body produced materials in abundance, certain of which thickening to the point of no longer being able to pass, creating a block, others of which, on the contrary, flowing without stopping, preventing anything from entering.

"Can you tell me about the treatment you have been under, specialists you have been to?"

"Yes."

About that I was able to speak: I could enumerate the doctors and the remedies, I could tell about the blood, about its soft and tepid presence for more than three years between my thighs, the two curettages I had had to stop its flow.

The bleeding, with its variations in rate of flow, was familiar to me. This anomaly was reassuring because it was real, it could be measured or analyzed. I loved to make it the center of my illness. And really, could such constant losses not be frightening? What woman would not have been driven insane to see her own sap run? How could one not be exhausted by the surveillance without respite of this secret spring, nagging, observable, shameful? How to avoid using the blood to explain that I could no longer live with others? I had stained so many easy chairs, straight-back chairs, sofas, couches, carpets, beds! I had left behind me so many puddles, spots, spotlets, splashes and droplets, in so many living rooms, dining rooms, anterooms, halls, swimming pools, buses, and other places. I could no longer go out.

4

How not to speak of my joy on the days when it seemed to dry up, only to show itself in its brownish traces, brownish, then ochre, then yellow. On those days when I wasn't ill, I was able to move about, to see, to get out of myself. The blood was finally going to creep back into its tender sac and stay there as before for twenty-three days. With this end in mind I used to try to exert myself as little as possible. I handled myself with the greatest possible precaution: not to hold the children in my arms, not to carry the groceries, not to stand too long before the stove, not to do the laundry, not to wash the windows. To move in slow motion, quietly, so that the blood would disappear, so it might stop its horrors, I would stretch out with my knitting, while watching over my three babies. Furtively, with a gesture of the arm, quick and adroit from habit, I went to check my condition. I knew how to do it in any position, so no one would notice it. Depending on the circumstances, my hand would slip down to my pubic hair, tough and curly, to find the warm, soft, moist place of my genitals, only to quickly take it away again. Or else it would slip just as easily up the valley between my buttocks and thighs, and suddenly plunge into the deep, round hole, only to quickly reemerge. I would not look at my fingertips right away. I would withhold the surprise. And what if there was nothing there? Sometimes, there would be so little on it that I had to scratch hard with my thumbnail the skin of my index finger and my middle finger in order to produce an almost colorless sample of the secretion. A sort of joy would come over me: "If I don't make even the smallest possible movement, it is going to stop completely." I would be motionless, as if asleep, hoping with all my strength to become normal again, to be like others. Again and again I made those weeks before, to the office of a famous professor of gynecology.

The specialist, wearing whites, in the American style, short jacket and pants, had penetrated me with his right hand, and, with the left hand, he pressed hard on my abdomen, one side, then the other, in the middle, pushing my insides towards the back of me, there where his gloved hands were palpating me. A little like a housewife about to clean out her chicken in one fell swoop. I expected my insides to respond with the soft sound of mud slopping, "pouff," "splash." The ceiling was white as a lie, with so immense a white as to abandon in it the deformed and used vagina, with a white deep enough to engulf within it the shameful pictures of my imagination.

The lengthy examination over, the specialist straightened up, removed his glove, and while I was still there with legs apart on the table, he said: "The only thing the matter with you for now is a fibroid uterus. But I advise you to get rid of it right away. Otherwise, you are going to have serious problems, and sooner than you think. Let's set a date for the operation. You'll see, everything will be fine afterwards. Let's get to the point; I'm operating next week. Which day do you prefer? Monday or Tuesday?" I said, "Tuesday." He indicated to me the procedure for the preoperative tests and for being admitted to the hospital. I paid his fee, said "Thank you," and went out.

I was almost thirty years old. I didn't want to have my reproductive organs removed. I didn't want the blood to run flowing from there, but I wanted to keep myself intact. The Thing rattled around in my brain. I fled down the carpeted stairway with marble columns, copper stair rods, mirrored landings. I found myself outside on the wide gray sidewalks that distinguish the better parts of town. I

7

ran, I hurled myself into the subway where the Thing took possession of me, this time driving its roots right there into my fibroid uterus. Fibroid uterus. What words! Caverns coated with algae flowing through the blood. Monstrously swollen artery. Pustular toad. Octopus.

For the mentally ill, words, like objects, are as much alive as people or animals. They palpitate, they vanish or expand. Passing through words is like walking in a crowd. Faces stay with you, as silhouettes which quickly fade from memory, or else as images that stick there, one doesn't know why. For me at that time, a word isolated from the mass of other words started to live, becoming an important thing, becoming perhaps even the most important thing, inhabiting me, torturing me, never leaving me, reappearing in my dreams, waiting for me to wake up.

I would open my eyes cautiously, emerging from the heavy chemical sodden sleep the tranquilizers had given me. First, I felt my body intact. Then I was conscious of the time of day and the sun. It was all right. I would rise to the surface of consciousness. One second, two seconds, maybe three: Fibroid tumors! "Squish," "splash," spreading out like a heavy oil paint on a white wall. Immediately there came the shuddering, and with it the pounding of the heart, and the sweat of fear. That was how my day would begin.

I must think back to find again the forgotten woman, more than forgotten, disintegrated. She walked, she talked, she slept. To think that these eyes saw, that these ears listened, that this skin felt, filled me with emotion. It is with my eyes, my ears, my skin, my heart that that woman lived. I look at my hands, the same hands, the same fingernails, the same ring. She and I. I am she. The mad one and I, we have begun a completely new life, full of expectations, a life which can no longer be bad. I protect her; she lavishes freedom and invention on me.

In order to tell about the journey, the birth, in effect, I have to remove myself from the mad one, to keep her at a distance, to split myself in two. I see the mad one hurrying in the street. I know the effort she makes to seem normal, to stop the fear behind a glance. I remember her as she used to stand, her head hunched between her shoulders, sad, at once absorbed by the growing agitation within and by the armor descending over her eyes, so nothing could be seen! Above all, not to fall in the street, not to be grabbed by the others, not to be taken to the hospital. She trembled to imagine she could no longer stifle the madness, whose swelling tide would one day breach the dikes and overflow, making her shudder and groan.

The route she traveled grew more curtailed. And then one day, she no longer went into the city. After that, she had to limit the space in which she moved within the house. The traps multiplied. In the final months before she was handed over to the doctors, she could live only in the bathroom, a somber white-tiled room, barely lit by a window in the form of a half-moon fanlight cut out of the shutter and almost totally obstructed by the branches of a large pine tree which scraped against the window on windy days. A clean room smelling of antiseptic and soap. No dust in the corners. Her fingers slid across the tiles, as if on ice. No decomposition, no fermentation. Nothing but that material which doesn't rot, or else rots slowly so as to convey no idea of putrefaction.

It was between the bidet and the bathtub where she felt most secure when she could no longer master her internal functions. It was there where she hid while waiting for the pills to take effect. Curled up like a ball, heels against buttocks, arms holding the knees, strong, tight against the chest, nails dug so deep into the palms of her hands they eventually pierced the skin, her head rocking back and forth or side to side, feeling so heavy, the blood and sweat was pouring out of her. The Thing, which on the inside was made of a monstrous crawling of images, sounds, and odors, projected in every way by a devastating pulse making all reasoning incoherent, all explanation absurd, all efforts to order tentative and useless, was revealed on the outside by violent shaking and nauseating sweat.

I think the first time I went to see the psychoanalyst was in the evening. Or was I still nostalgic for those late sessions at the foot of the dead-end street, sheltered from the cold, from the others, from the mad one, from the night? One of those sessions when I was aware of coming into the world? An opening up of the mind was making the pathway larger, more accessible, I understood. The mad one was no longer this woman who went to hide her trembling in the toilets of bistros, who bled on the sidewalks. The sick one who didn't want to be touched, to be looked at or to be spoken to. I began to accept her, to love· her even.

In the beginning, I had come to the cul-de-sac with the idea of putting myself in the care of a doctor who would not hospitalize me. (I knew that psychoanalysts do not readily put their patients in the hospital.) I was afraid of being put away as I was afraid of the operation which would have removed my organs. I'd run away from a sanatorium to come here, but I thought it was too late and that I would have to return to the hospital. I thought it was inevitable, especially since the Thing had by then acquired the trappings of a hallucination. Moreover, I had decided against speaking of it to the doctor. I thought if I spoke of it, he would send me back there. In certain moments, the presence of a living eye, looking at me, really there, but existing only for me (that I knew), seemed to me to be the evidence of genuine insanity.

I was thirty years old. I was in good health. Yet I could be locked up for fifty years. But for my children, I might let myself go completely, stop fighting, perhaps, for the struggle against the Thing was exhausting. More and more, I was tempted by the medication that delivered me to a nothingness which was dull and sweet.

Ever since I was a little girl, I had said to myself: One day I'm going to have children. Full of new life and strong, they had come into the world, each one different from the other. They were growing up well. I loved their laughter, I loved to sing to them.

Then disaster. The Thing had come back again and would no longer leave me. It absorbed me so completely that it had become my only preoccupation. There was a time when I believed I could live with the Thing, the way others live with only a missing eye or leg, with a stomach disorder or with kidney trouble. Certain drugs relegated the Thing to a corner from which it did not budge anymore. I was able to listen, to speak, to get about. I could go out and take a walk with my children, do the shopping, make them desserts, and tell them stories which would make them laugh. Then the effects of the drugs wore off more quickly. So I took a double dose. Then a triple dose. And one day, I woke up a prisoner of the Thing. I saw innumerable doctors. The blood began to flow without stopping. My eyesight was growing weaker. I lived in darkness, everything becoming imprecise and dangerous. My head was hunched between my shoulders, my fists were clenched tight in a defensive posture. My pulse went up to 130 to 140 beats per minute, all day long. I believed that my rib cage was going to break, my heart was going to spring out, palpitating, for everyone to see. Its agitated rhythm exhausted me. It seemed to me that the others could hear, and I was ashamed.

I had acquired involuntary obsessions, two gestures which were repeated a thousand times a day: checking the flow of blood, and taking my pulse, furtively, so no one could see. I didn't want to hear anyone say, "What is going on, you don't feel well?" My blood and my pulse were two barometers of my illness, two symptoms which could sometimes allow me to say, when I could no longer stand it: "I am about to have a heart attack. I have cancer of the uterus." And the waltz of the doctors would begin again. And death was ever more present with its putrid liquids, its disintegration, its worms, its gnawed bones.

Now I have it in mind to tell the story of my illness and am accorded the privilege of the supplicant to describe the awful images and painful sensations which procured for me the memory of past events. It seems to me that I am a director with his camera attached to the end of an immense arm, capable of descending to shoot closeups and of drawing back in order to take in the action of the scene. So it is for this first visit I see Paris lit up at night in autumn (was it in autumn?) and, in Paris, the Alesia district, and in this district the dead end, and on the dead end the little house, and inside the little house the softly lit office where a man and a woman are speaking, and this woman, on a couch, curled up, like a fetus in the womb.

But at that time, I didn't know that I had hardly begun to be born again and that I was experiencing the first moments of a long period of gestation lasting seven years. Huge embryo of myself.

I'd told the doctor about the blood and the Thing which made my heart pound. I knew I wouldn't speak of the hallucination. I was going to speak of the last days in the hospital. Then I'd have told everything.

The doctor listened attentively, yet nothing in particular in my long recitation caused him to react. When I was through conjuring up the scenes of anguish in the bathroom, he asked me: "What do you feel when apart from your physical malaise?"

"I'm afraid."

"Afraid of what?"

"I'm afraid of everything, afraid of death."

In truth, I didn't really know of what I was afraid.... I was afraid of death, but I was also afraid of life which contained death. I was afraid of the outside, but I was also afraid of the inside which is the opposite of outside. I was afraid of the others, but I was also afraid of myself who was other. I was afraid, afraid, afraid, fear, FEAR, FEAR. It was everything.

Fear had relegated me to the alienated of this world. My family, from which I had hardly emerged, had again secreted its cocoon around me, tighter, more and more opaque, as the illness progressed. Not only to protect me but also to protect themselves. Madness is unacceptable in a certain class; it must be hidden at any cost. Madness among the aristocracy or the lower classes is regarded as eccentricity or as a defect which can be explained. But in the newly powerful middle class, it is not admissible.

When the madness comes from inbreeding or poverty, it may be understood. But when it comes out of a comfortable life where there is good health and that poise conferred by money decently earned, in such a case, it is a disgrace.

At the beginning they murmured to me, "It is nothing, you are nervous. Rest, get enough exercise." In the end it turned into an imperative: "You are going to see the doctor. So-and-so is a friend of your uncle's and a great neurologist." The great specialist friend had ordered a course of treatment "under medical supervision." They had reserved a room for me high up in my uncle's sanatorium.

A room was set up in the attic with a big bed, the walls covered in fabric depicting a restful country scene. The shepherdess with her sheep and crook, the gnarled tree with its trunk and olive leaves. Shepherdess, sheep, tree. Soothing repetition of a pattern. A screen covered in the same fabric hid a comfortable toilet with its white porcelain angles rounded, reassuringly. Opposite, a table and chair and a small dormer window opening onto a line of trembling poplars, apple trees planted four in a square, one at the center, fields of grain stretching to the horizon.

Was the restful scene in my room at the hospital or at home? Was the restful scene on the fabric printed with large flowers with pulpy stems? Was there fabric on the walls, or was it painted a glossy blue? I no longer know how I got there or who drove me. I can recall the narrow wooden stairs leading up to the room. I can remember the proportions of the room and its furnishings, the window, the toilet.

I must have undressed, put on new pajamas, gotten into the soft, freshly made bed, stretched out, allowing my blood pressure and pulse to be taken, delivering myself over to the medication. Meanwhile, I closed my eyes in order to continue my internal struggle as I was outwardly letting myself go: I had stretched my body out at full length, my arms resting on the taut sheets, my hands open. Outside I was normal. Inside, I had to calm my heartbeat. They put on the arm band. I heard the quick puff of the ball they squeezed to inflate it, I felt it clasp me tighter and tighter, then I cringed a little from the contact with the cold metal disc placed in the crook of my arm. The doctor had insisted on taking my blood pressure, which was very low; they had taken it every four hours before giving me my pill. It was all the same to me if my blood pressure was so low. What I really cared about was my pulse, the insane beating of my heart. The procedure of taking my blood pressure gave me a little time to try to calm myself. They took off the arm band. Near me someone was moving.

Who was it? My uncle? The specialist friend? Someone else? I don't know. At the time, I was so taken up with trying to control myself in the war against the Thing that my vision was warped. I felt I was going blind, I was navigating by radar. Some kind of instinct kept me from colliding into people and things.

Finally, I felt the ends of the four fingers pressing against the inside of my wrist. Four soft little balls. They had no need to grope. Scarcely had they touched the zone of my pulse than the blood, churned up by the Thing, made me fight them. Hardly had the fingers felt the beating of the heart when they amplified it and made it resound throughout every part of my body. Ninety, one hundred, one hundred ten, one hundred twenty, one hundred thirty, one hundred forty.... In vain I hid the Thing, in vain, I shut everything up in order not to let it out, though it knew very well how to reveal itself through my veins and my skin. The bastard, it was there, it made fun of me, it would not obey me, it was beating like a maniac against fingers which let go. Now they knew. Again, someone moved about, making small inoffensive bustling noises.

"You are going to take your pill now. Only a quarter of a pill, four times a day for a week. Then the dose will be increased. It will do you good."

It was a woman who spoke, short, thin, with white hair. I saw in her eyes that she had taken in the message transmitted through the fingers. She knew.

I took the minuscule quarter pill and the glass of water she handed me, and I made it seem as if I were swallowing normally. There were weeks when I could no longer swallow the undiluted pills. My throat was so constricted, nothing would go down. I had the impression that I was suffocating whenever I tried to swallow. I closed my eyes and indicated by my attitude that everything was all right, I wished to rest. The small portion of the pill stuck in my throat. It was enormous, like a block. They went out.

Immediately I sprang towards the sink to spit it out, my fingers down my throat, provoking the spasms which would deliver me. Finally the little yellowish triangle came up, covered with phlegm, saliva, and ropy mucus. (Was the morsel of pill yellowish or pinkish? Was it the color of a pearl?) I was sitting on the bidet, trembling from head to toe, my forehead against the cool, hard edge of the sink. Time had no meaning. I don't know how long I stayed there without moving. I remember taking out the tampon that stopped the blood, which I began to watch gently flowing, drop by drop, rocking back and forth, all the while knowing very well that at that same time I was rocking the Thing. The drops of blood flattened out and became slightly diluted in the moisture on the white porcelain, eventually making a narrow, winding path right to the drain. It was an activity to watch the blood work its way out of me; it had a life of its own now, it could discover the physics of earth-bound things, weight, density, speed, duration. It kept me company and at the same time was delivered over to the indifferent and incomprehensible laws of life.

The Thing had won. There was only it and me from now on. We were finally shut in alone with our secretions— blood, sweat, mucus, pus, saliva, and vomit. It had driven away my children, the animation in the street, the lights in the shop windows, the sea at noon when there are small waves, lilacs in bloom, laughter, the pleasure of dancing, the warmth of friends, the secret exaltation of study, long hours of reading, music, the arms of a loving man holding me, chocolate mousse, the joy of swimming in cool water. All I could do was curl up in the bathroom at the sanatorium, there where it was cleaner, trembling in my own sweat. I shivered so that the sound of my teeth chattering made an idiotic clatter like machinery.

Luckily, the steps of the little stairway creaked. At the slightest noise, I would go back to bed and lie down as usual. I didn't like the woman with white hair and I never spoke to her. She carried in my meals on a tray and gave me the pills after taking my blood pressure and my pulse. I couldn't eat. I threw what I could of it down the toilet, the rest I threw down into the gutter which ran along the edge of the tiled roof under my window. I do not remember whether the time was short or long, any more than I do the difference between night and day. I was a prisoner. I looked out the window to consider whether or not I would be killed if I jumped. Yes. There were four floors to the ground below. But the roof hid what was down there. Would I crash into the glass enclosure or into the shrubs? I did not want to kill myself in this way. Moreover, death made me afraid, while at the same time it held out the only means of getting rid of the Thing.

I don't know how many days had gone by when I was seized by a violent need to escape. More than a week in any event, since the morning (I'm sure it was in the morning) the woman had me take half a pill, and I remember very well that I was supposed to take a quarter of one for a week and then a half.

Suddenly, I realized that I was in my bed, lying on my back like other people, and that my face was showing. That surprised me: there were so many months when I could only live, whether awake or asleep, in the fetal position, my body hidden under the sheets. While at the same time as I verified this change, I felt a heaviness at the nape of my neck, as if the base of my skull was weighing me down and my brain was made of lead. Then it came to me that this heaviness, though well defined, had been there for some time. At the same time, I recognized that the Thing was not the same anymore, agitated, breathless, weak; it had become thick, gelatinous, sticky. It was not so much the fear that inhabited me as the despair and the disgust. I didn't want any of it. I don't know what instinct made me prefer the exhausting struggle with the Thing when it was enraged to coexistence with it when enfeebled, sticking to me with nauseating abandon.

In the course of the morning—my head more and more painful and heavy, buried in the pillow—I made a connection between my present condition and the pills. I was reminded of a conversation between the psychiatrist friend and my uncle. They spoke of a new treatment, of a "chemical electroshock," difficult to control but promising much better results than the standard electric shock treatment. They held forth in front of me as if I were a piece of furniture. And the fact is that at that point, I had taken absolutely no interest in what they were saying. I thought simply that the door was shut. I was going to be locked up, which was as it should be since I was incapable of living like the others, incapable of bringing up children. I couldn't take it anymore. I wanted them to deliver me from fear, from the Thing, whatever the cost.

However, on this particular morning in the sanatorium, I had figured out that the price was going to be enormous and that I did not want to pay it.

It was decided! I wasn't going to take any more of their disgusting pills. When the lady came I would pretend to swallow the pill and instead would spit it all out the window. In the gutter!

And that is what I did.

In searching through the memories of this period I am amazed that all I find is that great indefinite terrain of debris of people and objects, beaches strewn with indistinct morsels of my days and, all of a sudden, hard-edged constructions, precise, entire, and brilliant. In the course of my illness, there were moments more intelligent, more lucid, than I had ever known. I have heartrending memories. Without my madness I would never have discovered certain pathways of the mind. I was capable of incredible intellectual agility. There were times when my thoughts became sharp, subtle, and clear, which led me to a deeper understanding of my surroundings. I thought about those around me and saw them going in directions so different, so contrary, even so bad for them that I wanted to stop them and warn them of the danger. But, knowing I was ill, I thought my discoveries were sheer lunacy. How could I shudder at the idea of seeing the others so lost when I was like them?

So it was on that day I foresaw what was going to happen to me. However, I had never yet seen anyone "cured" by psychiatry. Since then I have seen a few: inoffensive, cautious, stuffed versions of themselves, humans with moist hands and the look in their eyes that moves between the flame and the ashes, the flame and the ashes.... I believe that the Thing no longer made them suffer but that it remained alive in them. It is still the Thing which is the driving force in them.

Even with my sick, heavy, painful head (this brain which the drug steals from me!), I understood it all. I wanted no part in such a fate. So I concocted the perfect escape plan, down to the last detail. To begin with, no more pills. Then to eat enough to get my strength back. To get permission to go out on the grounds. The rest would be easy. Above all I foresaw that without the drug the Thing was going to assault me with anxiety, the shivering, the shaking, the fear, and the sweat. I'd begin to have trouble seeing, to bleed like a stuck pig. Too bad. I had to get out of there! I had only twenty-four hours to play out this little comedy. After that, I might not be able to leave, my strength once again mobilized in the struggle with the Thing. For I suspected that I wouldn't be able to get back my bag full of tranquilizers, sleeping pills, and the little things that I was in the habit of taking: lumps of sugar for stomach cramps, mints to make the tongue less pasty and the throat less constricted, aspirin to soothe my aching head, a deodorant so as not to be overwhelmed by the stench of my perspiration, Tampax, Kleenex, cotton balls to stem the flow of blood, dark glasses to hide my glance from others and to protect my eyes from the insupportable light. This bag also had money in it which I needed since I was out in the country. It was impossible, therefore, to take a bus, or a train, or a taxi. I had to find another way. I would find it. I would go to the village and call a friend. (They knew me at the post office. "The head of the hospital's niece... she'll pay tomorrow." I had done it before.) I would be lost if I asked for my bag, of this I was certain. They must not have the slightest suspicion. Fortunately, I knew the grounds where I came to play when I was little and where often since then I had taken my children for walks. I knew of openings in the fence I could slip through without being seen by the guards. They didn't know why I was there; this sanatorium was not reserved for the mentally ill. Only my uncle and aunt and the nurse were in on the secret. But the guards might have talked, and my uncle might learn of it. My whole plan would be ruined. It was different with the people at the post office. They were not in constant contact with the staff.

I'd start tomorrow. The day after tomorrow I'd be gone. Only my pulse could betray me. Would the effect of the medication go on long enough? For the twelve o'clock medication, I was sitting up in bed. The nurse came in.

"Good morning."

"Good morning. It looks as if you're feeling better today."

"Yes, I feel better."

The blood pressure, the pulse, the glass of water and the half a pill on a little tin tray. For several days, it was no longer worth the trouble to delay it. I swallowed normally. The half-moon wedged cleverly under my tongue against my teeth, while the water went down.

A smile, and she was gone. The pill in the gutter below.

Now it is afternoon. I am standing in the bathroom: "It's a nice day."

"Yes, it's a beautiful day," the nurse said.

"I want to see my uncle, I feel like going out."

"Take it easy, I don't think it's possible. Not in the middle of the treatment."

"Could I see my uncle? I feel like reading."

"Certainly."

The blood pressure, the pulse, the pill down the gutter. Several minutes later my uncle appears: "So it seems you're feeling better, you want to read! I brought you some magazines and detective stories."

"I'd like to get a little exercise. Could I go for a walk on the grounds tomorrow?"

"I have to ask the doctor who's treating you."

"Call him. I know it would do me good. I want to do it."

"I'll call him; anyway, he's supposed to come and see you the day after tomorrow."

"I'm not going to stay here all the time without moving. You know I'm feeling much better."

A big smile. He is sitting at the foot of my bed. He hardly dares to look at me.

To give himself something to do, he studies my chart on which every day they put down my blood pressure, my pulse and the doses of medicine that have been given me. He knows it by heart. The nurse takes it down to him every morning.

"You look better. I'm really happy. I'll let you know what your doctor thinks later on."

My doctor! I don't even know his name!

Waiting for my uncle to come back, I decide to freshen up. I brush my hair for a long time, front and back, then I brush my teeth. I'm exhausted, out of breath. I keep a close watch on the Thing, but it doesn't stir. I've installed myself on the bidet to watch the blood flow. Since I am here, it is a favorite activity. It makes me think of the sea and the waves lapping against the shore with a sigh. I think of the planets unchangingly spinning in their orbits.

At the first creaking step, I pull myself together and sit down on the chair in front of the table, a magazine open in front of me. In a low-cut dress, Gina Lollobrigida is smiling, her teeth revealed. My God, how can that woman be so happy!

My uncle comes in, still dressed in his white coat which tightens a bit across his stomach, and the small white hat he wears in the operating room.

"Your doctor has given his permission. You can go out for a walk tomorrow. He is very pleased that your condition is improving so rapidly. It seems this new treatment sometimes has the opposite effect on patients; it makes them listless, it gives them migraines. The nurse will go with you. Your aunt has asked if you would like to have dinner with us."

"No, not tonight thanks. I've already had dinner and I'm going to sleep. I would rather tomorrow if the walk goes well. Thank her for me. She'll understand, won't she, if I don't come?"

"Of course. You know, she never doubted for a second you'd come out of it in a hurry. It is not in the nature of the family. You were too exhausted to want to raise your children alone. That is all. Her chief concern is for your mother, who is wild with anxiety. You know how fond they are of each other. They spend the whole day on the telephone. Your poor mother doesn't even have the energy to go out. The children exhaust her."

"I'm going to feel better very soon. You must reassure her. It's not going to drag on."

"You know, what I'm going to say about it... it is mostly for your mother's sake. The poor woman has been through enough, she deserves a rest... I am talking to you like a... grown-up. You're not going to make a mountain out of a molehill."

"No. No. I understand what you're saying but I'm going to get over it, I know it. I really do feel like I'm getting better."

"Goodnight, my grown-up."

He kisses me on the forehead and leaves.

I don't want to think about my mother. I don't want to think about my children....

Then everything is confused. The Thing is taking hold of me with such ferocity. I don't think I am strong enough to fight it for very long without any drugs to help me, without anything; I am defenseless. And yet, I am getting past it.

I went out without the nurse. I ran in the fields (I try to remember if the wheat was high, but am unable to). I got my friend on the telephone: "Promise me to come tomorrow at this time? At the junction of the main road and the little one, where there's a sign for the sanatorium, one kilometer before the village on the left."

"You can count on me, I'll be there."

In the evening, sitting in front of the TV between my uncle and my aunt, for I had decided I would go there after all, it seemed to me that we were in an enormous aquarium. They were the gentle fish peacefully feeding on seaweed and I was an octopus.

Above all my aim was not to provoke them, not to do anything to displease them, not a word, not a gesture.

I didn't know that I was never going to see them again. I knew only that I was about to deceive them and that it upset me. Especially these two, who were the most successful branch of the family. In abandoning them, I was abandoning the Good. But that was the road I had decided on. Thinking about it, I had never been normal like them. I might just as well disappear and release them from having to deal with me.

The following day the car was there. We started up right away and I was able to let myself go, body trembling, teeth chattering.

"Are you sick? What do you want me to do?"

"Nothing, Nothing. You can do nothing for me. Take me to Michèle's. Don't worry, I'll get over it. Call the sanatorium later, tell them I am safe, that they mustn't look for me. But don't tell them where I am. I don't ever want to see them again."

The next day I entered the cul-de-sac for the first time. Who called the doctor? Did I call him? Was it Michèle? I no longer know. She knew him and I had heard of him. I must have called him myself. (At Michèle's place, I got hold of some tranquilizers and managed to stifle the Thing.) I just don't know.

There, I had told it all.

I had wanted to talk about the blood and yet it was above all the Thing about which I had spoken. Was he going to send me away? I didn't dare look at him. I felt all right there, in that small space talking about myself. Was it a trap? The last of them? Perhaps I shouldn't have trusted him.

And then he said: "You were right not to take those pills. They are very dangerous."

My whole body relaxed. I felt profound gratitude towards this little man. Perhaps there was a path between myself and another. If only it were true. If only I could talk to someone who would really listen to me!

He continued: "I think I can help you. If you agree, we can begin an analysis together starting tomorrow. You would come three times a week for three forty-five-minute sessions. But, should you agree to come here, it is my duty to warn you, on the one hand, of the risk that psychoanalysis may turn your whole life upside down, and, on the other hand, that you will have to stop taking all medication right now, whether for your hemorrhages or for your nervous system. Not even aspirin, nothing. Finally, you must know that an analysis lasts at least three years and that it will be expensive. I'm going to charge you forty francs a session, that is to say one hundred twenty francs a week."

His manner of speaking was serious and I felt he wanted me to listen to him and to think about what he was saying. For the first time in a long time someone was addressing me as if I were a normal person. And for the first time in a long while I was behaving like a person capable of assuming responsibilities. Then I understood that little by little they had taken all these responsibilities away from me. I was no longer a nothing. I began to think about this situation and about what he had just said. How could my life turned upside down be worse than it was? Perhaps I would get a divorce because it was from the time of my marriage that the Thing established itself inside me. Never mind, I'll get a divorce or I won't get a divorce. Besides this, I couldn't see what else could be changed in my life.

26

As for the money, that was more difficult; I didn't have any. I lived on the money my husband earned and what my parents gave me.

"I have no money, Doctor."

"You will earn it. You will have to pay for your sessions with the money you have earned yourself. It is better that way."

"But I can't go out, I can't work."

"You'll manage. I can wait three months, six months until you find a position. We can arrange something. What I want is for you to know that you will have to pay me and that it will be expensive. The sessions you miss will be paid for the same as the others. If it doesn't cost you one way or another, you won't take the analysis seriously. This is common knowledge."

His tone of voice was dry enough, as though he was someone involved in a business transaction. Not any commiseration in his voice, nothing of the doctor or the father. I didn't know that in agreeing to begin imme- diately, he was taking three more hours a week out of his own life which was already invaded by his patients. He made no allusion to the additional fatigue or to the fact that he was making an exception because he saw how ill I was. Not a word of it; on the contrary. On the face of it, it was a simple bargain. He was taking a risk, he was allowing me to choose. And yet, he knew that but for him, there were only two solutions for me: the psychiatric hospital or suicide.

"I agree, Doctor. I don't know how I can manage to pay you, but I agree."

"Very well, we'll begin tomorrow."

He took out a little notebook and he showed me the days and the hours when I had to come.

"And what if I hemorrhage?"

"Do nothing."

"But they already put me in the hospital for this, they gave me transfusions, curettages."

"I know it. Do nothing, I will expect you tomorrow.... There is one thing I want to ask you, however: try not to pay attention to what you know of psychoanalysis; try to avoid any reference to this knowledge; find equivalents for the words in the psychoanalytic vocabulary which you have learned. Everything you know can only hold you back."

It was true that I believed that I knew everything about introspection and that, in the core of my being, I felt this treatment would have no more effect on me than cauterizing a wooden leg.

"But, Doctor, what is the matter with me?"

He made a vague gesture of the hand, as if to say: "What use is diagnosis?"

"You are tired, troubled. I believe that I can help you." He took me to the door. "Goodbye, Madame, I will see you tomorrow."

"Goodbye, Doctor."

# Chapter II

It was a difficult night following this first visit. The Thing was rumbling inside me. For a long time, I had been in the habit of going to sleep only when put to sleep by a massive dose of drugs. But the little man had said to me: "You will have to stop taking all medication."

I was in my bed, oppressed, suffocating, covered with perspiration. If I opened my eyes I experienced the decomposition of the outer world, of objects and the air. If I closed my eyes I experienced the decomposition of the inner world, of my cells and my flesh. This frightened me. Nothing or no one could stop even for a second this degradation of everything. I was drowning, I couldn't breathe, there were microbes everywhere, maggots, pustules, and acids were gnawing at my insides. Why this existence which feeds on itself? Why these agonizing periods of gestation? Why is my body aging? Why does it produce stinking liquids and stinking matter? Why my sweat, my shit, my piss? Why this dung heap? Why the war of everything that lives, of every cell, to decide which one will kill the other and gorge itself on the corpse? Why the ineluctable and majestic round of phagocytes? Who is controlling this perfect monster? What inexhaustible driving force keeps the rat race going? Who is shaking up the atoms with so much power? Who has his eye upon every pebble, every blade of grass, every bubble, every baby, with unfailing attention, only to bring them to the putrefaction of death? What is stable other than death? Where to take one's rest unless it is in death, which is decomposition itself? To whom does death belong? What is this soft, enormous thing, indifferent to beauty, joy, peace, love, that lies down on me, suffocating me? What is no less fond of shit than tenderness, making no distinction? Where do others find the strength to endure the Thing? How can they live with It? Are they crazy? They're all crazy! I am unable to hide myself. I can't do anything, I am in the power of the Thing which is coming after me slowly, inexorably, which wants to feed off me.

Life's putrid current swept me along, whether I wanted it to or not, towards absolute and compulsory death, which was the real horror. This inspired in me an overwhelming fear. Since there was no other fate in store for me than to fall into the ignoble belly of infection, to do so as quickly as possible was all that was left to me. I wanted to kill myself and get it over with.

Towards morning I finally fell asleep, exhausted, curled up in a ball like a fetus.

When I awoke I was drenched in my own blood, which had seeped through the mattress and the box spring and was dripping onto the floor. He had said, "Don't do anything, I'll expect you tomorrow." Six more hours to wait; I couldn't last that long.

I stayed motionless in my bed, stiff as a corpse. I expected the worst. Two horrible memories came back to me in every detail, two disasters, two waking nightmares. One time the blood had flowed in such large clots that it might have been said that I was producing slices of liver, one after another, with an absurd obstinacy; as they passed through me they caressed me gently, softly. They had taken me to the hospital for an emergency curettage. Another time, the blood had come out of me like a red thread which wouldn't stop unwinding—an open faucet. I remember the shock of seeing it, and how it terrified me: "At this rate the blood will drain out of me in ten minutes flat." Again, the hospital, transfusions, doctors and nurses covered with blood, throwing themselves on my arms, my legs, my hands, trying to find a vein, struggling through the night. Then, in the morning, the operating room and again, a curettage.

I was not aware of the fact that in having surrendered to the blood I was misrepresenting myself, I was concealing the Thing. At certain times this cursed blood invaded my existence so completely that it left me exhausted, again more fragile in the face of the Thing.

At the appointed hour I was at the dead end of the cul-de-sac, bundled in cotton pads I had put together to form a kind of diaper. I had to wait a while, since I was early. The person ahead of me came out. Like the day before, I heard the opening and closing of the two doors. At last I entered and said right away, "Doctor, I am bled dry."

I remember very well having chosen the words because I found them beautiful. I also remember that I wanted in my look and my posture to communicate the pathetic. The doctor answered me quietly and calmly: "Those are psychosomatic disorders. That doesn't interest me. Speak about something else."

There was a couch there. I didn't want to lie down on it. I wanted to remain standing and fight. The words that this man had just uttered were a slap in the face. Never had I encountered such violence. Right in the face! My blood didn't interest him! If that is so, then everything is destroyed! He took my breath away. I felt as if I were struck down by lightning. He did not want me to speak about my blood! But of what else did he want me to speak? What ELSE? Apart from my blood there was only fear, nothing else, and I could no more speak of it than think about it.

I broke down and cried—I who had been unable to cry for so long, who for so many months had sought in vain the comfort of tears. Now at last they flowed freely, dissolving the tension in my back, my chest, and my shoulders. I cried for a long time. I reveled in the storm.

As soon as the door had closed again behind me, after that first session, I was reminded of the blood and I thought the doctor was a madman, a charlatan, one of the worst. What witchcraft had I allowed to trap me? Now I had to act quickly. I was going to get a taxi and see a real doctor.

The driver was talkative, or perhaps he found me a little odd. In any case, he didn't stop speaking and I continually caught his eye observing me in the rearview mirror. In these circumstances and especially given the way I was bundled up to go and see the doctor, it was impossible for me to make one of my brief and secret verifications of the blood. The more we drove towards the address of the doctor I had given him, the more imperative it became to make the verification. I was getting upset, aggressive. I wanted the driver to stop and at the same time to continue driving. He didn't know what was going on with me. Finally, on the edge of the seat, I put my left arm on the back of the seat in front of me, my head resting on my arm. I made it seem as if I was listening to what he said. Meanwhile, I rummaged under my dress with the right hand, undid the zipper, tore at the diapers fastened by diaper pins until I got to the source of the blood. I ascertained that nothing remarkable had occurred. The hemorrhage was no worse; if anything it seemed to have let up a little. Difficult to say. Only an hour earlier, before leaving, I had been bleeding heavily.

Suddenly I changed my mind, disconcerting the taxi driver by giving him Michèle's address. Then I hid in the back of the cab. Perhaps I could wait it out until the day after tomorrow.

I ran up the stairs four at a time, clutching my clothes that I had torn to ribbons. Quick, to the bathroom. The soiled rags on the floor between my feet, me on the bidet. The bleeding had stopped! I could not believe my eyes.

I didn't know, I couldn't know it, not on that day, that the blood would never flow again without stopping for months and years. I believed that it had only stopped flowing for a few seconds. I wanted to savor it, as I had my tears. I washed up and lay down naked on the bed, legs apart. Pure. I was pure! I was a sacred vessel, the altar for the blood, the receptacle of tears. Clean, shining!

The doctor had said, "Try to understand what happens to you, what provokes, attenuates, or accentuates your crises. Everything is important: noises, colors, odors, gestures, atmospheres... everything! Try to proceed by the association of ideas and images."

That day, clumsy as I was in the manipulation of the analysis, it was still easy enough for me to establish a link between hemorrhaging and the blood stoppping, with the doctor's slap in the face at the center of it: "Your blood doesn't interest me, tell me about something else...," and my tears.

That night, liberated from the blood, my mind ventured forth as if on a holiday into facile reflections, simple calculations and restful thoughts — activities of the mind which I normally regarded as a playground in which I might not linger, under pain of being captured by the Thing. I could only fight it off when I was at the peak of my intelligence or in the farthest reaches of my imagination on the path of the infinite, the unknowable, the mysterious and the magical.

In this way, quite unthinkingly, with the freedom of a spring and the simplicity of an egg, I realized I had been subjected to dozens of tests and there had never been any evidence to indicate something abnormal in the various bodily functions. Not with respect to hormones or the circulatory system, the organic or chemical. I understood my blood was the life buoy which allowed the doctors and me to keep afloat on the sea of the inexplicable. I bleed, she bleeds. Why? Because there is something wrong, something physiological, something very serious, complicated, fibromatous, introverted, lacerated, abnormal. The tests reveal nothing, nothing significant; however, one doesn't bleed like that without a reason. The doctor has to open you up and have a look. He has to make a long incision in the skin, in the muscles, in the veins, open up the flesh of the belly, the viscera, and take hold of that hot, pinkish organ, cut it away and eliminate it. Then there won't be any more blood. No gynecologist, psychiatrist or neurologist had ever acknowledged that the blood came from the Thing. On the contrary, I was told the Thing came from the blood. "Women are often 'nervous' because their gynecological equilibrium is precarious, very delicate."

That evening it was apparent to me that the Thing was the essential element: it was all powerful.

I was made to face the Thing. It was no longer so vague, although I didn't know how to define it. That evening I understood that I was the madwoman. She made me afraid because she carried the Thing inside. She at once disgusted and attracted me, like those magnificent reliquaries in a religious procession enclosing the remains of a saint. The gold, the precious stones, these beauties to contain a skull with rotten teeth, shinbones yellow with age and dried blood! Around it the priests with their censers, their canopies, their banners, the stultified crowd chanting the response in procession behind those vile and stunted remains! The lamentation and the ecstasy which come from so many wagging tongues and vacant eyes and bended knees, and from all those fingers entwined with the rosary! Madness!

It had become impossible for me to comprehend the division of lives into years, months, days, hours, seconds. Why did people do the same things at the same time? I no longer understood anything, the lives of those around me made no sense.

Hostage to a hostile or indifferent universe to which I was accountable, I accused myself of bad deeds and I did penance for them. My thoughts were so entangled that the more the years went by, the more I had the impression of sinking into evil, or imperfection, or the indecent, or the unseemly. I was never able to be satisifed with myself. I looked upon myself like so much garbage, an anomaly, a disgrace, and, what was worse, I believed that I had allowed myself to be overrun by error because of an evil nature. With a little courage, willpower and by taking in the advice lavished upon me, I might have been on the side of the angels, or so I thought. But by being cowardly, lazy, mediocre, and low, I was in the wrong camp, irrevocably. I was the lowest of the low! My body had thickened and sunk in upon itself. I believed that I had become ugly inside and out.

And then, that night, because the bleeding had stopped and the doctor had spoken to me as if I were a normal person, I looked at myself in another light. What had that small man set into motion? What instinct propelled me?

I began to doggedly follow my new path. I was like the honeybees whom nothing can distract from their task, solely occupied in choosing the best pollen. The honey would be my equilibrium. Nothing else interested me. I thought of nothing else. It did not cross my mind to telephone my uncle. It was only much later that I told my husband.

# Chapter III

Autumn, winter. The cul-de-sac was forever damp, full of puddles, poorly lit. It happened sometimes that I would cross paths with the clients who preceded or followed me, bundled up, hugging the walls and hurrying. We exchanged glances we considered anonymous, but we knew all the while that we were the sick and that we shared the same doctor, the same couch, the same ceiling, the same flawed tapestry, the same stupid gargoyle on the top of the same fake beam on the other side of the couch. We belonged to the brotherhood of the lost and the trapped. They also moved between suicide and fear, as though between two policemen.

I knew also that the words which I came there to pour out in torrents three times a week were not their words, that they had their own stories, no less painful and ridiculous, incomprehensible to others, unlivable.

The first three months of my analysis, I lived with the

idea that I was having a reprieve, it was not going to last, they were going to discover me and take me back there. And yet the blood no longer flowed except when I had my period normally. The anxiety subsided, increasingly slackening its grip. But I still hadn't spoken of the hallucination, fearing it would condemn me to a psychiatric hospital, were it known.

I still maintained a defensive posture, head hunched between the shoulders, stooped over, fists clenched, on the lookout from within through my eyes, my ears, my nose and my skin. Danger was everywhere. I had to figure out a way to see without seeing, hear without hearing, feel without feeling. What really counted was the struggle with the Thing that had rooted in my mind, this filthy hag whose two enormous buttocks were the lobes of my brain. Sometimes she propped up her big ass in my skull (I felt her settling in), and, head down, she manipulated the nerves which constricted my throat and stomach and opened the floodgates of perspiration. She made the icy air circulate, and then started to run, terrorized, hallucinating, incapable of screaming, incapable of speaking, incapable of expressing herself in any way, until drenched in cold sweat, trembling throughout her entire body, she was able to find some clean, dark place to curl up in like a fetus.

Since the start of the analysis, I had let myself be swept away by the mad one less and less often. I observed it. The Thing didn't like me to look at it like that, from the outside, and, after a moment, it let go. It continued to stay there, sad, downcast, nostalgic even for the days of its agitation.

Monday, Wednesday, Friday. The three stops on my route where I could bring my yield and communicate with someone about it. It was the only point of contact with the lives of others. Each week, the great distance between Friday and Monday seemed impossible to get beyond. All day Sunday I would wait, guarding my strength, sheltering myself from the world. Monday I would go back to my cul-de-sac, again invigorated by an immense joy and a bottomless hope.

At first, I spoke about my first encounters with the Thing, referred to simply as anxiety. Then I spoke of the principal elements of my life, the full extent of my existence, as I understood it.

My first anxiety attack occurred during a Louis Armstrong concert. I was nineteen or twenty. Armstrong was going to improvise with his trumpet, to build a whole composition in which each note would be important and would contain within itself the essence of the whole. I was not disappointed: the atmosphere warmed up very fast. The scaffolding and flying buttresses of the jazz instruments supported Armstrong's trumpet, creating spaces which were adequate enough for it to climb higher, establish itself, and take off again. The sounds of the trumpet sometimes piled up together, fusing a new musical base, a sort of matrix which gave birth to one precise, unique note, tracing a sound whose path was almost painful, so absolutely necessary had its equilibrium and duration become; it tore at the nerves of those who followed it.

My heart began to accelerate, becoming more important than the music, shaking the bars of my rib cage, compressing my lungs so the air could no longer enter them. Gripped by panic at the idea of dying there in the middle of spasms, stomping feet, and the crowd howling, I ran into the street like someone possessed. It was a beautiful cold winter night. People were snug in their houses. I ran, and the sound of my running reverberated like a horse galloping in the echo chambers of the avenues, boulevards, and back streets.

"I'm going to die, I'm going to die, I'm going to die."

My heart was beating to the rapid tempo of the music. I remember a camellia in bloom, glistening, full-blown, in its concrete tub on a street corner, just before plunging into the tunnel which led to the university. The beauty of those thick, glossy flowers! I was running, they were already far behind, and yet the heart of one of them that I had glimpsed for a fraction of a second stayed with me, keeping me company in my race, as calm as I was agitated, svelte in appearance but torn apart inside. The brightly lit tunnel was reassuring. Cars swept by me on this well-traveled route into the city. Pedestrians hurried along its sidewalks. At the far end, a neon sign flashed on and off coquettishly. But nothing could appease me. And so I continued to run.

When I got home, instead of taking the elevator, I ran up the stairs four at a time all the way to the fifth floor. And it was there, at the front door, that I became conscious of the enormous physical effort I had just made. And I said to myself, "If I had heart trouble, I'd be dead, I wouldn't have been able to do a fraction of all this." But the thought failed to relax me. I went to my room to catch my breath and collapsed on the bed. I was alone, my eyes closed, nothing mattered but the beating of my faltering heart: "I'm going to die; I do have heart trouble." And the anxiety that I encountered for the first time took hold of me, covering me with icy perspiration. My muscles were trembling grotesquely, playing with me as though I were a dog. I called my mother, who was sleeping in the next room. Once, twice. I no longer remember how many times I called her, louder and louder, "Mamma, mamma, mamma!" My mother came into the room, disheveled and swollen from sleep. Her bun had come undone, her chestnut hair fell away from her scalp and even from her shoulders, in long locks going every which way. I thought that the spectacle I offered her would shatter the composure which I had perceived in her green eyes, and that she would dissolve in my fear and keep her child *in extremis* company, her big, grown-up daughter who was dying! Instead, she got herself dressed and did her hair. With a look of compassion, she came to sit near me on the bed. She took my hand and made herself comfortable. She had the same expression when she visited the cemetery, at once sadly tender and lamentably smug. "It's an anxiety attack, it's nothing, don't be afraid, it isn't serious, it's your nerves."

I didn't like her composure. Neither did I like her control nor her readiness to accept the situation. How is it that what I was enduring was nothing? How could this wave of slimy liquid crashing down on me, full of hooks and blades and decomposing material, not be anything? For me it was life-threatening. I was sure of it. To see her respond to me as she had responded to the dead only increased my anxiety. I was suffocating. The small amount of air I managed to take in whistled a ridiculous piercing note.

"I can't breathe, I'm going to die."

"No, no, it's your nerves. Your pulse is rapid, but good. Believe me, you are not going to die."

I didn't like this complicity between us. I had tried so hard to win her love and attention. I had waited so long for just that look which now fell softly on my dark eyes, my curly hair, my potato of a nose, my mouth, my chin my broad shoulders and strong body. It was as if she were making my acquaintance and at the same time recognizing me. I didn't want any of it in such a state. I had wanted it before, while running in a race, diving off a diving board, laughing, winning prizes. I wanted her to be proud of me then. It was my strength which should have come from her, not this malaise and the fear. In the warmth of her attention, this complicity, this intimacy which she offered me that night, I understood that she had conferred death upon me at my birth, that what she wanted me to give back to her was death, that the bond between us, a bond I had tried so hard to discover, was death. This filled me with horror.

Following this attack, the days dragged on, heavy with anxiety and the fear of a recurrence. I went to see the doctor with my mother. He confirmed her diagnosis: "It's nothing, it's your nerves. You must have had a little tachycardia, and certainly you have a slight tendency to swallow air." "A little," "slight." The words were so minimal! And yet what could be worse than what I had experienced? Can one suffer more? Is there any greater human misery? They began to talk about serious cases of tachycardia, and of air swallowing encountered in the course of their medical careers. Mine was nothing by comparison with those unfortunates. They looked at me with a sort of gentle mockery, they patted my cheeks and my hands: "Come on, it's nothing at all, you are young and in good health." The doctor confessed to me that he himself sometimes swallowed air, and he told me his trick for stopping it quickly. You had to get on your hands and knees, raise one leg or the other slightly, according to how you felt, rather like a dog pissing against a lamppost. The purpose was to encourage the passage of the gases, which in excess amounts pressed on the diaphragm and produced the sensation of choking.

Affectionate comments were underlined with smiles, and such words as "youth," "love," "marriage," punctuated the rest of their remarks. I knew what they meant and so I lowered my eyes and let them talk.

I had the sense then that what I had learned at the university about psychology, and particularly psychoanalysis (my two years in the physiology of the nervous system at the Psycho-Technical Institute), provided me with the ability to define and classify myself, to understand. I knew I suffered from the divorce of my parents, who fought over me until my father's death. I knew that my mother unconsciously resented my birth. (I was born in the middle of their divorce proceedings.) For this reason, I scarcely knew my own father. And as a consequence of the dissension between them, I was aware that there were sexual complications. I thought I knew all about them. Though at the same time, it seemed, I had decided to remain a virgin.

Several months went by. There was no repetition of the first anxiety attack. Then on the night I chose to lose my virginity I had another milder attack.

Seeing the boy naked with an erection, feeling in my hand his penis, smooth as silk velvet, warm as a fresh loaf out of the oven, I felt a tremendous joy. There were tears in my eyes. He was so beautiful. All his muscles, his skin, his hair, seemed to be there only for the simple purpose of brandishing his erect member. Spreading my legs and kneeling between them, gently he set about to devirginize me. His determined look made me understand that nothing would stop him, that there was no choice but to submit, that what he was doing was useful, necessary and in perfect harmony with the deepest part of me. I reproached myself for an instant for having been kept so long a prisoner from the profound undulations traveling through me from my heels to my neck. Nothing shocked or surprised me, even when the rhythm became brutal and I felt within me the collapse of a silken barrier I never knew was there. Afterwards, he was so tender, even to the point of fragility, as if he had given all his power to me and I was filled with gratitude.

While I didn't have an orgasm, there was no disgust in me: on the contrary. Alone again, I washed my blood-stained sheets. It was a warm night and they would soon be dry. I stretched out on the bare mattress in the darkness. I couldn't sleep; I was thinking about the boy whom I had picked out for his skill. He was known to be a lover of women. I had heard he was in love with an older married woman, which made me feel that he would take this rite of initiation seriously. And there I was, certain to make love with him again tomorrow, and looking forward to it.

And yet, my pulse was rapid. I had difficulty breathing. I understood the importance of the event, I knew that by this act I was setting in motion my whole little inner sea, even creating a storm. I was over twenty. Not only was I a virgin until that day, I had never even had a flirtation. (Except for a kiss in broad daylight, my head tilted back in the sand, only long enough to feel on my lips a touch of sweet saliva tasting of Gauloise cigarettes. A little memento hidden like a dried flower between the pages of a thick book when I was fourteen.) These limits allowing for so little in the way of experience were in accord with my mother's rules. There was, of course, no place for masturbation. My siestas and my nights were often hellish, as I lay flat on my stomach on the cold tiles of my bedroom floor, trying to escape from the softness of my body, trying to escape from the scent of thyme and jasmine, and the dust of the Mediterranean, the irritating noise of the cicadas and the tender notes of the Arab flute, overwrought to the point of howling my desire and my need.

And then, suddenly, I had decided on my own to overcome the prejudices of family and class, and the colossus of religion, to have sex with a boy I didn't even love, with whom there couldn't even be the excuse of either passion or reason. Quite simply, I wanted to do it because I felt like it.

When the anxiety attack came I recognized it immediately. But this time it seemed more normal, less frightening. I knew very well that I was entering the world of sex by the wrong door, as did the women my father entertained at his house. My mother called them "whores," and the memory of the vulgarity of that word in her mouth made me tremble. I caught a glimpse of a few of them long ago. They were leaving as I arrived. My father pretended to be seeing some ordinary callers to the door. His smile was forced, his gestures overly polite. He knew how to control himself. The way they swung their hips to cross the threshold, the goodbye with a look in his direction, indicating an awareness of me, said it all. Every time, I felt a distressing intimacy between them, a frightening complicity, a whiff of unimaginable pleasures. This staggered me. My father's mistresses made fun of my mother kneeling at her prie-dieu. Her virtue... their vice... my vice... an angel, devils. All of it came back to me and kept me awake that night. And then there was something else, I didn't know what, which played on my heart and made it beat fast.

My bedroom, once a guest room, still smelling of mold and gloom, looked out on a small back street where there was a livery stable. In the early morning a man came to line up the horses along the sidewalk, putting them in harness, hitching them to the old-fashioned coaches which would soon carry tourists under the palm trees bordering the sea. I can remember the sunrise and the day as it dawned, separating the venetian blinds into stripes, first gray and black and then yellow and black. The horses' shoes struck the asphalt ever increasing blows as the mounting heat restored the flies to their daylight activities. The smell of fresh dung came up at me. My white night was over. I made the bed with clean sheets. Nothing to see, nothing to know. I didn't try to make sense of what I was doing. I went out and took off in the direction of the beach; the sand was already hot. It was enough, however, to sink your feet just below the surface to recapture the coolness and the damp of the night that had just ended.

The twelve years that followed were gnawed at by the slow gestation of the madness. I had less and less of a desire to move about, to express myself, to throw myself into an action or a thought. The more I tried to find my own way, the more I despaired of finding it on the ground which my birth had given me. I became heavy, slow, dense, with moments of agitation which they called my "impetuosity." I was looked upon as a sensible and well-balanced person. During this period, I passed my exams, plunging into sexual life as one dives into water believed to be cold. While I didn't find it cold, I didn't take the liberty to swim in it according to my fantasies. I got married, I taught in lycées. I had three children. I wanted to give them happiness, warmth, an attention that I had never had, a father and mother always there, in love.

Instead, day after day, the sluggishness, the viscosity, and the absurdity of existence became fixed in my mind, before becoming the Thing.

# Chapter IV

First Paris winter. Sun never shining. Trees without leaves. And, like an old refrain, the wayward advance to the cul-de-sac. It is in the obscurity of the fog, the emptiness of the cold, the spiritlessness of the rain, and the dullness of the clouds that I come here to experience once again the dazzling heat, the sweltering streets, the impetuosity of childhood and the explosion of my adolescence. An entire population of ghosts accompanies me. In the rutted and narrow passageway, memories rush in behind me which are precise and alive, palpitating, derisive.... They jerk about as far as the couch and pass in parade like a procession of carnival wagons.

No man intervened in my early years. I was in the hands of women: my mother, my grandmother, the maids and the nuns who were my teachers.

Of my father, whom I had known little because he

didn't live with me and died during my adolescence, I held on to the memory of a dandy, with spats, hat, and cane. A small moustache, fine hands, a dazzling smile. I was afraid of him. I knew nothing of the male universe. His place, his bathroom with his razor and shaving brush, his bedroom with his drawers full of shirts and his cuff links, attracted and disturbed me. His huge bachelor's bed covered in panther skins made me stop and think.

He called me his "little minx." He treated me like a little woman, not like a little girl, which made me uncomfortable.

In my childhood, I would visit him with my governess. Later on, I went by myself to have lunch in between morning and afternoon classes at the school. These were trying meals. When he didn't frighten me he wearied me. I had to pay attention to how I moved and to the words I chose. Often he would reprimand me, and I understood through these reprimands, that it was my mother he wanted to get at. My mother, who was raising me, dressing me, educating me. Yet I felt he loved me and wished me no harm.

My schoolwork was so important to him. He would tell me to learn everything: Latin, Greek, mathematics, all of it.... Though I did well, I never would let him see either my report cards or my exercise books. I knew I was protecting my mother, who had custody, and that I was taking her side. As far as he was concerned, my schoolbag was locked, my strongbox, my treasure, my credibility. So it was I who kept my father at a distance and forbade him access to my world. And I did it knowingly.

I saw my parents together on only three occasions, the first of which was my Holy Communion. There they were, in the same room, at the same table, separate. The attention he lavished on me was bothersome. On that day, I would have preferred only my mother's strict eye upon me, as I cut into the elaborate cake of many layers, covered with little cream puffs. I might have done a better job of it.

The second occasion was my initiation into the French Girl Scouts. It was out-of-doors; other parents were there. Mine were close together, but did not speak. Their attention was on the ceremony. I remember the brilliant autumn sky on that day. I was twelve years old.

The third occasion was towards the end of his life, when I was about fifteen years old. He had been spitting blood. He thought he was dying and sent for my mother.

TUBERCULOSIS! Bogeyman of my childhood. My grandfather dead of consumption, my uncle in the sanatorium, my sister dead at eleven months of tubercular meningitis, my brother who reacted badly to his tuberculosis skin test, and was developing curvature of the spine.

B.C.G., Koch bacillus, thoracoplasty, pneumothorax, phrenicotomy, cavity, pleura, sputum, the Leysin TB treatment center in Switzerland, X rays, vaccine, Calmette and Guérin.

So many words, so many miseries, all because of my father and his disease and because of the Great War in which his lungs were rotted out by gas.

"All the same, he could have taken better care of himself before marrying me. He didn't even warn me. It's shameful, it's dishonest."

The war, the trenches, my father under a pile of soldiers who had been gassed, kept from death by the thickness of the layer of corpses, his chest consumed.

"I saw his X rays, it's quite simple, his lungs are like sponges."

myself from what I had come to hear and to see. I knew that old war machine by heart. It intrigued me. Inside it, I had the feeling I was in danger, and yet I didn't hesitate. It was a short-winded box, closed by a recalcitrant folding gate. When you rang for it, the cables bristling from its roof grew taut, lashing the air, and started forward, hoisting the cabin by fits and starts, while a cylinder of steel, very strong and dripping with black oil, gave a powerful thrust to help it rise. The precise and steady ascent of this splendid lubricated column seemed incompatible with the uproar ringing throughout the abode.

This contraption stood guard over the house of my father and made of it a region accessible only with difficulty, a little dangerous even. I knew everything about it except the dimensions of the hole into which the column of steel would bury itself, which I imagined dizzily. And sometimes, I imagined that this hole wasn't so deep, and that the column coiled itself up in it like a spring.

It happened once that I made peepee in this elevator, for at my father's, I didn't dare ask to go to the bathroom. One day, unable to hold it in any longer, knowing it would be another two hours before I could get back to the Turkish squatters at my school, I had gone ahead and peed right in the middle of the old box. I might have enjoyed this relief if the shaking and trembling of the elevator had not interfered with my aim, so that my shoes were filled. In order to be able to perform comfortably, I had ended up by stopping between the third and fourth floors. But—disaster!—my urine had soaked the thread-bare carpet right through to the floor, and spread out in a spray of little drops which resounded interminably against the metal plate which held the steel column at the ground floor. The instant I heard the first rain I pushed the button for the fifth floor, but by then I couldn't stop. In my fear and in the shame of my behavior, it sounded like a waterfall. By the time I reached my father's, I was drenched.

That little girl, that elevator...how far away it all was! That discussion between them changed everything. It was the first time I had really seen them together. I had just realized that I was born of their wretched desire and their enmity. Suddenly I had grown old. All of a sudden, everything around me was old.

There ought to have been another setting for this sudden swallowing up of childhood into the past. There ought to have been a blue sky in spring or autumn, and an ocean sparkling with little waves, smells. Stupidly, I thought first love, the first kiss even, would make me grow up. Not at all; this was it—this conversation between two strangers who happened to be my parents. It was the blood from the hemorrhage, my mother's bitterness, and the elevator—which was becoming darker and darker as the day was drawing to its close, in Algeria where the sun sets so quickly.

Right in the middle of my daydream, point-blank and a little bothered, my mother had appeared on the scene: "Oh! That's where you've been. I was looking all over for you. What were you doing on the stairs? Has anyone seen you? Come along, let's go, he's fine. It was all a pretense, as usual. He won't get me here again! What a farce!"

I knew that he wasn't going to die. I knew that she was irritated. I understood that I was completely in the dark about their history.

And then a few months later I saw them together again, but on this fourth occasion, he was dead.

It was a boiling hot summer day when I learned of his

death. It was afternoon. I was with my friends, a group of teenagers together on a shaded patio. We were waiting for the heat to die down so we could play. It had been such a short time since I had gotten permission to go without my afternoon nap that when I saw my mother appear, I started to defend myself in the old way. In one second my apparatus of excuses, explanations and lies was at my disposal; the mechanism of childish deceit wasn't rusty yet. So that when she planted herself in front of me, dressed as if she were going to town, awkward and embarrassed, looking a little strange, and after a moment, when she said to me in a pitiful tone, "Your father has just died, go and dress, you must come back to Algiers with me," I relaxed. I saw the beautiful sky, the dazzling sea, the succulents with their pink and yellow star-shaped flowers. I was relieved. She didn't come there to deprive me of all that. The rest didn't concern me. Moreover, why this compassionate tone of voice in a matter concerning my father, about whom she had never been anything but spiteful? Because he was dead? Did death make him small, miserable, lamentable? He was the same to me: a stranger, a bachelor, boring, a little frightening and embarrassing with his awkward gestures meant to draw me to him. "Come and give me a kiss, my little minx." Usually my mother called him by his last name, "Tell Drapeau he still hasn't sent me my alimony." "Ask Drapeau to buy you some shoes," etc. Today she said "your father," as if he were her husband, as if they were a couple. You would have thought that they were bound by death, that death had made of them a family. This I could not imagine. It seemed to me false, and unhealthy, although I couldn't say why. I didn't dare look at her, I was longing for her to leave.

And still she stayed. I thought: "If, into the bargain, she cries, I'm getting out of there fast." No, she didn't cry; she was upset, she was waiting for me. "We have to go back to Algiers, and make all the arrangements."

It was odd to be driving at that time of day in the height of summer. Moreover no one was out there in the countryside. I saw the perfectly aligned rows of vines reel past, the avenues of eucalyptus, the copses of sea pines, the thickets of reeds, the aloes lifting their long flowering stalks into the colorless sky, the prickly pears crowned with fruit and, on the hillsides, set out as if on the flat before me, rectangles of cypresses enclosing small orange orchards. Through the rear window I could see the red dust we raised whirling so high and far that it eclipsed the entire countryside.

We had closed the windows so as not to choke on the dust. The heat was appalling. Who was driving? I don't know. Impossible to remember. At any rate, it was someone who didn't speak.

We were in the eye of the hurricane. Traveling so fast made the car noisy and the insanely agitated dust was our escort. Before us the landscape, weighed down by the heat, seemed paralyzed by the trembling of boiling air.

In this context, she got to talking: "We received the telegram a little while ago, after a delay of eight days on account of the postal strike. So your father's body is arriving this very afternoon. Nothing is arranged.... We could have rented a mortuary chapel. There's a very good one on the waterfront. But we received word too late. We'll have to set it up at the house. Late as it is, I was able to get the undertaker to go and get Maurice's body from the ship and deliver it to the fifth floor. The thing is, the coffins are unloaded only after the passengers and the freight, last of all! It'll be late...what a story!"

What is that supposed to mean, "your father's body," "Maurice's coffin," "the mortuary chapel," "the undertaker?" Above all, what is the meaning of "Maurice's body?" And then what she referred to as "the house" was not hers, not mine, not the "house" but "his" house. It was the house of a man who lived there with his souvenirs of travel, a collection of African masks, weapons, his razor, and that huge bed covered with panther skins in which I knew he must have carried on with his "tarts," as my mother called them.

There was incredible confusion and bustle in his apartment. The living room had been emptied of its furnishings "in order to get the coffin in it." Was a coffin as big as all that?

"The Church of Saint Charles is sending over the kneeling chairs."

Kneeling chairs here! So near the great bed, the razor, and the weapons?

"They're going to set up cots in the back bedrooms."

"Cots? Who for?"

"Why, for the family, of course. We're going to keep watch all night."

The family? But he didn't have any, he was alone. What my mother called the family was her family, the family that weighed him down for so long. They were coming here? It seemed improper to me. He never saw them. He wouldn't have wanted them to set foot in his house. He had told me on several occasions that it wasn't my mother who destroyed his family. It was them.

The hallways and other rooms in the apartment were obstructed by the furniture from the living room and the dining room. It had been reduced to a place of confusion, as in the wings of a theater where, because my father was a person of influence, everyone was getting ready to receive the city's notables who were going to file past them. Here and there, there was the agitation that precedes a funeral, complete with mourning crape, the sparkle of amethysts, the glistening of tears, and the crying of the jays.

Then they opened the double doors in the entryway. People began to whisper and to walk on tiptoe. The apartment was packed and padded, cold, ready for the macabre and worldly reception. It smelled of floor polish. There were flowers everywhere. The good smell of bourgeois cooking emanated from the pantry and the kitchen. They were preparing a potluck supper for those who were keeping the vigil.

From the landing, I kept an eye on the undertaker's assistants hoisting up my father's coffin, an object of heavy oak with bronze handles on the sides and a bronze crucifix on the lid. Numerous black men were busy, huffing and puffing, while commenting on the maneuvers required by the sharp turns in the staircase. They were put out by the elegant grillwork, the acanthus leaves, the scrolls and curlicues of wrought iron which protected the old, decrepit elevator, which was once more useless, too fragile really to hold the coffin; through which my peepee had passed so easily. It would have given way.

They kept climbing. Five interminable floors. And my father in there like a package. They set him down finally on the black-draped trestles. My mother, very dignified, very busy, gave orders like an expert. She showed me to my place — a solitary prie-dieu in the front. Wreaths and bunches of flowers were brought in. Because it was summer, they were made up of zinnias for the most part, dry flowers without a scent in splendid shades of mauve, ochre, carmine and gold. I remained there, on my knees, and I was bored in this contemplation. I had been taught not to turn and look at people in the street or in church. And I didn't dare look at who came and went. The rugs and the drapes absorbed the noises, leaving only rustlings, imperceptible fumbling, creaking from the prayer stools, and incomprehensible sniffings.

Since I had to stay there, I did. I thought of other things, of the beach I had left, my friends. How would they look at me when they saw me dressed in black, a color for grown-ups. I almost dozed off, my head propped up between my hands, my elbows on the back of the kneeling chair.

The odor of the plants came up at me as if summoned by the heat of the night and the flames of the tapers. Mixed with the perfume of the foliage in which I could detect cypress, asparagus, fern, elder, trees and plants whose branches are used to make the framework of wreaths, there came another odor, stale, a little nauseating. I tried to define it. It could not be the zinnias; those are dried flowers, smelling like dust. This odor is something else which isn't vegetable. A restlessness was born in me, something I couldn't define. An odor of standing water, of swamp? Yes, but barely perceptible: not so violent or precise. An intimate odor, embarrassing even. An unknown human odor.

My mother came towards me. With one hand on my shoulder, she leaned over me, speaking low, her face right against my cheek.

"Are you all right?"

"I'm all right. Don't you think there's a funny smell?"

Her hand pressed harder, she gripped my shoulder,

moving it back and forth as if to rock me.

"It's because he's been dead for several days. And in this heat! While it was being moved, the coffin must have knocked against something, there may be a small crack. I've already spoken to the undertakers about it. They'll take care of it, don't worry."

"Don't worry?" About what? The fact that you could smell my father rotting? Because that's what it was, decomposing flesh!

My dashing father with his cane and spats, shoes polished, nails manicured, teeth gleaming, smelling of eau de cologne. My father rotting away like on the day after a storm, when the sea throws up its carrion onto the sand, attracting large pestilent bluebottles. From his polished shoes, his starched collar and cuffs, his trousers impeccably creased came the juices of death. My father reeked, my father was crawling with worms! It was unbearable. I left, I ran to the farthest room and threw myself face down on a cool bed made with sheets that smelled fresh from the wash. With my head in the pillow I wept, I sobbed. To drive away the rot I tried to focus on living images, laughter, happy times, summer skies, the little waves at midday, somersaults in the grass and the boy I loved who took me in his arms and kissed me. I drank his sweet saliva which retained the taste of cigarettes and toothpaste. I fell asleep.

This would be the first and last time I slept at my father's, near him.

That is where the solitude began.

This man I didn't know, of whom I had seen so little. He was, without my wishing it, however, my only ally. I had never counted on him and now I had to go on without him, which made a great, inexplicable void. Something tenuous and disturbing had disappeared forever. Today I know where the emptiness came from: I no longer had the certainty of pleasing someone no matter what I did, as well as having been deprived of tenderness. Even when he had me do homework, his voice, his eyes ready to criticize, there was a kiss which I refused, but which was nonetheless a kiss for me.

From that time on and even now, a sudden urge to run, impelled by joy, by the desire to be loved and protected, to take refuge in my father's arms would come over me. He would cradle me, rock me from side to side. We would dance together shifting from one foot to the other in a slow and tender rhythm: "There, there, my daughter, you are safe in my arms. Relax, my big girl, rest." He would scarcely be any taller, my face up against his. How would he smell? How strong would he be? I do not know

For me, Father is an abstract word without meaning, since Father goes with Mother, and those two persons in my life are unconnected, far from one another, like two planets obstinately following their different paths in the unchanging orbits of their separate existences. I was on the mother planet, and, at regular but distant intervals, we would intersect the path of the father planet, shrouded in its unwholesome nimbus. Then I would be ordered to to shuttle between the two, and, as soon as I had set foot again in the realm of the mother, as soon as she had retrieved me, she seemed to accelerate her course, as if to carry me away more quickly from the ill-fated father planet.

When I too became a solitary planet, obedient like all planets, and began to follow my trajectory through the great blue-black skies of existence, for a long time I tried to get closer to the Father. But, not knowing him, weary, even a little sad, I had to abandon my investigations. I know that I know nothing of the paternal side of men, if indeed there is one.

In the dead end of the cul-de-sac, stretched out on the couch, looking up at the ceiling, my eyes shut, the better to establish communication with the forbidden, the unnamable, the unthinkable, I would find my father at last, thinking that his absence—his nonexistence even—had opened up in me a kind of deep and hidden sore in whose infections I would find the germs of my illness. So I applied myself to gathering up all memories of him, the merest thread of an image.

For a long time I had two recurring nightmares in childhood and adolescence. In one of them I relived a scene which had actually taken place: it was at the zoo at Vincennes.

In order for me to really see the lions and tigers, my father had set me down on a parapet overhanging the deep moat that separates the wild animals from the public. He held me securely. In reality I was greatly afraid but didn't show it. In the nightmare, what I feared took place: I was falling into the moat and when I awoke, I was suffocating with terror at the moment the animals were coming after me to rip me to shreds. I was six or seven years old.

In the other nightmare, I was younger—two or three years old. (Certain times I was only a few months old.) I was perched on my father's shoulders; we were lost in a snow-covered pine forest. The snow, which I had never seen save in photographs, made this place even more beautiful, extraordinary; I had the feeling that it was forbidden me, that I couldn't stay there very long. And yet we couldn't find the way out. The weather was menacing and we went around in among the black pine trees, finding only other black pines and our own tracks in the snow. My father held my ankles; I felt his head warm between my legs. He was laughing, he wasn't nervous at all. But I knew that night was about to fall and that we were lost forever... I awoke drenched with perspiration.

So it was I discovered that the Thing was a part of my universe since I was a baby, and that my father could do nothing to protect me from it. He had only the dimensions my mother had given him. My father is a complete stranger, never a part of my life.

Sometimes I look at the few photographs that I have of him towards the end of his life, the way I had known him, looking for all the world like a million dollars. I prefer the others, taken when he was young and his character was still inchoate. Difficult, stubborn, and proud, he'd run away from his parents' big house in La Rochelle and had found himself a job in Paris as a laborer on a building site when he was fifteen. He'd sworn never to set foot in his house until he had his engineer's degree in his pocket. A degree he would have earned on his own. In one picture I see a young worker in heavy boots, and trousers which were too long and too big, as if they were held up by string, sleeves rolled up, shirt open at the chest, his head tilted, laughing in the sun, in the back joists and beams. In his hand he holds a bouquet of wild snapdragons. To whom was he going to give them?

He had gone to night school, had passed all his examinations. All, while continuing his life as a worker. He ended up becoming an engineer at the government engineering school. He liked to talk about that time, of the troubles he had as the young son of parents who were well off, living the backbreaking life of an apprentice. He rubbed the skin off his back under the weight he carried, and in the evening after work, while the men gathered around a fire amid the rubbish and scrap iron, they heated big cauldrons of water, which they would then pour over him. Then he could take off his shirt which blood, as it had dried, had glued to his shoulders. He told me the others laughingly called him the Prince because of his fine hands and his delicate skin. He had a nostalgia for the camaraderie and the hard life. He never fully reverted to bourgeois life. It could be seen from the way he would grab a tool. My mother said: "He's not one of us; you only have to see him eat." And it is true that at meals he leaned over his plate a little, as if he wanted to protect it with his arms, regarding what was on it with great seriousness and satisfaction. Food shouldn't be wasted. He didn't like that.

I don't know how I came to have at home in a drawer his engineering diploma, a license to operate a motorbike as well as an operator's license for gasoline-powered vehicles, letters of recommendation from bosses in the course of the years, apprentice, workman, foreman, and, finally, engineer. One photograph from this period: on a tennis court delivering a backhand shot. It is apparent that the ball surprised him as he was moving back and caught him off balance. His body is at the same time stretched way out, as if uncoiled from the tip of his toes to his hair, and supported by that long racket, all his strength concentrated in his right wrist, his left arm flung up against the sky, a beautiful hand, fine and strong.

This was in the time before he had tuberculosis, when he didn't know my mother. Looking at his fine hands, his dazzling smile, his slender, muscular body, I think he would have pleased me.

# Chapter V

"Talk, say whatever comes into your head; try not to choose or reflect, or in any way compose your sentences. Everything is important, every word."

It was the only remedy he gave me and I gorged myself on it. Perhaps it was my weapon against the Thing: that flood of words, that maelstrom, that mass of words, that hurricane! Words swept away distrust, fear, lack of understanding, severity, will, order, law, discipline as well as tenderness, sweetness, love, warmth and freedom.

Vocabulary was like a word game, thanks to which I reconstituted the image of a little girl sitting very properly at a big table, hands on either side of her plate, sitting up straight, not touching the back of the chair, by herself, across from a man with a moustache who offers her a piece of fruit, smiling. Crystal saltcellars with silver tops, Sèvres china, the bell that hung from the chandelier and on which Columbine and Pierrot waited to sound the buzzer back in the pantry when they were made to kiss.

The words made the scene come alive. Once again I was a little girl. Then, when the image became obliterated and I again became a thirty-year-old woman, I asked myself, Why the rigid posture, hands folded on the table-cloth, the back of the chair forbidden to touch? Why the boredom and embarrassment while facing my father? Who forced it upon me? Why? There I am on the couch, keeping my eyes shut tight in order to retain my hold on the little girl. I was really her and me. Then everything was easy to understand. I began to see clearly the outline of my mother's grip on me.

To find myself, I must find my mother and strip away the mask and penetrate the secrets of family and class.

I closed my eyes: I was the little girl lying in her bed, the sheets taut, a crucifix on the wall above her head, eyes turned towards a closed door, her dolls arranged according to size. In the room, a wood fire dying in the hearth which gave birth to volcanic transports, exploding the shadows.

Waiting for my mother. I struggled against the sleep which might have made me miss her coming in there. I was good. "If you're not good, I won't kiss you goodnight."

I began to speak of my mother, never stopping until the end of the analysis.

Over the years I explored the very depths of her being, as though she were a dark cavern. Thus did I make the acquaintance of the woman she wanted me to be. Day after day I had to weigh the extent of her desperation to create what in her opinion was a perfect being. I had to measure the force of her will to distort body and mind, to make them take the path she decided upon. It was between the woman she had wanted to bring into the world and myself that the Thing had lodged itself. My mother had led me astray to such a point that I was no longer conscious of what she had done so profoundly and so well, nor did I understand.

What I now remember of my mother is having loved her to distraction in childhood and adolescence, then having hated her, and, finally, having abandoned her just before her death, which, moreover, put a stop to my analysis.

Warm nights when I was young and couldn't sleep. When, after tossing and turning in my bed, after reading until my attention was exhausted, I would get up in search of nothing in particular. I wandered through the large, sleeping apartment, in the corridor shaped like a U: one branch of it ran along the bedrooms, the base giving access to the living and dining rooms; the other branch ran through the pantry to the kitchen. I knew the place so well that I didn't need a light. Moreover, I always liked walking in the dark, and during that period the darkness and the mystery were well suited to the feeling of being on edge or to the anxious excitement which children sometimes experience without being able to really say what it is. All that lay ahead of me, all that I longed for and feared!

In my blind wanderings, lamentations really, it happened more than once that, after passing the first turning in the corridor, I was drawn from my solitude by a far-off light which cast red and gold streaks on the glass doors to the living room. One of these reflections, deformed by a flaw in one of the little panes, became circular, like a sort of eye, distorting the purity of the transparent glass. These glimmerings indicated that my mother was in there.

I advanced more quickly and more silently. I came into the entryway opposite the door that opened onto the work area. I stopped at the frontier of night. At the end of the corridor, I saw her bathed in light, which was the more dazzling in contrast to the deeper shadow in which I found myself. In her hand a large glass of wine. She was motionless, sad, and calm. She looked far away, very far away. She would drink in great gulps, sometimes, closing her eyes. I had the impression that it did her good. The glass emptied, she went into the semidarkness of the pantry, opened the refrigerator, which gave off a gay and reassuring light, took out a bottle, filled her glass, turned out the kitchen light, and then, feeling her way, went towards her room, her viaticum in her hand. She locked her door. I knew she wouldn't stir from there until the following day.

While she was alone in the light of the kitchen, I saw her drink her white wine and I wanted to be the wine, to do her some good, to make her happy, to attract her attention. I promised myself that I would find her a treasure.

I thought so much about treasure during the siestas, I would begin to perspire with excitement. It's in the ground that precious stones are found. So, I went out into the riveting sun, the air as thick as jam. I went out through the French doors, closing the shutters behind me, and took off among the vines. Crouching, I scratched at the ground. I scratched until it hurt, until I had the sensation that my nails were coming off. I looked for pebbles which did not look like the others. I would fill my pockets. In among the pebbles, perhaps there were diamonds, emeralds or rubies. What a surprise she would have! Her face would relax, she would kiss me, she would love me.

The blossoms of certain flowers attracted me, particularly the canna and arum lilies. What I saw in them, looking closely, gave me vertigo: velvets of gold and fire, drops of elixir, damasks and satins. These could only be fabulous jewelry boxes. I'd tear the flowers apart and find nothing. In the evening, before the spectacle of the ravaged plants, she'd say, "You don't like flowers, I love them; you mustn't ruin them."

I was gasping for breath, before the little piles of pebbles which I took from my pocket, my mind in a frenzy of excitement, my heart rejoicing at the idea of the marvels surely contained therein which were going to light up her life! My mother said: "Don't drag such filth into the house." There were also reeds and bamboos. The sheaths formed in the spaces between the rings in their stems seemed to me to be coffers for rare objects. The mandarin buttons which she collected ought to be found. There I would rip open the leafy, sharp-edged shafts, exploring each little tube. There I would find white cotton wadding and sometimes tiny, fragile offerings which took up the entire orifice. But nothing else, nothing, nothing. When I had had enough of these accumulated deceptions, I would take the heart of the plant, at the end of the shaft, and make of it a student flute. The other children would imitate me and we would set out, a small but deafening band, for games of hide and seek or tag.

Never did the mandarin buttons or the jewels or the nuggets leave my mind completely.

At least I got good marks in school.

As the years went by and my understanding increased, I knew beyond the shadow of a doubt that our grounds were not auriferous or diamondiferous. I came to know that reeds could not contain mandarin buttons, for these were made of ivory and were not to be found in our part of the world, but belonged to officials who had lived in China a million miles away from here. I came to know that the beauty of flowers for those who had a taste for them was a treasure in itself.

To compensate, I learned about the value and existence of money, barter, and trade. I started selling old books and bottles, collections of *L'Illustration* and *Marie-Claire* accumulating in the storeroom. I compared the sum represented by adding up my pennies to the price of the smallest mandarin button on display in the antique shops. The subtraction gave a disheartening result. I acquired an awareness of her tastes and needs. For my mother, who loved only "priceless things," there was nothing on the market within my reach. The door to her happiness was, therefore, closed to me, since I thought it could only be opened with presents. My love was not, apparently, the right key.

I took refuge unconsciously in the world of dreams, despising the blunders of my early years, the absurdity of my affectations and the folly of my hopes. All these fruitless efforts had made me reject myself; I was ashamed. But I discovered that in secret I could make up who I was for myself alone.

After school I devoted all my time to self-glorification, to creating some measure of self-esteem. Scarcely was I in the house again than I would go out onto the terrace and organize world championships, cosmic championships. Alone against the universe, but with a will to triumph and a need to express myself that made me fearless, I even longed for the confrontation.

There was nothing on the red brick terrace save for

some firewood and the sky above me. Thousands of swifts circled above my head, chirping shrilly. There must also have been the noises from the town, but I have no memory of them. I remember only the sky, the swifts, and the red surface on which I drew a hopscotch court. All the girls in my class, in my school, everyone was there, down to the last one. We'd see who'd win.

The choice of a marker occupied me the most. The best marker was a Valda cough drop box filled with mud. But, playing frantically, the way I did, the metal wore out very fast, and the bottom would come apart like any old tin can. Having no pocket money, this was serious. It meant waiting for the next family member to catch a cold, and meanwhile, for want of something better, playing with whatever can I could find, which compromised the championships.

For each person I represented, I played with equal passion and power. When it was my turn I shook with fear. I often played better for the others than for myself.

"Go on, miss!"

This time the young lady was me! My ankle bone became rigid. An ankle bone whose flexibility was the guarantee of victory. I was on the watch to see the rules were applied with extreme severity, especially when it was my turn. I was not interested in any half victory. The merest overlap of a shoe on a line meant elimination. Several times I had tried to cheat, playing for myself, but triumph turned to ashes in my mouth. When I got to "heaven" it was really heaven. I could put both feet on the ground and relax. I would calculate what my chances were. It never occurred to me that I was the one who played for the girl who was momentarily in the lead; I had to be the winner. I'd take off again, hopping on one foot.

When they came to find me for dinner it would often be dark, but I saw the white chalk lines that outlined my field of battle perfectly. The swifts had taken off with the sun.

I organized handball, jacks, jump rope, and yo-yo tournaments, whichever game was played the most in the playground at my school.

When I got to be the world champion, I met with such satisfaction I understood perfectly what my mother said about the benefits of Communion. She was secure in the knowledge that Christ, once having entered the heart of a person, gives happiness, goodness, wisdom and peace: exactly what I felt after winning an exacting championship.

For I had taken Communion and was very attentive to the sanctifying effects of the Eucharist. It hadn't happened for me. Quite simply, I dreaded the idea of the tiny little man with long hair and a goatee wandering in the caverns of my heart. At the same time, I was very apprehensive on his behalf about the passage from the mouth to the heart, that formidable toboggan run of my larynx. They had taught me in the catechism that the Lord was to be found in His entirety in the tiniest crumb of the Host. As it was wartime, and economies had to be made in all things, the priest divided the wafers in four. Logically, the smaller the piece, the smaller the creature it contained and the worse its chance of getting lost in the complications of my organism.

I was very preoccupied with what went on inside my body. When I was a child, my mother had told me, "If you swallow a cherry stone, a cherry tree will grow in your stomach." I deduced from this that if I swallowed a grape seed a vine would grow inside me, an apricot stone, an apricot tree, etc. I payed attention when I ate fruit, and if unhappily I let a stone slip down, I would not be able to get to sleep. I could feel the tree growing inside me; I waited from one minute to the next to see branches heavy with fruit spring out of my nostrils, my ears and my mouth. I felt my fingers changing into roots. After vomiting, I was able to get to sleep. Much later, I was aware of my mother taking me in her arms, cleaning my hair, changing my nightgown, sheets, and pillowcase. I was in a state of beatitude, perfect happiness. I heard her say to the nurse: "She can't be digesting the noodles in her soup. Look, they're still intact."

I fell asleep in her arms, held close to her. I was the happiest little girl in the world.

But the championships and the experience of victory had given me a value I had never had. I felt worthy of my mother and her severity. The kisses and caresses I had longed for and didn't receive were for silly little girls! I knew how to fight, how to show generosity, honesty, and, in a word, goodness. Wasn't that just what she wanted of me? And I would be better still by practicing my religion, to which she was so attached, and that was how I decided to go to morning Mass with her.

I was at the age when adolescence begins to bite into the mind, to mold and soften the body. I walked near her in the early morning; our footsteps resonated on the asphalt. We would say little to one another. My schoolbag was heavy. All the heavier, since, with my championships and my mother in my head, I hadn't had time to do the homework for the day. I would do it a little later, when I came out of church, on my way to school in the bus and then the streetcar.

"Are you quite sure you haven't eaten or drunk anything?"

"Quite sure. Even when I brushed my teeth, I was careful not to swallow any water."

"That's good. How long is it since you've been to confession?"

"Ten days."

"That's a long time. Don't you go to confession with your school?"

"Yes, tomorrow."

"Well, you'd better not take Communion today or tomorrow either. We're late. You wouldn't have time to go to confession before Mass."

At confession I always said the same thing: "Father, I've lied, I've been disobedient, I've been greedy, I said bad words." No matter how I racked my brains, I couldn't come up with anything more. This wasn't possible, however, since my mother had said that even saints sinned at least seven times a day. So much the worse for me; I didn't dare look at the priest. I would blurt out through the wooden grille: "I have lied, I have been disobedient, I have been greedy, I have said bad words."

"Is that all?"

"Yes, that's all."

"You have not sinned against purity, my child?"

"No, Father."

"Never?"

"Never." I didn't know what he was talking about.

"That's good. Recite the Act of Contrition."

Now that was a bit of bravery. I knew it by heart, both the old way and the new. During the war they had changed the words to simplify them. I liked the Church modernizing itself!

"My God, I am very sorry to have offended You who

are infinitely good, infinitely kind, and because sin displeases You. With the help of Your Holy Grace, I firmly resolve, not to offend You anymore, and to do penance."

"For your penance you will say three Hail Marys and three Our Fathers; go in peace, my child."

Penance is recited on the rosary. First the crucifix, followed by the small beads on the end of the free chain for the sign of the cross and then the series of Hail Marys. At my house there was quite an assortment of rosaries in gold, silver, crystal, amethyst, fake ones, rosaries from Lourdes, from Jerusalem, from Rome, rosaries blessed by the Pope, by Monsignor so-and-so, by the sainted priest of Ars, my grandmother's rosary, my great-grandmother's, my mother's, her wedding rosary, the First Communion rosary, the betrothal rosary, the twentieth-birthday rosary. It took a special technique to get to the last bead at the end of the prayer. I hardly ever made it. Either I had gotten to the last bead with half the prayer left to say, so that I had to roll the bead for a long time between my thumb and index finger, or else I had finished and I still had three beads left, and I would have to calculate; one bead for "ah" and one bead for "men."

During the Mass she was very withdrawn. She stayed on her knees almost all the time. I imitated her, and when I went out of the church, the straw of the prayer stool would have planted deep furrows in my knees. I watched her, to do as she did. I saw her beautiful profile, her straight nose, her well-defined mouth, her eyelids closing on green eyes, her gray veil resting like mist on wavy hair, her hands like a queen's, folded, long, white, exquisite, her nails, polished and filed.

There was hardly anyone in church: a few old women

half hidden in the shadows of the side aisles, and the two of us in the front row of the nave, on the family prie-dieu. At that hour she acted as sacristan, made the responses and rang the little bell. We even sang. We had low-pitched voices, both of us. The Consecration, the Communion, those intense moments in which I was unable to feel the intensity, which made me lower my head from shame even more. That made me pray even harder. Thinking of every word.

"*Introibo ad altare Dei. Ad Deum qui laetificat juventutem meam.*

"*Ecce agnus dei, ecce qui tollit peccata mundi.*

"*Domine, non sum dignus ut intres sub tectum meum. Sed tantum dic verbo et sanabitur anima mea.*"

I was doing Latin, the translation was simple: "Lord, I am not worthy to receive you under my roof; only say the word and my soul will be healed."

If only He'd say the word! Fill me with grace! So that she'd love me! Nothing but the sun rising like a miracle, making the stained glass window behind the altar reflect the light. The Christ with feet and hands crossed, His side pierced, hung poised in the glowing air with His skinny thighs and embroidered loincloth.

Afterward the mad race through the gardens of Galland Park, an open book in my hand, my schoolbag open, my uniform in disarray. And then history homework, math homework and in the streetcar, the translation into or out of Latin on my lap. Everything shaking, jerking about!

"Young lady! Your exercise book looks like a dust cloth!"

And for good reason! As if I had the time to make my hyphens straight, to write titles and subtitles in different

76

colored inks and to put in the date!

"And it is badly written!"

It was true, the streetcar wasn't helping any. Handwriting was like religion: I tried hard, but it just wouldn't come. I would have given anything to make "D's" like Solange Dufresnes, or "M's" like my mother. Moreover, I made blots and scratched words out, my fountain pens never working.

"It's too bad, your homework is good, but I am taking two points off for carelessness."

I didn't care. She didn't look at my grades. At least, she only looked at the bad ones, her pretty finger following the column of figures stopped at the ones below A.

"C! You got a C (or a D or an F)."

"It's only in sewing."

"But sewing is important. You have to know how to do hems, to say nothing of sewing on your buttons. Really, I wonder what we're going to do with you. I'm afraid we have a slattern on our hands."

A slattern! A slattern was like scullion, squamous, squeamish, squalid, scabrous. It was something limp, fermented and slimy. That didn't at all resemble the picture I had of her which I myself wanted to resemble. A little while before, after the Mass, she smelled of lavender. Her overweight body with broad hips but slender, good-looking legs was tightly buttoned into a gray-blue gabardine suit with clean, impeccable lines. Her walking shoes were polished. She was going to take a bus which would carry her to the upper reaches of the city, where she would gather up street children at one of the bus terminals. Everybody knew her there: ticket collectors, conductors and inspectors. They held a little reception for her every morning, giving her little bouquets of anemones, jonquils, or pansies, depending on the season, homemade cakes made with love. Newborns were presented to her, wrapped haphazardly.

Before leaving me she had made a little sign of the cross with her thumb on my forehead, as if saying goodbye to me. "Go and work hard."

I would start running towards the school, leaving her behind to the poor, who crowded around her, happy to be in her presence.

I imagined the mark on my forehead was a stigma, visible to everyone, resembling dense moss, rounded as a cushion and soft to the touch, as a scar which invades the letters engraved in stone on old, damp tombs.

On its own, religion was lacking in significance. I never had faith or was in a state of grace, though not for want of prayer, begging God to send manna from heaven to appease my anxiety and guilt. For, of course, I didn't possess the Christian virtues which had been described to me. In the course of these meditations, to which I was often subjected (I attended a convent school, and had a mother who was so involved herself in religion), I was so terribly bored. I couldn't think. If, for example, I was told to meditate for a quarter of an hour on the subject of Christian charity, I'd begin like the others. I put my head in my hands and said to myself, "Love one another, it is truly good. Yes, we must love one another, it's true, and it isn't easy, because there are those one has no desire to love, and there are others one would like to love, but who won't allow it." And that was as far as it went. I began to think of other things. I'd try to concentrate on the fabric in my dress, the weave of the cloth. But every time, my mind would wander and I'd think about what I was going to do at recess, or after Mass, or next Thursday. I couldn't stop myself from thinking about such things and I was ashamed. I tried to stop myself and really suffered from this inability to deliver myself from this distraction. As I was persuaded that Paradise and God's forgiveness were to be obtained only through sacrifice, suffering, difficulty and misery, I inferred logically, that I would go straight to Hell, and at that very moment even God was knitting his brow and weeping from the vexation I was causing Him. I was in a bad way when I came out from such soul-searching: I'd wounded God, whom my mother loved, to whom she sacrificed everything. There was no resolution.

If I could not conform within, I had to conform without. Correct my behavior, be polite, a good student, clean, virtuous, obedient, economical, obliging, modest, charitable, and honest, all of which I was able to do, more or less, often less, because I loved a good time. I got my clothes dirty and my hands, I scratched myself, my exercise books were full of ink blots and erasures. All the same, I was good though not very presentable, and made an obvious effort to lead a truly religious life.

In fact, the only time I came to have a religious attitude was in moments of ecstasy created by objects or anecdotes. Something very concrete. Stories of miracles, for example, when Jesus walked on the water, when He caused fish and loaves to multiply, when He healed the sick and raised the dead, etc. These stories made me dream. I really loved Jesus as someone who could do things, someone I would really like to have known, someone, moreover, with whom I would gladly have walked the roads of Galilee. Yes, I would have liked to go to Paradise and find Him there, and see Him perform His hocus-pocus. In much the same spirit, I loved the moment of the Consecration when the bread and wine are transformed into the body and the blood of Christ. One day I had remarked that the Host in no way resembled the bread. My mother explained to me how and why they made the wafers, and that it was only Protestants who ate bread for Communion. At once I believed that I had sinned by wanting bread, and I began to regard the Host as though it were a large, round, crusty loaf such as one sees in certain paintings depicting the Last Supper. In any case, I was very happy on Easter Day. I found the little morsels of brioche which they gave out at High Mass for the occasion delicious. I also loved religious music. Certain chants overwhelmed me, particularly the Stabat Mater on Good Friday. I had a low voice, and the girls' choir always sang very high. In order to get my voice in their range, I had to wrinkle my brow and find the music as far down as my toes, which gave me vertigo and a light migraine headache that I very much appreciated. It seemed to me such discomforts were a sign of mysticism.

The only meditations which had been really full of reflections were those in which I plunged every night after saying my prayers on my knees before the crucifix that hung on the wall at the head of my bed. The cross was made of ebony; Jesus was in ivory, as was a kind of scroll above his head bearing the inscription *INRI*. The nails were bronze. This object was given to me as a present on the day of my First Communion. For my edification my mother had itemized the precious materials which had gone into it. "It's a very beautiful crucifix, you know. It's very valuable. It's a genuine work of art." Nothing is too beautiful for God. So every night I admired the ebony, the ivory, the bronze and the tortured Jesus. For a long time I would contemplate the nails. Those in the hands I imagined having gone in easily; they had slid in between the bones. But those in the feet must have been more difficult. Surely they must have been driven in any which way. It made my feet hurt. And the crown of thorns! Impossible to put His head back. It would have bumped into the cross and that would have driven the thorns even further into the skull. He'd known how to assume the best possible position, head tilted forward, His beard on His chest. The triangular wound on his side didn't inspire me very much. His torso was so thin, with ribs protruding like an abandoned hull or like poor dogs sniffing in the garbage. It was the thinness that gave me pause for thought, not the wound in the shape of a triangle, barely showing in the ivory. On the other hand, the legs were quite muscular. They were the legs of an athlete. And then the modest cloth covering the genitals was something else! Those beautiful legs, the mystery behind the rags...I didn't linger overly long in that zone, and yet, it brought tears to my eyes when I thought He died for me. To conclude the ritual, I would stick the nails into the ends of my fingers. They were bound to do a little harm. I think I would have liked them to draw blood. It never happened. Then quickly I made the sign of the cross, a sort of magical confusion, and with one quick somersault, I was under the sheets, which retained the sweet smell of laundry detergent, my head on the feather pillow, which I hugged lovingly. Even in the middle of summer I wouldn't risk the exposure of a leg or a hand outside the bedclothes, lest the evil demons who were under my bed grab me and carry me to Hell. In my grandmother's old catechism I had seen two big illustrations: the death of a Christian and the death of a sinner. The Christian was half sitting up, supported in his final agony by angels with beautiful wings. His eyes were

ing noise of cicadas.

Happy memories were attached to the farm like garlands to a Christmas tree. Why? Was it because I spent my vacations there, where time was more my own than during the school year? Was it because the space was limitless? The farm was Algeria, the city was France.

I loved the red furrows planted with vines, the rows of eucalyptus trees, the wild yet sparse vegetation in forests of stunted pines, pepper trees, gorse bushes, and arbutus, and the dry soil where tufts of thyme grew. Beside the vast arid spaces the fertility and riotous growth of the irrigated areas was offered up for me daily like a festival.

Over the vines and as far as the horizon floated the smell of freshly turned earth. The gardens from morning to night were an ecstasy for the nostrils: jasmine, orange, fig, datura, cypress, and, last of all, after the evening watering, after the earth had opened its heart to the coolness, the subtle, joyous perfume of the marvels of Peru. It was the same for the colors. Discretely in the red-ochre background of the rich agricultural land, the green-black of the vines, the gray-green of the olive trees, the beige of the vine-stock, and the trunks were aligned under the same worn-out blue of the too brilliant sky. But near the ponds there were pinks, yellows, indigo, white, bright rose, orange, violet, emerald, turquoise, sapphire, amethyst, diamond. I wanted to dance in the middle of it with little bells on my feet and hands so that the whole world might hear my satisfaction.

The house was squat and imposing, built by the original ancestor from Bordeaux who had wanted it to resemble the houses of his own country: simple, practical, solid, and grand. In the beginning, it was a fortified farm surrounded by walls sixteen or seventeen feet high. When

I knew it, only one section of the high walls remained, on the side of the courtyard through which one entered by an enormous gate made of massive timbers. Inside the living quarters, the rooms were vast and opened out onto the others. The huge living room, which ran the length of the front of the house, was furnished for adults who loved to drink port wine, smoke Havana cigars and listen to classical music. Through its bay windows you could look beyond two romantic mock pepper trees, showering their serrated leaves and their bunches of round red blossoms, and the beautiful vineyards to the horizon.

Slow yet attentive service was provided by Arab domestics who wore embroidered vests, white trousers, loud silk neckerchiefs and gold sequins on their tattooed foreheads while serving the meals on festive occasions. Their bare feet made no noise on the black and white tile floor. Their hands, red with henna, respectfully manipulated the family silver.

Between the earth and the sky, on the triangular pediment of the dwelling had been carved the date of construction: 1837.

There were vast gardens there. First, a garden to walk in, with flower beds, parallel plantings of clipped rosemary, arbors; one in the form of a gazebo was overrun by a jasmine with huge star-like blooms. That was the jasmine Youssef, the gardener, picked on those evenings when he went out whoring, God knows where, in the empty countryside. He would put a few tightly bunched sprigs above his left ear against his silk tarboosh, leaving a trail of perfume wherever he went. He was close-fisted with them and would only give these flowers to me from time to time. This garden bored me a little. While I found it beautiful, it was far too formal for me. I preferred the garden that had the cutting flowers and plants and the vegetables.

Early in the morning, my mother would prepare flat baskets and pruning shears and we would start off.

I loved these early mornings in the still cool greenness of the dawn. We would lay bare new flowers and leaves which the night had made ready for us. Sometimes we would wait a week or more for a rose or dahlia to bloom. Each morning we would make a prolonged stop before the bud, checking on its progress. Tightly closed at first, it slowly grew larger, with a small opening at the top to display its colorless petals, still tightly furled and stuck together. Then, one fine morning, the bud began to burst in places, like the brassiere of the Spanish laundress who couldn't manage to conceal her great breasts.

"When it opens we'll put it in the bouquet with French marigolds. The yellow will go well, as will the other paler roses, the ones with a pearly sheen that grow beside the row of almond trees. I think it's going to be even more beautiful than last year."

And so, absorbed and satisfied, we gathered the flowers which would revive or change the bouquets in the house. Sometimes, in the entrance hall, she would make a flower arrangement more than six feet high, with medlar branches and sprays of yucca with their pyramids of thick white flowers.

Flower arranging was part of the education of a girl with my background. My mother excelled at it, and, as for me, I loved the scents, colors, the shapes, and the mysteries in the hearts of flowers in which I used to think I'd find mandarin buttons when I was little. I never stopped hoping that one day I would find something to make her still more happy and beautiful, something which would take away this lack of understanding between us, my inability — I never knew why — to satisfy her completely.

It was during these lessons in flower arranging that I got along best with her. She taught me how to place flowers in a vase. First she showed me how to choose the vases according to the flexibility of the stems that we were going to arrange in them. She showed me how some combinations were impossible or very difficult because of the flexibility of certain flowers, which would not go with the stiffness of some others.

In the course of the morning, we never failed to spend considerable time in the vegetable garden, which smelled of celery and tomato plants.

Vegetables are like precious objects! Eggplants, melons, pumpkins, peppers, tomatoes, cucumbers, broad beans, zucchini, green beans, fresh, swollen, gleaming with health, sending out their bright or dark reflections from the depths of their heavy foilage. Parsley, carrots, turnips, radishes, lettuces, onions, shallots, chives, chervil, in broad, orderly rows, smooth or scalloped, breathing out the smells of good cooking, the family table, suggesting peace, warmth. The garlic blossoms crowning their long stems, displaying delicate pinks above reds, violets, and greens.

After, there were the orange trees, bearing throughout the seasons, tangerine, lemon, grapefruit, the medlar trees under which we would stop to taste the fruit full of juice in which the cool of the night was captive still.

When it was the season, we would always end our tour of inspection in front of the large shaded bed of violets, from which we made round, perfumed nosegays. The long hands of my mother searched nimbly under the broad leaves sparkling with the dew, picking out the blossoms.

# Chapter VI

French Algeria lived out its agony. It was at the time when, according to specialists, the war in Algeria was a military victory for the French. The best of our soldiers, those who had just taken a terrible beating in Indochina, organized the great search-and-destroy campaign on the stony soil of that mountain country: the boys of the constituency, the youth of Saint-Malo, Douai, Noanne, and elsewhere besides (they will be marked with a red brand, like beasts of an accursed herd) with their helmets and boots, their automatic weapons and armored vehicles, each of them having received orders to wipe out as many as possible of the skinny and fanatical partisans. The children of France fell in hand-to-hand combat, while vomiting up their guts and their patriotism; even more of the others fell. Finally, the fighting ended for want of those who could fight. The partisans who had managed to get away sought refuge in the towns, where they had become heroes, and as in the fairy tales, words fell from their lips like diamonds and roses in the casbahs and the poorer quarters.

So the French stopped fighting. For the Ministry of War in Paris, there was no more war in Algeria. No more artillery, or bullets, or machine guns, or hand grenades, or napalm to be sent over there. In the bookkeeping of French economy, there was, as in a bathtub, a dead calm. The electrodes, the open-handed blows, fists in the face, kicks in the belly and the balls, cigarettes put out on nipples and pricks, whatever could be found, merely kindling. Torture, that didn't count, and because it didn't count it didn't exist. Torture was a figment of the imagination, nothing more.

And yet, for French Algeria, it was the same humiliating and shameful agony. The degradation of everything was in the blood of civil war which ran into the gutters and overflowed onto the sidewalks, following the geometric patterns in the cement of civilization. The end was accompanied by the age-old ways in which Arabs settled accounts: bodies disemboweled, genitals cut off, fetuses hung up, throats slashed.

It seems to me that the Thing took root in me permanently when I understood that we were to assassinate Algeria. For Algeria was my real mother. I carried her inside me the way a child carries the blood of his parents in his veins.

What a caravan I led through Paris into the cul-de-sac! What an absurd troop! While lacerated Algeria showed her infected wounds in the full light of day, I revived a country of love and tenderness where the earth smelled of jasmine and fried food. To the doctor's I brought with me the workers, the employees, the "domestics" who peopled my childhood! All those who made a little girl of me, who knew how to laugh and run, to steal candied chick-peas or pickled broad beans from old Ahmed's tray, to sing the *Laroulila*, to dance to the drums, to brown the fritters and to pour the mint tea.

In the town and on the farm I was a solitary child. After morning Mass, my mother left to care for the poor in the dispensaries of the city or in the mud huts of the countryside. Weary and exhausted, she did not return until evening. All day long she'd given injections and applied dressings, listened to complaints and gratitude, not to mention having liberally offered her patience, her attention, her knowledge and her love, all for the greater glory of her God. In secret, she baptized the dying: "At least, their lost souls could be recovered."

When she got back to the house, there was nothing left but a desire for sleep and a feeble instinct to do her duty; and not a scrap of patience left. I who was the privileged one, who lived under her roof, had no excuses at all for my weaknesses.

"If you had seen the misery I saw today, you would get down on your knees and pray to God to thank Him for having given you all that you have.

"When someone is lucky enough to have what you have, there is only one thing to do: praise the Lord, help others, and don't think about yourself.

"If you were to live just one day like the poor people I visit every day, you'd understand how lucky you are to be going to your school and you'd always be first in your class.

"If you knew what it is not to have any shoes, you'd take care of the ones you have." (The same went for dresses, coats, sweaters, etc.)

"There are people who have nothing to eat; finish what

you have on your plate; don't make a mess of your porridge; finish your calves' liver!"

She had achieved such a level of self-sacrifice and generosity of spirit that it was impossible for me to keep up with her. Her goodness, the sacrifices she made every day of her life, raised her so far up above me that it was discouraging.

So I found my way to the kitchen, the stables, the garden or the cellar, and it was there that I managed to live. I went to be with those who made life beautiful, those I loved and who loved me in return.

Without them, I know that I would have walled myself off internally; all my outlets would have been blocked by an inability to please my mother or to make her love me, by my complete and utter inability to understand her world, and by my conviction that I was ugly and bad.

Fortunately, because of the divorce and my mother's work, I didn't really have a family life. When I was very young, during the day, I saw only my Nanny, who was, in fact, an affectionate and ugly Spaniard. On me she lavished all the love she was unable to give to the *caballero* of her dreams. She covered me with kisses and cradled me, murmuring *"madre mia"* or *"pobrecita"* and *"ay, que guapa!"* She had three sisters who worked as chambermaids and laundresses for my mother and grandmother. They lived on the floor above. Jeannette, the youngest of the sisters and also the prettiest, used to practice incessantly for tango contests. Thus, fandango sessions were organized daily, with clapping hands, stamping heels, castanets, and *olé*'s in acid voices. She would wind up by its handle an old gramophone hidden in the linen closet, and with her sister Elyse, who acted as her cavalier, she would rehearse to the tempo 1,2; 1,2,3, a choreography made up of expert turns, perilous spins, and rapid advances winding up in reverse, on a note, in absolute immobility, one foot frozen in the air behind her, her paralyzed profile turned towards her cavalier (he staring fixedly at infinity), Jeannette's arm pulled up towards the ceiling by Elyse, who put everything she had into it.

Without ever having been asked, I never spoke of these sessions to my mother, who returned in the evening tired, beautiful and sad. In the entrance hall, she put down her prayer book and her mantilla on the tray for mail; she would recover them on her way to early Mass. Nanny worshipped her. She was already in her service, unimaginable for me, at the time when my mother was living with my father. Nanny knew everything. Once my mother was in the house, the atmosphere became hushed, silent and a little dramatic. I took my dinner in the pantry. I ate very correctly, as much to please my mother as to avoid a scolding from Nanny, who, the rest of time, laughed a lot no matter how I behaved. My mother looked in, in effect, to see how the meal was going. In bed I waited for her to kiss me goodnight.

Often I would hear whining from the bedroom. Through her door would come little noises, the rustling of tissue paper mingled with faint sobs, and sometimes a lament: "Ah, my God, my God." I knew she was on her bed, unwrapping the relics of my dead sister: slippers, locks of hair, and baby clothes. Nanny would then behave as though she were in church. She would cross herself, mumble prayers, her eyes suffused with tears. As for me, my heart was hard as a stone. On those nights—just as when I swallowed a pit and was afraid to feel a tree growing inside me—I would throw up my dinner and when my mother came to say goodnight, I was bathed in the liquid of my soup and the curdled bits of pudding. She would call Nanny to the rescue. "Don't you think this child vomits a lot?" Once again I had to be washed and changed, and while Nanny was remaking my bed I would fall asleep in my mother's arms. I still remember the ecstasy of drifting off to sleep tight against her, in her perfume and in her warmth.

A few years later when the war had come, I was approaching adolescence, and we had left the city for several months. We left partly out of prudence—"The Italians are going to bomb us any day now"—mostly for reasons of economy. The wine business wasn't doing well: "Wine doesn't sell anymore." This was nothing to be ashamed of since all the other growers were in the same boat. Our retreat even had something of the heroic about it: "One must sacrifice for one's country. Let's live like the peasants."

The city payroll was cut back. Nanny was now a chambermaid and her sisters were passed back and forth between friends and relations.

So lock, stock, and barrel we went to the farm, which was happiness as far as I was concerned.

In the morning I would pile into the old carriage driven by Aoued, along with the children of Kader and Barded. With the children of other workers in the area we found ourselves all together in one room in the village schoolhouse. I worked very hard in that school, and yet it seemed to me that I did nothing but amuse myself. The teacher rapped knuckles with a ruler, and from time to time, when his wife called him for one reason or another, he told us to take a rest because we were growing. Then he had some of us stretch out on the tables, others on the benches, and gave the order not to say a word in his absence.

Then on the way back to the farm, suddenly the familiar rooftops were visible through the branches of the eucalyptus trees, there, at the end of the little valley surrounded by vineyards. Bijou, the horse, was very old and let enormous farts. Right after, his tail rose up and revealed his behind, which would bloom like an enormous pink dahlia. Immediately he let go a succession of odorous droppings and we laughed until there were tears in our eyes. Aoued didn't approve, either because we were not polite in taking notice of this occurrence, or because he didn't want us to make fun of Bijou. He threatened us with his whip, which he would crack above our heads, calling us "sons of bitches" and "children of whores." But because the whole of it was delivered in Arabic, it was understood that he was not addressing himself to me.

In the early years of analysis, I always behaved in the same way: I doled out in small measure my fear and quickly I compensated for it with laughter, pleasure, happiness, a touch of nostalgia.

I had begun to speak of my mother, and of how difficult it was for me in childhood to make her love me. I poured out memories which were a little sad and recited the catalogue of attentions, expressions, and gestures of which I had been the object, moments we had spent in relative harmony at Mass, among the flowers. Unconsciously, so as to protect myself and not be so much raw meat on display, I pushed aside the essential element.

Was it as if my fear, once expressed, would destroy me? Or as if my fear, once expressed, would take away my importance? Or when it was revealed, would it show itself not as fear but as a shameful sickness?

At the time, I was not capable of answering these questions. I was not even capable of posing them. I was a hunted animal; I understood nothing about people.

It took at least four years of analysis for me to learn that when I changed the subject or wouldn't speak, it was not because I had exhausted the subject but rather because I had come up against an obstacle and was afraid to go beyond it. It was not the effort involved that stopped me but what it masked.

There was no risk in speaking of my father. Of my mother, I had spoken only in a cursory way, to engender a little pity. Never had I spoken about the hallucination, never about the beastliness between my mother and me. Concerning the hallucination, I spoke only of my fear of going back to the hospital because of it. I continued to be afraid. What if I were denied access to the cul-de-sac? But as for the corpse between my mother and me, I had no explanation to give, either to the doctor or to myself. I wasn't looking for any. I didn't speak of it. That was all.

When I got there, I'd close my eyes and the trifles, which had their importance, to be sure, yet were not at the heart of the Thing, would come alive.

The little man said nothing of any importance. He opened the door: "Bonjour, Madame." He'd have me come in. I'd lie down on the couch and talk. At a certain point he interrupted me: "I think the session is over." Out of the corner of my eye, I had seen him look at his watch two or three times before speaking, as if he were refereeing a game. I stood up: "Au revoir, Madame." Nothing else. His face impassive, his eyes attentive but without sympathy or involvement. Later, he would sometimes pick out a word from the jumble of my monologues and say, "Such and such a word, what does it make you think of?" I would take the word and unravel the thoughts and images attached to it. Most of the time, this word was the key to open a door I had never even seen. This gave me confidence: he really knew his job. How did he manage to seize upon the very word that was needed? I admired him.

But, at the beginning of the analysis, he never intervened.

Sometimes I left his office terribly agitated, caught up in the madness: he had stopped me in the middle, before I had said a quarter of what I wanted to say.

"I don't want to leave now. You interrupted me in the middle of a sentence. I haven't said anything yet."

"Goodbye, see you Wednesday."

His face stiffened, his expression was severe, his shiny eyes locked into mine, unmovingly, as if to say, "It's no use insisting." I found myself back on the street alone, choking with anguish, in the grip of the Thing. I thought he was evil; he was pushing me to suicide, murder. Inhabited by a demented passion, I dragged myself along the length of the wall. "Kill myself, kill him. Kill somebody. Throw myself under a car, my flesh splattering all over the street. Go back to his house and split his head open, his filthy brain oozing all over his ridiculous little best suit!" I started to cry, and when I got out of the cul-de-sac onto the street, I felt better. I wasn't even afraid.

I would learn much later that the mind doesn't just present itself at the gate of the unknown. It isn't enough merely to want to penetrate the unconscious so that consciousness can enter. The mind procrastinates. It goes back and forth. It delays. It hesitates. It keeps watch. And when the time has come, it stands motionless in front of the gate like a setter, paralyzed. Then the dog's master has to come and flush the game.

Now that I was free of these embellishments in whose resurrection I had taken such satisfaction, I realized that I had avoided coming to the point. I was annoyed with myself for not plunging right into the waves of the Thing, thick with filth, horror, putrefaction, and the unendurable. For I thought that to get well I had to confront it, tackle it. And yet, what came to the surface at the doctor's was rather sad, really rather nice, sweet even, and sufficiently touching to move a sensitive soul to tears.

Then came the day when, having continued to sort out faded memories, I made an imperceptible but important departure.

I still spoke of my the search for gifts worthy of my mother. It was always during the siesta that my mind was inflamed by that subject.

The child came to join me in the cul-de-sac. I was looking for skin tanned by the sun, tousled blond hair, curiosity, and her desire to please. One more time she lay down beside me, in me.

The doctor's office is my room. I am ten years old. On the ceiling is a little tan lizard who lives there during the day. It is the only active creature in the house at this hour, when everyone is resting. It stalks insects in the ribbons of light projected by the sun through the slats in the shutters. Its webbed feet resemble vine tendrils. It seems to be asleep. It isn't really. Suddenly it darts forward at full speed to snap up the fly which it ingests with movements at the throat like a turkey gobbling. A little while ago it lost its tail in a nocturnal scuffle, for it does go out at night. Gradually, its tail has grown back, until now, it is almost normal. I would like it if I grew a tail too, like a boy.

It is always during these wretched afternoon siestas that such ideas come to me. When we bathe in the irrigation pond, where the water is so warm it feels thick, Kader's son amuses himself by flipping his spigot until it becomes stiff as a finger. Then he struts about, hips pushed forward, proudly preceded by his periscope. The others make fun of him. But I am envious. I would have loved to have something like that instead of my smooth fruit at the base of my stomach. If I had a tail, I would go around stark naked, and I would plunge it into the beautiful yellow rose or the swelling buttocks of Henriette the cook, when she bent over in front of her oven. Wham! Just thinking about it I would get hot all over.

I am hot in my bed, my sheets and pillow are too soft. I rub myself against them, I can't help it, while trying to find the sleep which doesn't come. The other day I saw Aoued leaving his quarters, a towel around his stomach. A moment before, I had heard him laughing with his wife behind the door. He was on his way to the pond. It was time to let out the water from the pond; his towel stuck out in front of him as if it were pushed by a tent peg. It was quite clear to me that it was his spigot which had gotten big and was standing up. When he came back, he locked the door and I heard nothing more. When I grow up I'll get married and fool with my husband.

Oh, Lord, forgive me, I am unable to come close to You; my head is full of sin. I don't like to wear gloves. They make me perspire. I don't like to wear underpants. They give me a wedge. I don't like to wear shoes. They bother me (I'm hardly past the cellar wall when I take off my sandals, hide them in the vines and run barefoot with my friends, all the way to the forest). I get bored at Mass. The most shameful thing of all, Lord, yes. I accuse myself of being bored at Mass, of having often looked at the blond boy from St. Charles' School during the retreat for my First Communion. I accuse myself of losing buttons, breaking zippers, mislaying hair ribbons and barrettes, and having dirty hands. Oh, God, I accuse myself of being incapable of reading the books of the Comtesse de Ségur, with stories about feudal lords; poor Blaise and the proper little girls. I accuse myself of not being interested in Andersen's tales, in stories about fairies, will-o'-the-wisps, and children lost in the snow. I would rather go to Youssef's *raima* where I get lice but where old Daiba bakes cakes and unleavened bread from hard wheat, and tells stories. All the farm children go there. We settle down around her fire and listen....

Old Daiba, with an eye on her simmering stew, told us, in the sort of plaintive monotone used for reciting litanies, of sudden flights on winged horses prancing all the way to Allah's Paradise. She lifted the lid of her earthenware pot, releasing every time the famous smells of mint and spices, and took up again the account of the punishments inflicted on some unfortunate by a serpent from the tombs in the neighboring cemetery. She kept her fire going with a round fan of braided raffia, stringing together the adventures of black giants who shook mountains, fountains springing up in the desert, and genies inside bottles. Slowly, she offered each one of us a pastry dripping with honey, which she ladled out of an enameled bowl, decorated with yellow crescent moons and large red and black flowers. Even the prospect of having my hair washed and my curls combed out with a fine tooth comb, which was torture, couldn't prevent me going down there.

"You have no self-control. You'd do anything to stuff

yourself with that old woman's swill."

The attraction was not Daiba's cakes so much as Allah's white horse galloping across the sky with his shoes and wings of gold. But that I didn't speak about.

Unable to sleep, keeping track of my sins, got on my nerves. Then, carried along by an evil current, I would do worse.

I had been making a horn, a sort of tube wider at one end than the other, by wrapping a sheet of paper, or, better still, of construction paper, around one of my fingers. Then, hiding it under my clothes, in the silence of the sleeping house, my bare feet making no sound on the tiles, I made my way to the bathroom and I locked myself in.

It was much larger than the usual bathroom. And, as everyone but my mother was fond of reading there, it could be said that the bathroom was an annex of the library. Arranged on its shelves was a collection of back numbers of *L'Illustration*, *Marie-Claire*, dictionaries, Larousse and Littré, in I don't know how many volumes, telephone directories and detective stories. The throne was a bowl of immaculate white porcelain, framed by a comfortable toilet seat of oak, polished by use and waxed daily. In the afternoon, the sun entered directly through a narrow window in a thick wall which opened out on the courtyard. I loved to crouch in the alcove made by the dormer window. The center of the farm was at my feet: around the courtyard, paved with large, irregular, shiny stones, were the living quarters of the farm workers and the stables, behind which the six eucalyptus trees of the entryway rose high in the sky. And above the pink tile roofs of the grain silos I could see the gently rising slope of a hillside planted with vines and crowned by a forest of sea pines.

The forest was a paradise. Not only did it smell of thyme, mastic and resin all year round, but, depending on the season, it sent into the very bedrooms long breaths of broom, wild hyacinth, daisies or immortelles. Its soil, composed of the red earth of the area mixed with shiny sand, was soft underfoot. This was the domain of the farm children. We built forts and organized games of hide and seek which made our hearts pound, or when the donkeys and the mules were not needed for work in the fields we took them on expeditions. Thicknesses of empty potato sacks provided us with saddles on their lumpy backbones. I preferred the forest to any other place in the world.

In spite of my mother's instructions—"Stay at the edge, where I can see you from the house!"—I would charge in with the others all the way to the clearings and the thickets which only the children knew about.

The boys played Tarzan, swinging from tree to tree, uttering terrible cries or dropping down from the branches onto the back of a donkey who, as a rule, took the game badly, and, after bucking once, wouldn't move an inch. The boys fought among themselves, organizing little battles in which they would roll on the ground, arms and legs all mixed up together in the sand, trying to grab hold of each other's already tattered shorts. They ended up naked, and when the fight was over, they hid, snickering, making funny faces at the girls, pink and gray buds dangling between their legs.

I was envious. I could do what they did. But I didn't. Girls weren't allowed to, so, with the other "squat pissers" (that's what Kader called us), I picked flowers and tidied up the forts while waiting for a mixed game to be organized.

Just thinking about it while crouching in the bathroom dormer excited me. The sun beat straight down and made me sweat. After a moment, I'd leave my hiding place, find the paper tube hidden under my blouse, and piss standing up like the boys, or try to, aiming through the cone. It wasn't easy.

At the end of the cul-de-sac, reliving these moments, feeling them exactly as they'd happened twenty years before, I understood that the motions I made to fit the tube to my body, the fumblings to find the source, were the same as what I did when checking the flow of blood: furtive movements, the merest contact, imperceptible motions back and forth, slight tugs, all done absentmindedly with an indifference to the rest of my body, part of me elsewhere, as if what I was doing had no importance, whereas all thought was really concentrated at my fingertips.

But, instead of experiencing the blood as a punishment, I would feel down at the base of my calves a powerful sensation, a sort of pinching, tingling on the borderline of pleasure and pain, progressively spreading to my thighs, and invading my stomach. And finally, because I had lost all control, I was peeing hot urine over my fingers. My body was seized by a rocking, a pitching, a sort of creeping motion which made me arch my back violently, bringing me an extraordinary joy that frightened me.

As soon as it was over, I was ashamed. I threw away my cone of softened, wet paper, and pulled the chain to send it far away. I got out of there. I felt guilty and unworthy of my mother, of the world, of the farm, of my family, Jesus, the Holy Virgin, everything. I had to do something to redeem myself; I would find treasure. I promised Jesus not to do it again, and, as I never managed to keep my promise, I felt more and more guilt every time.

I opened my eyes. Everything was just where it should be: the doctor at my head, a little to one side, the gargoyle on the top of the fake beam (What an idea, to set an imp in a room where only the mentally ill come! Was it done on purpose?), grass cloth on the walls, the abstract painting, the ceiling.

Nothing had changed, and yet I looked at everything differently, more boldly. In fact, I had encountered myself for the first time. Until then, I had always organized the scenes of my past in such a way that others—my mother, in particular—had the leading role. I was merely the submissive performer, a nice little girl who was being manipulated and who obeyed.

I remembered the incident of the paper spigot very well. It hadn't fallen into oblivion; I just didn't like to think about it. Twenty years later, the memory still awakened in me a terrible shame which I didn't try to explain. Twenty years later, when I had made love, had "adventures," I was ashamed of having wanted to do peepee standing up! I was not ashamed of having masturbated, since until that very day, I hadn't acknowledged what I was doing. The little girl masturbating among the dictionaries, the sunlight caressing her behind, didn't exist. She was born on the doctor's couch at the end of the cul-de-sac.

At the time of the paper spigot, I didn't know the expression "to jerk off," and knew nothing whatever about masturbation. When the boys were playing with themselves until their spigots became stiff, we said among ourselves that they were "touching themselves." The matter of girls "touching themselves" never came up. And besides, what could they have touched? They had NOTH-ING to touch. Later, when I learned what masturbation was and how women are made, it never occurred to me to make the connection between masturbation and the paper spigot. And yet it was obvious why, until that day, I had felt a deep disgust for masturbation, a kind of nausea which made me dangerously ill.

I discovered that I preferred to be abnormal and ill rather than normal and well. At the same time, I disco-vered that there was something for me in the illness and that I was partly responsible. WHY?

This first genuine "why" was the tool that I would use as pick and shovel to turn over the field of my past until I had exposed it to the light of day.

In any case, looking back on it now, what pleasure I took from my pleasant little orgasms of another time! How moved I was to meet a child full of the juices of life, who wanted to play with herself, who did play with herself, and who found pleasure doing it. (My mother was not completely wrong to call me mule-headed.) That child reassured me: I existed, therefore, and not only at the mercy of others. I could fool them, make fun of them, escape them, protect myself from them. What joy! I would find the way again. Henceforth, I was certain of its exist-ence, though I was still a prisoner. Yet I had held onto the means of freeing myself, since the child who masturbated was me.

As I got up, I said to the doctor, "You shouldn't keep that gargoyle in your office, it is hideous. There is already enough horror and fear in the minds of the people who come in here, no need to provide any more of it."

If was the first time I addressed him other than as a patient.

He did not reply.

That day I discovered that this confusion, this madness which made me flee into the heat in search of nonexistent treasure, was even then the Thing. If my heart beat so fast it wasn't only because of my flight; if I perspired like that, it wasn't only the heat; my suffocating was the fear and the sweat caused by the Thing. My shame and guilt had already become a part of the Thing. It was there, to torture the little girl running, twisting her ankles in the dry clumps of earth cultivated with grapevines.

# Chapter VII

At the very next session I spoke about my mother's villainy.

This took place a very long time ago, at the threshold of adolescence.

She was perched in the leather armchair like a hen about to lay an egg. She had sought the most comfortable position for a lengthy stay, plumping up the cushions underneath her, resting her head on the back of the chair. Her luminous eyes were green as waves, her brow serene as a beach. Her features were refined, though somewhat angular.

Her very rich and tempting body was not of a piece with her face. She was sheathed in an impeccable pajama of white shantung, very wide on the bottom so that the fabric fell in folds around her legs, which she had just crossed. I saw her slender ankles, where all her youth had remained, and her well-shod feet, supple and long in white sandals.

It was 1943. She was beautiful, she was my mother. I loved her with all my heart.

I was not in the habit of having tea with her. Normally I went to look for my afternoon snack in the pantry when returning from class, and went outside to eat with the farm children. Something out of the ordinary must have happened for me to be there wearing dress-up clothes, as if I were paying her a visit in this living room, which was for me a formal room I went into only to say goodnight and to greet family visitors.

I was sitting in a chair identical to hers. Between us there was a low table on which were scattered in studied neglect articles of silver: boxes for makeup, pills, or smelling salts, ashtrays, little ramekins full of anemones. They surrounded the base of a tall old lamp whose parchment shade gave off a light the color of honey, at once joyous and intimate.

They came in to serve the tea. Its aroma, interspersed with that of the Craven A cigarette my mother was smoking and the hot toast, forms a precise unit in my memories, so that any one of them encountered anywhere summons up the others, and I relive the scene one more time: she and I before the fire long ago, drinking tea. More than thirty years ago now.

She was in no hurry to speak. Alternately she would take a puff of her cigarette, inhaling deeply, and gulp down tea. She put her cup down and with a languorous movement of the arm let her long hand trail over the articles strewn across the table between us like a comet. She took one of them, smoothing the flat of her thumb over it slowly, as if she were caressing it, and put it back in its place.

She had a serious expression, like that of an initiate, which she put on to receive certain of her visitors: priests, nuns, ladies of good works, doctors. To some extent her behavior raised me to the level of an adult and allowed me to understand that she was going to speak to me as a woman and an equal.

A few words and an occasional reference to the visit we had just made to a doctor in town were enough to let me know that it was a medical conversation we were going to have. This was not displeasing to me. I had my share of curiosity on that subject.

When I was little I liked to operate on my dolls. At first, I opened them up, but the hollowness of their bodies and the simple Y ending in the two balls that I found in their heads disappointed me. Not to mention the scandalized expression of my mother when Nanny showed her the results of my operations.

"Why did you do that?"

"..."

"If I catch you at it again, I'll take away all your toys. There are children who have nothing to play with. What a shame to ruin your dolls."

From then on I performed my operations with colored pencils for surgical instruments. I undressed "my children," while saying reassuring words to them, even though I knew I was going to hurt them. To operate, I had to be alone, absolutely alone. I began by drawing lines on the bodies of my babies, great colored slashes starting at the neck, passing between the legs and ending in the back above their behinds. I made several of them, using different colors. I imagined their bodies were open, gaping, palpitating, a sacrifice. Then in black pencil I would violently attack a spot, making a circular scrawl, the pencil going round and round very fast and pressing very hard. I told myself that the operation had failed, that now I had to kill my children. The excitement would make me perspire. When it was over, quickly I got my dolls back into their dresses so that no one would see what I'd done to them. I was ashamed of myself.

Because of such memories, medicine was linked to mystery and remained a questionable though enticing pleasure. What was my mother doing all day with the black bag she never let out of her sight, in which hypodermics, a small scalpel, tweezers and scissors were kept?

Medicine exerted an attraction for me. But I preferred to be the one to operate. Nevertheless, on that afternoon I was stretched out naked on the table, examined all over by the doctor, and I was discussed in private, after having been sent out to the waiting room. I would have liked nothing better than to hear their conversation. But because of a lady who was waiting there with her sickly son, I hadn't been able to go and listen through the door but had to sit still like a good little girl, my hands on my knees, looking at the six seams on the back of my white gloves. And yet, the annoyance and vexation of not knowing what they were saying created such tension that, knowing I could do nothing to stop it, I dreaded the shrill cry that would come from my throat if the situation continued over too long.

When the door opened, I started so violently the doctor asked me, "Were you sleeping?" I smiled and nodded acquiescently, to make him think he had guessed right. I didn't say "yes" because I was unable to lie in the presence of my mother.

Kader waited for us down below with the car. He took

off his cap, held the door open for us, and we rode all the way to the farm without saying a word. It was as we were pulling in to the courtyard that she spoke to me.

"Come and have tea. I have something to tell you."

And so there we were, taking little sips of the boiling hot tea, looking at the fire.

"Are you always as tired as you are this summer?"

"No, Mama, I'm only tired now and then."

For months I had been suffering from dizzy spells, the sensation that my body was becoming very weak, very light, and that I was falling, falling, and there was nothing to do about it.

"Did you know that the doctor thinks you're about to become a young lady and this is what's troubling you? It is true that you are not ahead of schedule and that it should have happened already. Otherwise, you're in perfect health. There is absolutely nothing wrong with your lungs, which is what I feared most."

A young lady! How could I suddenly turn into a young lady? They were the older girls who put on stockings and makeup as soon as they turned the corner of Rue Michelet and stood in front of the bakery "La Princière" simpering at the boys, making dates with them. How could I become like them! The doctor must be mistaken.

"Do you know what it means to become a young lady? Have your friends talked to you about it? There must be someone in your class to whom this has happened. I am even certain that you are the only one to whom it hasn't happened. Though you may be ahead in your classwork, you are certainly behind for the rest."

I didn't know what she was getting at. I sensed her embarrassment and confusion, and the effort to master them. What did she want to say to me?

"I suppose you know little boys are not found under cabbage leaves, or little girls among the roses."

I knew by her tone of voice that she was making fun of me.

"Nanny sometimes says that storks bring babies, but of course I know it isn't true. Once when Barded's wife was expecting a baby you told me she was carrying it in her stomach, and that it's the parents who order children. But I don't know how they do it."

"It's only a manner of speaking. All the same, you must have some idea about it."

In my school there was a group of girls, at the center of which reigned Huguette Meunier. They gorged themselves on dirty stories during recess. I didn't like to mix with them, but they kept talking when they were in line. Huguette Meunier said boys made babies with their spigots. Sabine de la Borde insisted a man only had to stick his finger up a girl's behind to make a baby. Some of the others said it came from kissing on the mouth.

In fact, over the last year or two, I had isolated myself. I didn't have much to do with the girls in my school, at any rate, not for that sort of thing. So I didn't have a very clear idea about sex. It was a thorny subject which attracted and frightened me enormously; I never talked about it with anyone.

Besides, such things were shameful, and there was surely no question of my going into them with my mother. As to whether I was a young lady or not, it was a question of age, and I wasn't the right age yet.

"Look, don't be silly. You said yourself a minute ago that you knew that women carry their babies in their stomachs. If you're afraid you'll shock me if you admit to knowing more, you're mistaken. I find all of that perfectly natural. I know very well you're not going to remain a child forever. You're going to become a woman.

"You know that the woman's role is not only to bear children, but also to bring them up in the love of our Lord.... God subjects us to trials which we must accept joyfully, as these make us worthy of drawing closer to Him.... You are about to face the first trial, since you'll soon be having your period."

"..."

"You really don't know what that means?"

"My period? No, Mama, I don't know what that means."

It's true I didn't know. In school the girls never spoke about it and outside of school, my only friends were boys.

"Well, one of these days you'll see a little blood on your underpants. And this will happen again every month. It doesn't hurt, it's dirty, and no one should be aware of it, that's all. You mustn't be afraid when it happens. Just let me know, and I'll show you what to do so as not to dirty anything."

"When will it happen? Did the doctor tell you?"

"He doesn't know exactly, but he thinks it won't be long...within the next six months. Do you know what it means to have your period?"

"No, Mama."

"I couldn't possibly go into all of it. I'm sure you understand. It's as embarrassing for me as it is for you. But I favor certain principles of modern education. Too much ignorance is harmful. I've always regretted not having known more about certain things. I think I could have avoided some serious mistakes. This is why I have decided to speak to you. The doctor was very much in favor of it. He agrees that old-fashioned education sometimes has its disadvantages.

"Well, little girl, having your period means you can bear children."

I looked at the carpet without seeing it. I was paralyzed by the situation, the conversation, the revelation. How is it that with the body of a child you can have a child in your stomach? When all you want to do is play in the forest and run in the surf where the waves make lacy foam, how is it possible to be promoted to the exalted position of motherhood?

I didn't feel capable of it. I was repelled, terrified and disgusted before the Lord's first trial. I didn't dare look at her for fear of her seeing the sacrilege.

The branches from the vines crackled as they burned in the fireplace.

The tea, the fire, the polished furniture, the thick pile rugs, outside night falling on the vineyards, the dogs barking, my mother: my whole life! A beautiful, bountiful, exemplary, warm world where there was a place for me. And I refused the difficulties of my role! I did not accept my condition: it frightened me.

At the farm, the cows and the mares who were expecting babies were the object of very particular care. Their offspring increased the herd and enriched the family. Yet I had never been authorized to attend a birth, and when the dogs mounted one another the adults did everything to distract me from the sight. I had seen enough of it, however, to spark my imagination. And the images beginning to form in my brain were shameful to me. I had always been told of someone base or criminal, "He behaved like an animal, like a beast, like a dog!" But these stories of blood, of children, were stories having to do with dogs! And was it my own mother who wanted to initiate me into this life and who spoke of it in my presence?

"Don't lower you head, don't be afraid. All women go through this, you know; they don't die of it. I admit that men are better off than we are. They don't even know about troubles like these. It is true they go to war.... I wonder which is worse...."

"And do you get it too?"

"Of course. I told you, all women do. One gets used to it. It's not painful, apart from the dirt. It lasts only two or three days, four at the most."

"Every month!"

"Every twenty-eight days as a rule. But having your period is one thing. Having children is another, although the two are related. The first is shocking at the outset, but one gets used to it, and it can be easily concealed. It's like breathing, or hunger, or any other natural function. You see what I mean? It's inevitable. That's the way we're made. We must respect God's laws. His ways are mysterious.... The second is more complicated, because it doesn't depend entirely on you.... You know that the second comes from living with a husband?"

"Yes, Mama."

"Who told you?"

"Huguette Meunier."

"Is she in your class?"

"Yes, Mama."

"What does her father do?"

"I don't know."

"I'll ask the principal. What did she tell you?"

"Well, that you had babies with your husband, that you carried them in your stomach...that it takes nine months."

"Well, that child knows a lot. And you want me to believe with all that she never spoke to you about periods?"

"I assure you, Mama, she never spoke to me about them. I don't talk with her much."

"I suppose it's normal she didn't say anything about them. We don't like to talk about them much."

That "we," linking Huguette Meunier and my mother, was something I simply couldn't cope with!

"Did she tell you that some women have babies outside of marriage?"

"No, Mama, she didn't speak about that."

Actually, Huguette Meunier talked about boys, not husbands. As she resembled a weasel, and since to tell the stories she would gather the girls together in a corner of the playground where we were hidden from the teacher on duty, I thought she was making it up to interest or amuse us.

"That can happen. It is so great a sin that the Lord never forgives it. A woman who commits this sin, and the child she bears because of it, are cursed for the rest of their lives. Do you understand me?"

"Yes, Mama."

"Also, from the moment you have your first period, you must never be alone with a boy again, still less with a man. You who love boys' games will have to control yourself. No more rides in the forest with Barded's sons! Is that understood?"

"..."

"If I ever hear of you hanging around after class picking up boys I don't know what I'll do, but I warn you you'll not stay here. You'll be in the convent within twenty-four hours."

"Why?"

"Because that's the way it is.... I don't have to explain....

One doesn't speak to just anyone, one has to get respect. That's it, period."

What an upsetting turn of events! I was aware, however, that I was at a turning point and, finally, I was proud of having been taken into the confidence of those around me. For basically I understood what she meant. I played the donkey because I wanted her to tell me more, but I was well aware of the difference between myself and the other children, and that in certain matters, there was no bridging the gap; no communication was possible between us. They knew nothing. I saw it in the way they ate, spoke, and played even. They were without any self-control and sometimes even smelled a little. I liked the farm children, but I knew that I was not one of them.

It was an initiation which my mother and I were engaged in. A significant transaction, the most significant perhaps. For it gave me a most precious piece of an invisible uniform designed to identify my caste to whomever I might meet. I had to be trained in such a way that my origins could be recognized at any time, in any circumstances. Dying, playing, giving birth, making war, dancing with my fiancé in a tavern or at the governor's ball, I had to wear the invisible uniform. It would protect me and help me to know and be known by my peers. It would instill respect in my inferiors.

"Please, Mama, why do Henriette's girls go to the beach on their own with boys?"

"Henriette is an excellent cook. I have nothing but praise for her work. But she raises her children in her own way. That doesn't concern me, or you either. Working people don't have time to look after their children's education. Anyway, it wouldn't do them any good. It might even be a hindrance to them later on.

"By the way, I don't much like your bringing these young people home. I know that your intentions are good, but you see, one day they'll envy you for everything you have and they'll never have, and they will be miserable. You have to know how to be charitable and to try to understand them. One day you'll be having young ladies your own age come over, and Henriette's daughters won't be able to come. You can understand; they would be out of place, embarrassed. If you get them into the habit of coming here, their feelings will be hurt. So learn to keep your distance, my love, while holding onto your generosity."

She had called the servant to take away the tea tray. We were alone again with the fire. I loved the fire and the glow that the cinders caught up and reflected on the walls of the room, radiant like stars and dying out all of a sudden.

It was then I asked a stupid question. A question to which I knew the answer, although no one had ever given it to me. But I thought today was a day for explanations, to bring it all out into the light.

"Mama, is it the same for Muslims as it is for us?"

"Obviously, we are all equal before God, subject to the same natural laws."

"Will you invite well-bred Arab boys, the sons of Sheik Ben Toukouk, for example, who are going to boarding school in France?"

"You do have a talent for asking stupid questions. What would people like that find to do here? They would be bored. They wouldn't feel at home."

It was aggravating. I didn't know how to talk. I always managed to do something clumsy. I shocked her. Often she would sigh, "Won't I ever get anywhere with you?"

When she was with people I didn't know and she saw me appear, she would warn them, "Watch out for my daughter, she's a wild one, like quicksilver." I felt her uneasiness. I understood that she was trying to excuse any possible clumsiness by so fine a word.

Quicksilver. It made me think of the flash of lightning that schools of fish emit when they change direction, the scintillation of their silver scales. Also the flight of pigeons releasing bursts of silver as they turned.

It was over. I thought she was going to ask me to leave. Instead, she took another cigarette, lit it, settled down in her chair. She blew the smoke out slowly. Her lips were perfect, well drawn, with two pointy crests above and a clean line lightly curved below.

Her green eyes had embarked on a sad dream. I couldn't bear it when she was sad. If only she had let me get close to her, if I had been able to console her, embrace her, caress her. But she didn't want it. Only the little pecks on the lips, the good mornings and goodbyes, nothing more. She reminded me of those royal pheasants in their cage in the garden. They strolled, hieratic, with stiff and leisurely steps, their russet cowls and plumage of luminous green and their long trains of gold and bronze. I would have loved to touch them, but, careful, they peck at you when you get too near them. They should not have been locked up, which is perhaps the reason they were bad. And what of my mother, was she locked up? Why no, she did as she pleased, she went wherever she wanted to go, she knew all the rules, she ran no risk of losing her way. And if the rules sometimes seemed like bars, it wasn't really like that — on the contrary. Often, she would say to me, "If you don't listen to me you won't make it." Which is how she got her way.

"I would like to speak to you about your father. I would like to tell you how you were born. I think it will help you to understand our conversation better, and help you avoid making the same mistakes.

"He doesn't have the same background as we do, despite his birth. He comes from a good French family, entirely correct and without pretensions. He broke with his family very young, to try his wings. You know he is French, from La Rochelle. But God knows where he'd been before ending up here! It's better not to know. He's much older than I am, as you know....

"He's a very handsome man. As they say, he has a lot of charm. From the moment he got here, he was the darling of the town. An engineer, French, a good talker, attractive in every way, and I admit I was very flattered when he asked to marry me. Despite the age difference, moreover, your grandparents had given their approval. He had a wonderful position, the factory was doing well at that time.... Let us render unto Caesar that which is Caesar's. He went to night school and got his engineering degrees by the sweat of his brow. But during his years as a working man he unlearned everything he had been taught at home, exchanging good habits for bad. He's an adventurer, in fact, but I didn't find that out until it was too late.... If you only knew what a goose I was! After all, he is your father. I don't want to speak ill of him in front of you...and yet, if I speak to you this way tonight, it's because I want to do you a favor. I want you to really get it into your head that when you lose your social position you court catastrophe. One cannot marry just anybody."

A black moustache over white teeth, a high forehead, slick black hair, black eyes laughing, supple, well-cared-for hands gripping me: my father. Carrying a cane and wearing spats, he tips his hat in the grand manner to the ladies on the street. Whenever we met he was happy to see me. Too happy even. He looked at me laughingly, holding me against him. He was attentive to how I moved and to what I said. He itemized my features: "The nose, eyes, and hands are the same as mine. You are like me, my little minx!" That made him laugh even harder. When I was there nothing existed but me. It bothered me.

I dreaded the Sunday afternoons I had to spend with him once a month. I found the lunches during the week enough. But when I finally had the courage to confess that I didn't like spending Sundays with him, she pointed out to me: "It's the law; if you don't go there he won't pay me my alimony, which as it stands is ridiculously small." And, moreover, at the end of those afternoons I was given the task of picking up "my mother's envelope."

It was Nanny who effected the transfer of power. Before leaving me at my father's door, she repeated once again the injunctions of my mother: "Don't blow your nose in his handkerchiefs. Touch him as little as possible. His illness killed your sister. And don't forget to ask him for the envelope."

On those Sundays he would invariably take me to his tennis club, where he immediately went off to play a match ("Your father is a marvelous player"). Then he went into the clubhouse, where he played bridge with sporty-looking men in white flannel trousers, Lacoste shirts, and shetland sweaters. There were invariably women there whom I found overly familiar, draping an arm over his shoulder, addressing him by his first name, making him laugh by whispering sweet nothings in his ear.

I detested it there. Not only because I was terribly

bored but because I was more ashamed there than any-where to be the child of divorced parents. For my mother, the divorce was a misfortune and a trial. With my father's laughter and his obvious taste for women, the fact of divorce became something scandalous.

When I was at the tennis club, I spoke to no one, and hid in the bushes behind the women's locker room. I would not move from there until nightfall. If it rained, I would seek refuge under the clubhouse veranda. My father, who wasn't used to children, never looked for me. He believed I was having fun in the clubhouse or on the grounds and found it quite natural to see me by the car when it was time to go. In the car, he'd invariably say, "We've had a nice day together, haven't we, my little minx?"

When we got to where we lived, my mother and I, I said (having rehearsed this phrase during the entire drive), "Mama would like her envelope."

He would pretend to have forgotten completely—how lucky that I had thought of it—and would start searching through all his pockets, even though he would always find the envelope in the same place. He handed it to me jokingly: "Children cost a lot of money!"

I didn't like it when he said that because I knew the amount of his child support had not been increased since the divorce, that is to say, since I was born, and that it wasn't enough to buy me a pair of shoes.

Now that the war had broken out, and my family was having money troubles, which I was old enough to under-stand, child support had become a constant subject of discussion.

"If you think I can afford to buy you this or that on what your father gives me...."

I was so afraid of hearing those words I never asked for anything. All through the war I wore shoes two or three sizes too small, so that my feet are permanently misshapen. Everything was hard to find, and clothing in particular was exorbitantly expensive. My mother, exasperated beyond endurance by my rate of growth, the change of seasons, and the new school term beginning, verified that I couldn't get into my clothes from the year before. Then she would pick up the telephone and in my presence call my father. With vehemence, she'd say: "I want you to be a witness. I have to have a witness to go before the judge to ask for an increase in child support. Someone has to tell him what a cross I bear. You will bear witness that I am being bled to death—and haven't anyone to help me!"

She put me near the telephone, dialed the number, and right away I heard the voice of my father, distorted by the instrument.

Today, I am certain she did it intentionally, for whenever I made a move to distance myself from the telephone she would abruptly gesture me back.

"Look here, your daughter has grown some more. I can't buy her clothes on what you give me. She needs a coat, a skirt, two sweaters...."

For a long time they would argue bitterly. Again, their anger would come to the surface. She would fling in his face the cost of my upkeep. He would answer her by saying there was nothing he'd like better than to take me to live with him. She would counter that it was the last place for a girl of my age to spend time. He would reply that she was the one who asked for the divorce, and in so doing, forced on him this bachelor's existence. She would explode into tears, say that she didn't know he was ill when she married him and that had she known, she wouldn't have done it. Indignant, he would say he'd been cured at the time, that it was a wound from the war which was the cause of it, and that it wasn't his fault if the disease returned without his knowing it. She would whimper that her daughter was dead. He would lower his voice to say that he loved her and it was because he loved her that he hadn't dared say he was sick. He was repentant. He had lost everything: his firstborn, his wife, me, everything.

It was appalling! The phone calls were torture! Sobbing, my mother would hang up. Then she'd shut herself up in her room, where I listened to her crying interminably.

At times like these in adolescence I began to think of suicide.

She spoke only for brief periods. The rest of the time, it could be said that the fire held her attention. She was brooding.

"In a few words, our life had finally become intolerable. Ever since the death of your sister, I had a horror of your father. I was very young, barely twenty; I had never seen a corpse. When I saw my baby in such a state, it was terrible. And that it happened in a hotel room. Your father's doctor had sent me to Luchon to take care of the baby. The doctor who was in cahoots with your father exiled me there so that the child would not die in Algiers. From the outset, they knew the child was doomed. The doctor hadn't told me her illness was tubercular in origin. He hadn't told me that your father had tuberculosis. I didn't know it. Your father never said so. If I'd known, I might have been able to do something, to protect her;

she'd still be alive. He killed her. In marrying me, he was entering our social world. He had money, he was an engineer, he was handsome. With a girl as pretty as I was, from a good family, he had everything he wanted.

"So I lost my head when I saw my dead baby in a strange hotel, in a detestable country. Bereft of family and friends, sunless. I went crazy. He was right to send me far away. If he'd been there I would have killed him!"

The intensity and ferocity with which she was looking at the fire allowed me to trace two straight lines from her eyeballs to the flames. Two murderously sharp swords with which to transfix my father.

My heart pounded and my mind made little leaps here and there like a bird. I was crazy. My love for my mother was in danger because it was not equal to the level of pain. What could I do? How was it possible to take the weight off her? How could I change that expression? I sat on the edge of my chair and leaned over towards her.

"Mama, you mustn't hurt yourself."

Her expression didn't change, nor did it shift even when she murmured: "Ah! you don't have any idea, you didn't know her. She was an extraordinary child."

For a long time she sat motionless, caught up in her memories: the life of her child, the death of her child, the cemetery.

She cried. A few tears slipped furtively down onto her cheeks; they were only the overflow from the pool of sorrow where her inner tears fell ceaselessly. On her face two delicate, satiny tracks remained now, as if two snails traced paths through her scented face powder.

Night had fallen and here and there the lights in the living room illuminated the nearest branches of the mock pepper trees along the front of the house, the foliage of which also wept the tiniest green tears.

We stayed there without moving until the fire interrupted our silence with its radiant explosions. She had gotten up and poked the fire, which had given birth to still more showers of sparks, and she pushed together the glowing embers before adding another log.

"You know that divorce is forbidden by the Church, except in cases of absolute necessity. Nothing in the world should make us stray from the Lord, who died for us on the cross. He is always near us, even though we do not see Him. He and our guardian angel try to protect us.... It took courage for me to ask for a divorce. I went to see the Archbishop of Algiers. I made my decision only after he assured me that, provided I never remarried, I could get a divorce while continuing to receive the sacraments. With God's help and confidence in His love it is possible to defy public opinion.

"I could have left your father after my baby died, but I didn't dare.... It was such a scandal. I didn't have the courage; I was too young.

"Your brother was born two years later. I trembled for my new baby. I was afraid to see him die. I am still nervous about his health, he's so thin.

"Then there were problems at the factory. When I was married, my father put in some capital as well as my dowry into your father's business, which was going very well. Some complicated things happened which you wouldn't understand. The arguments between them continued on a daily basis. I was the go-between for the two of them. Each one spoke of the other in an unflattering way. I couldn't take any more of it: my father on one side, my husband on the other.... Your grandmother became involved.... You know the way she is. She made scenes. I suffered terribly. In the middle of all that, your father had a relapse. He left for Switzerland. He spent two years in a sanatorium. When he came back it was worse. While he was away his business went downhill. I begged him to pay my father back, at least.... At the factory there were twenty-five mechanical saws; he called me the twenty-sixth.... He could always find something to laugh about! Even though there was nothing funny. We had lost our baby. She was tubercular, to the very marrow. The factory was no longer worth anything.... After all, my whole dowry was involved, I had a right to an opinion. One day I'll have only a small part of the land, which will belong to your uncles; I had to ensure my own future, and your brother's... yours as well, to be sure, but you hadn't been born yet.

"Our fortune isn't immense, but it goes way back. The first of our forebears to come here was a poet. He lost more money than he earned. What remains has to be preserved. Because of it, we can still do good; we can help our workers. "

My mother spoke of the workers in the same way as the saints, with fear and respect. Both were necessary for the proper practice of her religion. By giving charity to the workers while praying to the saints, one ended up in Paradise.

A few workers lived year-round on the farm with their families. They had running water and electricity in their living quarters, which opened onto the big courtyard They lived and died there, succeeded by their offspring. I played with the children of Barded, who played with my mother, whose father played with my grandmother, and whose grandfather played with my great-grandfather, and so on for the last hundred years. I knew more about the births and deaths and marriages of their family than about my own, some of whom lived in France, too far away, in the cold, unknown. The workers were entirely under our protection. We shared everything, save blood, money, and land.

The first colonists labored to make the land arable. They drained the swamps, which swarmed with adders and malaria mosquitoes. They drained the salt water which saturated the coastal plains. Later, they washed the salt out of those plains to make them fertile. They killed themselves toiling under the sun like the legendary pioneers. In the house, above the precious bed which had come from the old country, they built with their own hands the crucifix, surrounded by their children and servants. To the former, they bequeathed their red land and a zest for continuing to work it (for it was becoming beautiful, with its vineyards, its orange groves, its gardens). To the latter, they bequeathed security (they would never go hungry, they would never want for clothes. When they grew old they would be venerated as ancestors are venerated; when they became sick they would be cared for), and much more, if they remained helpful and trustworthy. Everyone cried, the servants perhaps even more than the children. Dividing up this land wrested from sterility wasn't easy to do. That's how it was, from generation to generation.

When my grandmother arrived at the farm for the grape harvest, it was like getting ready for action before a battle. Kader, who drove the limousine, wearing his chauffeur's jacket and cap, sounded the horn the full length of the alley of olive trees leading from the road to the house, raising the maximum of dust. It was in a reddish cloud that he made his triumphal entry into the courtyard, which had been washed down with streams of water, scoured, swept, brushed, and strewn with flowers. The workers with their wives and children, who had been excitedly waiting for hours, formed the escort for her car. As my grandmother would get out, everyone rushed over to touch her and kiss her hands and her clothing. She was the old one, the mother, even for those who were older than she was. She'd laugh, listen to what they had to say for themselves and, in turn, gave the latest information concerning each of her sons. She'd look around, see that everything was as it should be, clean and immutable. She had been born here. They had all known each other forever.

The vintage was the event around which the whole year turned. The men had worked hard to make it beautiful. In town, one looked out through the window every day for rain, hail, wind, and sun. One knew that behind these manifestations of nature there was, back on the farm, the immense expanse of vines in rows which suffered or flourished. From a distance, my uncle stayed in touch with the workers, directing their activities so that the crops might be well cultivated, pruned and sprayed.

The moment the crop was fully ripe, it was known they'd be hiring for the grape harvest. Several hundred men would have work for about ten days.

The grape pickers came in little groups. They had often walked for days to get there. In the morning when the big gate was opened, they were to be found settled in among the eucalyptus trees. There they would meet cousins and friends. It was always the same families who provided seasonal labor.

During the harvest, there was an uproar in the courtyard, beginning at four in the morning. Horses and mules were brought in to draw the grape carts. The cellar was illuminated like a cathedral in the night. The immense vats, the hose, the tubing, the copper faucets were polished and shining. The teams going to work in the sections of the vineyard at the farthest remove were piling into the wagons and disappearing into the darkness. By the time they got there, the sun would be up. Dawn with its red sun came quickly, in that season, lighting up the faces under the straw hats and tarbooshes. It came only a little ahead of the flies and the cicadas. Then you could see the plains and valleys full of men doubled over, working like slaves to relieve the vines whose clusters of grapes hung like swollen udders even to the ground.

Every morning around ten o'clock, my grandmother would establish herself under the olive tree near the cellar. In spite of her sunbonnet, she would open an umbrella over her head as a further protection from the sun, for like most of the family, she was a redhead. She wore lightweight clothing made of white linen or mauve or blue muslin, which floated about her shoulders and her bare arms. A table and a heavy scale would be set up in front of her rattan armchair. She was there with mint tea to welcome the small Arab landholders in the neighborhood whose vineyards were too small for them to have their own wine production. So they sold their grapes to my grandmother. Certain of them were even older than she was. They had gotten dressed in order to come and see her: white trousers, white tarboosh, a white shirt with a vest of yellow or mauve or black satin, and a great cape which gave off a smell of cleanliness. At their waist in a little leather sheath hung a *mouss*, a little knife which served both to slice the bread and to settle accounts. They'd arrive with a few baskets of grapes, sometimes with a whole cartload. They'd touch my grandmother's outstretched hand with the tips of their fingers and then kiss their own forefinger. She would do the same. Afterward, they'd exchange little taps on the shoulder and back, laughingly. They knew each other well. When she was a little girl she would barter her rings and bracelets for the date cake or the rye bread which they carried in a big plaid handkerchief. In this way, they had retained their habit of exchanging treasures. Today they were bartering their grapes, their entire year's labor, for a few banknotes and coins. They watched the weighing closely, sitting down cross-legged on the ground near her. Scarcely speaking, they rolled a cigarette. As connoisseurs, they watched the goings and comings from the cellar and the quantity of grapes from other sellers. So it was that they knew what was going on in the entire region, hundreds and hundreds of kilometers.

The farm was the center of the world.

The burning hot days went by exhaustingly for the men. The countryside was in the grip of a fever for profit: the vintage meant millions for some, a few coins for others. The tall vats filled one by one. The first vats were already starting to ferment: a thick, reddish foam was forming on the surface. Soon there would be new wine. A little semi-sparkling wine, high in alcohol, which would be used to cut the French wines. The workers didn't drink any (religion forbade it) but they knew that it was on the quality of the wines they were making that all their lives depended. The men working in the wine cellar had grave, attentive faces. They had to be scrupulously clean, and if outdoors there were dust, flies, the smell of horse droppings, must, and sweat, indoors it was cool and clean as in a laboratory. Everything was washed down continuously by pressure hose. The walkways between the vats were scrubbed with stiff brushes. The great copper wheels which closed the doors to the vats gleamed far off in the shadowy gloom. The noise of the machines which conveyed the grapes, pitching them into the wine press, crushing them and squeezing them, was infernal.

One morning it was all over. No more noise, no more goings and comings. But from the barest beginning of daylight there was furtive activity, murmuring, muffled, and fluttering sounds. The atmosphere quivered like dragonfly wings. Preparations for the feast of the grape harvest were underway. First would come the *couscous* and the barbecued mutton. The pits were already dug and the wood gathered to make a brazier there. The mutton, cut up, skewered and impaled on stakes, leaned against the entrance wall, ready to be roasted, any number of them! The women gossiped over the *couscous* as they were preparing it in the courtyard. Excitement was in the air. The men were not supposed to see them without the *haik* or veil. Yet they did all they could to attract their attention. The youngest went to spy on the boys from among the reeds in the garden, or even through the cracks in the big gate, only to be scolded by the matrons responsible for their virginity.

In those days, there was a lot of talk about the generosity of my family. It was known in the country that the harvest feast was particularly sumptuous at our house. I felt gay among the women, nibbling on raisins and toasted almonds.

For the digestion, there would be a long siesta after the meal in the shade of the eucalyptus trees. Then the fiesta meal in the shade of the eucalyptus trees. Then the fiesta prepared by the workers would begin, with singing and dancing and enormous bonfires as soon as night fell. From the windows of the great living room, the entire family threw packages of tobacco, toothpaste, cakes of soap perfumed with patchouli, little celluloid looking glasses, combs, toothbrushes, and junk jewelry to the workers. Unprecedented luxury.

"Finally, I asked for a divorce. Your brother was four years old. It was a dramatic summer. After having pushed me into it, my parents were now terrified to see me leave my husband. It isn't done in our family. But I couldn't take it anymore. I lived in perpetual fear, not only of having your brother fall ill, but of losing my fortune. I was firm in my resolution. I left your father's house.

"It was only when the divorce proceedings were underway that I realized I was pregnant."

In truth, this is not how it went. We were not in the living room at the farm in front of the wood fire. Her entire monologue, all the particulars, the revelations and the instructions she gave me about the condition of women, the family, morality, money, were told to me in the street.

We were on the slope of a very long street, the name of which I have by chance forgotten. The street led from the main post office to the Hotel Aletti, having on one side buildings and on the other a walkway, which at the beginning of the street overlooks the Rue d'Ornano from a great height, and at the end slopes down to the same level.

I think she preferred to tell me what she had in mind to tell me, what (in her view) I needed to know, somewhere other than in a place which was consecrated to our life.

Kader was not there waiting for us with his delicate nose and flaring nostrils, which he used to wiggle for my amusement. Kader with his white uniform and collar, the reverse side of which was blue, and his cap, which he would put on my head when we were alone with Nanny and when he sat me on his lap to drive the car. Of course, the car wasn't there either, with the jump seats I loved to fold up and down and the little mahogany compartments containing flasks with silver stoppers, which I never saw except when they were empty. It was war. There wasn't any gasoline.

We were on a downtown street, a street full of noise and passersby. What I saw, for my head was lowered while she spoke, were the cement squares of the sidewalk, and, on the surface of the squares, the residue of the city: dust, spittle, cigarette butts and excrement. The same sidewalk on which later would run the blood of enmity. And, twenty years later, the same sidewalk on which I would be afraid of falling, driven into a corner with death, by the Thing.

When I thought about it later, I'd eliminate the street and create a more reassuring framework to be able to endure the memory of that unprecedented interview. I was often reminded of all she'd said and, over the years, a setting emerged in which I had some influence and a chance to escape. I recalled her slightest words, the merest change in her expression whenever an overly long silence caused me to raise my head in her direction, to see what she was getting at. Not at any price did I want to remember that we were really on the street. I'd seen too many things there and heard them and felt them.

Until the war I'd only seen the street through the windows of the car.

I was in my last year. I had gone to school all by myself. Such unfamiliar freedom! So many people brushing up against me, jostling me.

The Mediterranean street! The boys whistling, hips swaying in response, permanents, violent perfumes, heavy makeup, strutting in rhythmic cadence. The beggars crying out their miseries as they scratch their scales, "*Ya Ma! Ya ratra moulana! Ya, ana meskine besef! Ya chabe, ya zina, atténi sourdi!*" They reveal stumps, sores, rotting teeth, scabs, blind, suppurating eyes and varicose veins: "*Ya chaba, ya zina, atténi sourdi!*" The women uncover babies bitten by flies and rock their deformed bodies while softly chanting "*Ya chaba, ya zina, atténi sourdi!*" Through an opening in their rags they bring out one more rag, this one streaked with blue veins, which they give to the baby to suck avidly. Sexy mannequins in shop windows. Men who, without breaking stride, spit thick spittle on the sidewalk. From the terraces of bistros the aroma of morning coffee. Lovers kissing in the corners, entwined in each other's arms, in their own world. Flower vendors and the vendors of prickly pears and Barbary figs, impresarios with trained monkeys, "They jump, they dance, da da da da!" Gypsies caning chairs. And, mirrored in the shop windows, my own fleeting reflection: back arched, buttocks high, button breasts, curly blond hair, the long arms and legs of a girl who is not going to be little very much longer.

The traffic, the honking, the streetcar bells, the conductors cursing each other out, "You son of a bitch, you dirty bastard." "Go fuck yourself!" The street that has to be crossed in all this turmoil. And having crossed to the other side, the same.

Taking the first left or right, changing my route, finding a whole new scene. Pay attention to everything except to where I'm going, constantly bumping into the fig trees planted right in the middle of Rue Michelet. Getting to school, groggy, losing my balance, the contrast too great! What I was taught did not correspond to what I saw. Charity, good habits, hygiene, manners! I understood that there were two ways of living, our own and theirs. In our life I never succeeded, and on the street, which drew me to it, everything seemed easy. The shame of it all. I was afraid. I wanted to please my mother. I wanted to live her way, and yet I felt within myself a terrible force pushing me away from the path I was supposed to follow.

My mother's two gloved hands were resting on the granite balustrade, and she was peering into the distance, farther than the street which lower down opened to a rectilinear arch through the city, farther away than the harbor, which, lower down still, bristled with cranes in an uproar of activity, and farther still than the bay, white with heat, flat as a mirror. Farther even than the hills on the horizon. She was looking at the place where memories are intact, frozen in the past.

If I could have known the harm she'd do me, if instead of having no more than a premonition, I'd been able to imagine the incurable and ghastly wound she was going to inflict on me, I'd have sent forth a howling.... Standing firmly on my own two feet, I'd have found within myself the deep cry that I could feel welling up in me, driving up into my throat, into my mouth, from which it would have issued forth dully, at first like a foghorn, becoming sharp like a siren, finally swelling into a hurricane. I'd have shrieked even to death, never having heard the words she was about to inflict on me like so many mutilating swords.

There on the street, in a few sentences, she put out my eyes, pierced my eardrums, scalped me, cut off my hands, shattered my kneecaps, tortured my stomach, and mutilated my genitals.

Today, I know she was unaware of the harm she did me and I no longer hate her. She was discharging her madness onto me; I was the sacrifice.

"To find myself pregnant in the middle of the divorce! Do you realize what that means? I wanted to leave a man whose child I was going to bear! You can not understand.... To sue for divorce you have to reject a man so completely that you are unwilling to tolerate being alone with him. Ah! You're too young, you don't understand what I want to say! But I have to speak to you. You have to know, if only a few seconds, what has to be endured for a mistake!

"There exist evil women and evil doctors who can do away with a baby in a woman's womb. It's a monstrous sin which the Church punishes with hell-fire. In France, you can go to prison. It's one of the worst things a person can do.

"It is possible, however, to lose the baby naturally. A shock can be the provocation, or an illness, medication, even food. Then it's no longer a sin, it's nothing, it's an accident, that's all.

"But it isn't as easy as all that! When I think of the precautions with which pregnant women are surrounded! They can't get overtired, or go down stairs without holding on to the banister.... They have to lie down as much as possible! I tell you! It's a joke!"

What violence, vulgarity, and hatred informed the expression on her face and her choice of words so many years later!

"I went to find my bicycle, which had been rusting away in the shed for I don't know how long, and I pedaled off into the fields, into the land being cultivated, everywhere. Nothing. I rode horseback for hours: jumping, trotting. Nothing happened, believe me. Nothing. When I was through with my bicycle or I got down off my horse, I went to play tennis in the hottest part of the day. Nothing. I swallowed quinine and aspirin by the bottle. Nothing.

"Listen, well: when a baby has taken hold there's nothing you can do to dislodge it. And you get pregnant in a matter of seconds. Do you understand me? Do you know why I want you to get the benefit of my experience? You see how one can be trapped. Do you understand why I want you to be forewarned? Do you understand why I want you to know that you can not trust men?

"...After more than six months of treatment, I had to resign myself to the obvious."

She was looking at me now, and in one of those lovely gestures common among white people in the colonies, where European reserve and tropical sensuality mingle, she began to slide under their satin ribbon my ringlets which always were escaping.

"At last you were born, for it was you whom I was expecting. Almighty God surely punished me for having tried to tamper with nature: it was an occipitofacial presentation. You were born with your whole face forward, instead of presenting only the base of your skull. I suffered agonies, a great deal more than with your sister or brother. But the punishment wasn't all that bad: you were a beautiful, healthy baby. To get through, you must have rubbed your chin and cheekbones against me, as they were bright red. It almost looked as if you'd put on makeup. My goodness, how cute you were! Sister Césarien was there, of course, just as she was at all the births in our family. And she got you clean, wrapped you up, and even brushed the little bit of golden fuzz you had on your head. Then she settled you into your pretty cradle, crossed your hands on your chest, and you went to sleep. She said, 'See, Madame, she looks like a postulant,' and we laughed and laughed."

She was laughing then at so charming a memory: a little baby girl with makeup on, hands folded, eyes closed, like a little nun.... She leaned towards me, and in a rush of tenderness unusual in her, she tried to kiss me. But recoiling unconsciously, as if I lost my footing, I avoided her kiss and above all the proximity of her stomach.

If only I had been in the living room, as I imagined later, or if I'd felt nearby the presence of Nanny or Kader, perhaps I would not have fallen into that fissure in the earth that had just opened up. If I had been able to hear the dogs barking in the evening. If I had been able to hear the jackals answer from the forest. If she had been wearing something elegant, the perfume she put on at home.... But no. We were in the uproar of the street, constrained by the clothes we wore. Alone, face-to-face, we experienced this unprecedented encounter.

Until then, my life had been made up of only a series of efforts to divert myself from the path I made in her direction. I believed that once our paths had crossed I would continue to go forward with her, following in her footsteps. Instead, we had barely made contact when I speeded up so that my path would quickly move away from her. We had been created only to hinder one another. Our two lives formed one of those oblique crosses of the sort used to erase, cancel out, or to suppress.

The hatred didn't flower immediately. First, an infinite expanse of arid desert, heartbreaking and featureless, opened out before me. Throughout my adolescence I moved through this desert like an ox, dragging the ridiculous and heavy plow of my love for my mother, useless hereafter. Not until I was twenty did the blood come to pay me irregular visits. I was expecting my first child. Having a child in my womb made my mother revolting to me. That poor bitch.

I don't know what I was doing when the blood first appeared. Until my analysis I have very few memories that stand out after the admission of her failed abortion. On the outside, life was gray, drab, correct, complacent, dumb. On the inside it was heavy, secret, shameful, and increasingly terrifying. In my abdomen on the right side I felt almost imperceptibly that some sort of contact was being made, a little like sensing the look of a person one doesn't see. I had been pregnant a little over four months. Again, a few days later, there occurred that slender shadow of a caress like that of a finger touching velvet.

It was my child who was moving. Larva, tadpole, fish from the depths. Beginning of life, blind and uncertain. Enormous hydrocephalic head, bird spine, jellyfish limbs. It existed, it lived there in its warm water, moored to the great cable of the umbilical cord. Infirm, powerless, horrible. My baby! The one who arose out of the great desire I had had for a man and the beautiful movement we'd made slipping into each other, the perfect rhythm we found all of a sudden. From this sweet perfection, only a marvel could come forth.

138

I was going to make its acquaintance. It moved on its own when it felt like it, in a rhythm not mine. I was attentive, I waited for it. There it was! I stroked the place with my hand. One of its transparent fingers or swollen knees or misshapen feet or its monstrous skull moved imperceptibly, like a bubble rising to the surface of the marsh without even the energy to break through. It moved the way a shadow of a tree moves on a windless day. It moved the way the light moves when a cloud passes in front of the sun.

I knew how it changed position as the weeks passed and its movements became more vigorous, thumping, pedaling, turning.

But to my mother, these signs of life meant only that she had not yet been able to kill me. Ah! What a nuisance! And it goes on for so long: minutes, hours, days, weeks, months. There is so much time to get to know the little one who lives inside you. Is there any greater intimacy or promiscuity? Did each of my movements inside the womb remind her of the odious coupling of which I was the issue?

So she swung onto her rusty bike and rode off into the wasteland of refuse. I hope you're having a ball in there, my girl, my little fish, you'll see how I am going to snap your spine! Get out. Take a look. See if I'm up to it!

She mounted her old nag, and giddap! Do you feel the battering ram against your hideous body? Darling! This'll work up a fine storm to shatter a little submarine! No? This'll make some fine waves to drown the little diver! Well? Go away, you little shit, get the hell out of here!

Still moving? Here's something to calm you down. Quinine, aspirin! Sleep, little darling, sleep, little baby, let me rock you; drink, my beauty, drink the lovely poisoned brew. You'll see what fun you're going to have in the toboggan of my ass when you're well and truly rotted by drugs, drowned like a sewer rat. Death to you! Death to you!

At the last, powerless, resigned, defeated, disappointed, she let me slip out alive into life, the way you let slip a turd. And what about that little girl/turd coming slowly, face forward, towards the light she saw down there at the end of the narrow, moist passage, at the end of the tunnel? What was going to happen to her on the outside where already she had been so mistreated? Tell me, Mother, did you know that you were pushing her into madness? Did you question it?

What I have referred to as beastliness in my mother is not because she wanted an abortion (there are times when a woman is not capable of having a child, not capable of loving it enough); on the contrary, her beastliness consisted in not having followed through on her desire to have an abortion. Then, in having continued to project her hatred onto me when I was inside her, and, finally, in having chosen to speak of her wretched crime, her weak attempts to murder me. It was as if, having bungled it, she were starting up again, fourteen years later, without risking her own skin, in comparative safety.

And yet, it was thanks to her beastliness that, on the couch in the little cul-de-sac, I was more easily able to analyze the malaise of my entire former life, the constant anxiety, the perpetual fear, the self-disgust which finally blossomed into madness. Without my mother's acknowledgment I might never have succeeded in going back to the womb, returning to that hated and pursued fetus, which, without knowing it, I had found when I curled

140

up between the bidet and the tub in the obscurity of the bathroom.

Today, I no longer look upon "my mother's beastliness" in the same light. It is an important turning point in my life. I know why the woman did it. I understand her.

# Chapter VIII

"'Tube.' What does 'tube' make you think of?"

It was now a long time ago that my psychoanalysis had begun and I had been leaving the heavy baggage of my life with the little doctor three times a week. The office was full. I would lie down on the couch among the clutter and talk. I made sure the doctor was paying attention so that I was not speaking in a vacuum. He remembered everything I said. How was it possible? Did he take notes? Did he record my monologues on tape? I had scrutinized the silence, trying to detect the slightest sound of a machine, the hissing of a magnetic tape. Nothing. I had often abruptly turned towards him in the midst of one of my divagations, thinking I'd take him by surprise in the act of writing. There he was, impassive, immutable, his arms on the armrests of his chair, his legs crossed. He wasn't writing, he was listening. I would have hated it if there had been a device between us, paper, a pencil. He knew my stock of memories, the ghosts accumulating there, as well as I did. There was only my voice between us, nothing more. I didn't lie to him, and when I tried to mask a situation or prettify it or soften it (like the time I had begun by saying that I was in the living room of the farmhouse instead of on the street, when my mother was telling me her tale of woe), I always ended up by lifting the mask to tell the exact truth. I understood very well, without needing him to tell me, that if I concealed certain images it was because of an unconscious fear they would hurt even more when brought into the light, whereas, on the contrary, it was by lancing the wounds and cleaning them all out that the pain would go away.

Until the day when I took my courage in both hands to finally speak about the hallucination, and he said at the end of my description, "'Tube.' What does 'tube' make you think about?" Until that day I had never made a real expedition into the unconscious. I had gone there by accident, almost without knowing that I had been there. I had only spoken of events stored in the memory which I knew by heart, certain of which were suffocating me because I had never confided them to anyone: the paper spigot, operating on my dolls, my mother's wretchedness. By putting my cards on the table for a total, brutal, and cruel analysis, I had ended up by bringing to light the links that bound them. I can only state that on each occasion, while I perspired and appeared paralyzed and dumb, that in my mind there occurred extreme agitation made up of sudden advances and withdrawals in every direction at once, which I did not understand and could not control, and which terrorized me. It was the Thing.

I was convinced, the Thing had been there since earliest childhood. It made itself known every time I displeased my mother or thought I did. To make the deduction in the cul-de-sac, that the pleasures forbidden to me by my mother were the generators of the Thing, there was only one easy step. I became aware that, even thirty years ago, I was always afraid of displeasing my mother. At the same time I understood that the terrible blow she had struck in telling me about her unsuccessful abortion had left in me a profound self-disgust: I could not be loved, I could not please her. I could only be rejected. In this way, I experienced every departure, every misunderstanding, every separation as abandonment. A streetcar I failed to catch stirred up the Thing. I was a failure and as a consequence I failed at everything.

This was clear and simple. Why wasn't I able, on my own, to come to these conclusions and apply them whenever illness overcame me? It was because until then I had never spoken to anyone about them. Each terror had been experienced in isolation and immediately repressed as much as possible without ever having been understood. When I was of an age to judge my mother's principles (which were those of my class) and to find them, for the most part, evil, stupid, and hypocritical, it was already too late. The brainwashing had been completed, the seeds were so deeply buried they were incapable of ever reaching the surface. I never saw the signals "forbidden" or "abandoned," which I should have knocked down with a simple shrug of the shoulders. When I arrived in their vicinity, I found myself pursued by a loathsome pack screaming, "Guilty!" "Wicked!" "Crazy!" and the old Thing crouching in the darkest corner of my mind took advantage of my confusion, my despair, and my bewildered flight to spring at my throat and bring on a crisis. When I tried, but was unable to understand, for the simple reason that I had erased "forbidden by my mother," "abandoned by my mother," and had written in "guilty" and "crazy." Therefore I was crazy. This was the only explanation I could give.

It was too simple to be believed. And yet the reality was there: all my psychosomatic troubles had disappeared, the bleeding, the feeling that I was going blind and deaf. And the anxiety attacks were at greater intervals, no more than two or three a week.

Still, I was not normal yet. Though I had established certain routes through the city that I could travel without too many apprehensions, other ways of getting about in the world remained closed to me. I continued to live in constant fear of people and things. I still perspired a lot. I was still pursued, fists clenched, head hunched between my shoulders, and above all, the hallucination persisted. Always the same, simple and precise without the slightest variation. Such perfection made it even more terrifying.

I had alluded to it once in the first months of treatment: "You know, doctor, every once in a while, something strange happens: I see an eye looking at me."

"This eye, does it remind you of anything?"

"Of my father...I don't know why I say that, because I have no memory of my father's eyes. I know that they were black like mine. That is all I know about them."

And then I had spoken of other things without even knowing that I had avoided the danger by beating around the bush. I had taken another, easier road that was better marked. But all the same I understood the hallucination was the obstacle, it was there, and that one day, to move along, I would have to go beyond it.

The anxiety attacks born of "forbidden pleasures" and "abandonment" were henceforth easy to combat. I had become capable of driving them away before they had time to get a hold on me. But the others, the ones which continued to lacerate me and which still kept me from living in relation to other people, where did they come from and how would I discover their origin? I wasn't making any headway. The time had come to talk about the hallucination.

One day I felt strong enough to be able to do it. I had enough confidence in my doctor. I no longer thought he would send me back to the psychiatric hospital.

I settled down. Stretched out, my arms and legs extended, I wanted to be sure first I had access to my material: my mother, the red earth of the farm, all the shadows and the outlines, the odors and the lights, the noises, and above all the little girl who had so much to tell: "Every once in a while, something strange happens. It never comes during a crisis, but it brings on a crisis every time because it makes me so afraid. It can come on whether I'm alone or with another person or a number of people. Now that I think about it, it happens mostly when I'm with someone. With my left eye I see the person facing me and the decor of a room down to the smallest details, and with my right eye I see a tube just as clearly which advances to fit gently over my socket. When it's in place I see an eye looking at me from the other end of the tube. The tube and the eye are as alive as what I see with my left eye. This could only be taking place in the real world. It is on the exact same plane as what I am living through. The light is the same. The atmosphere is the same. What I see through my left eye has no less objective validity as what I see through my right eye. Except that the one reveals what is a normal situation while the other terrorizes me. I am never able to find the equilibrium between these two realities; I lose my balance, I sweat, I want to run away. It's unbearable.

"The eye looking at me is not like mine pressing against the tube. If it were, it would be dark inside the tube, it would be black at both ends. Therefore, inside the tube it's not quite dark and the eye itself is brightly lit, very close to the opening of the tube, very clearly defined, and very watchful. The eye makes me sweat because the look it fixes on me is severe, though it is not really provoking. It is a cold severity, with shades of contempt and indifference. It never leaves me for a second. It scrutinizes me intensely, never softening. Its expression never changes. If I close my eyes, it doesn't help at all: the eye is there, evil, cruel and icy. It can go on for a long time, several minutes even, and then it disappears as suddenly as it came. After I start to tremble I have an attack. I experience an enormous feeling of shame. I suffer more shame from the eye than from all the other manifestations of my illness."

There, I've said everything, I've given myself over entirely. I knew that I had come to an important moment in my analysis. If I didn't find an explanation for the hallucination I would never progress. I would never have a normal life.

It was then that the doctor said, "'Tube,' what does it make you think of?"

It irritated me to hear the words said. I saw what he was going to do with them: tube equals paper spigot, exit from my mother's womb. It wasn't that. If it was that simple I would have discovered it on my own. I had wanted to get up and get out of there. He exasperated me, this silent little jumping-jack with his imperturbability, and the peace of mind of the initiate.

"You remind me of the priests. You're no better than

147

they are. You archbishop of the ass! Because with you that's where we always wind up. It disgusts me, you disgust me. You're a disgusting character, the way you listen throughout the day to the filth of this one or that one. It's you who makes it happen. You stink! Why did you choose the word 'tube'? Such a word is not going to make me think of a bed of roses....

"Without even thinking, tell me what tube makes you think of."

"Tube makes me think of tube. A tube is a tube...tube makes me think of tube...of tunnel.... Tunnel makes me think of the train.... When I was little I traveled a lot. We used to spend all our summers in France and Switzerland. We would take the boat and then the train. In the train I was afraid to do peepee. My mother had very strict rules of hygiene. She saw germs everywhere...."

I was wandering, wandering. A little girl had come to join me. I was the little girl, I was three or four years old. I had just landed in France, in a difficult place where you had to behave all the time, to always say "Bonjour, Madame," "Bonjour, Monsieur." A place where I was not allowed to take off my shoes and go barefoot, a place where it was forbidden to say a word at the table and where I had to ask permission to go out. A place where I had to wash my hands twenty times a day.

It was summer. We were on the train, it was hot. I was bored, it was endless. I asked to do peepee. (For that I had to say, "Nanny, number one, please.") Nanny let my mother know of my having to do "numbeurreouane" (when it had greater consistency, she would say "numberretout"). Then they felt compelled to look for a particular bag among the luggage: the pharmacy bag. To me pharmacy meant nothing good, nothing but things which hurt or

148

stung, like the iodine or the ether, or pulled your hairs out, like the adhesive tape. Why did they have to get the pharmacy bag just to do peepee on the train? It was beginning to alarm me.

In the end they finally found what they were looking for among the hat boxes, suitcases, toilet articles, etc., and we went out into the corridor of the train. We proceeded, my mother in front, Nanny behind with the pharmacy bag, and me in the middle. I could stretch my legs, which was better than being in the compartment. When we got to the end of the car where the toilets were, we were shaken up as though we were in a salad washer and the noise was terrible! It was hard to stand up without falling. My mother and Nanny clung to whatever they could find, while I clung to their skirts. It was amusing. Less amusing was the smell coming from there. It was the powerful smell of urine, disgusting, unmannerly, and shameful.

My mother said to Nanny, "Hand me the alcohol. You clean the toilet bowl and the seat, and I'll clean the washbowl. We might as well use the occasion to wash her face and hands; she's already black from the coal smoke. Isn't it incredible how quickly that child gets herself dirty!"

With wads of cotton they began to fiercely clean the stinking place. My mother said, "The place is crawling with germs." They had already taught me that germs were those little creatures gnawing away at my father's lungs and which had already killed my sister. I no longer wanted to go peepee, but I was afraid to say so. It seemed to me that the toilets were swarming with invisible scorpions, minuscule snakes and wasps which couldn't be seen. The terrible shaking and the horrible uproar never let up.

Once the cleaning was done, they spread white gauze

on the seat. Now I could go peepee. Nanny took down my pants. I was wearing *"Petit-Bateau"* ones which buttoned onto a camisole with suspenders. One button on the stomach and one on either side. The front was fixed and the back could be let down, and a tape in the hem gathered it or let it out as one grew bigger, just as the buttons got sewn lower and lower on the camisole as one grew taller. "It's very practical," said my mother. Nanny was not of the same opinion.

There I was with my backside in the air. Nanny held me under the arms and lifted me up to put me down on the enormous seat, where I was torn apart. She held my pants up so that I wouldn't wet myself. She was trying to keep her balance while supporting my back. My mother looked at the scene with a critical eye: "Hurry up! You can see it's not so easy for us."

At that point the uproar became deafening (we must have changed tracks). Everything was shifting so violently I couldn't tell which end was up. I looked between my legs and saw at the bottom of the shallow bowl, at the end of a large round shiny pipe replete with its nasty contents, the ground with its surface of crushed stone speeding dizzily away. I was afraid, afraid. I was afraid of being sucked into this hole, possessed by my own peepee, and, after being shoved through the disgusting tube full of excrement shattered on the brightly lit tracks.

"I don't feel like doing number one now."

"Yes, you do. Now that it's set up for you, you can do it. Hurry up!"

"I don't want to, I can't."

"Ah! You'll be sorry for these moods of yours!"

Nanny, who knew me well, said, "I don't believe she'll do it, Madame."

In the confusion and the madness, I heard a sound which was regular, quick and clear: tap tap tap tap...

Taptaptaptaptaptaptaptaptaptaptap...I was four years old, I was thirty-four. I was still torn apart in the bathroom on the train, I was lying on the couch in the cul-de-sac. Tap tap tap tap tap tap.

I was no longer any age, I was no longer a person, I was nothing but this noise: tap tap tap tap tap tap tap tap...as light as a rhythm to count by, a lullaby... taptaptaptaptaptap... Where did it come from? It was a matter of life and death to know where it came from.

"Doctor, I have a headache."

A terrible pain, an intense soreness at the base of my neck, sharper than anything I had ever felt until then. My brains were being extracted by sudden brutal jabs.

Flashes of pain. The bewilderment of extreme suffering. Roots monstrously distorted, encompassing in their convulsions, skeletons of dragons, decaying carcasses of octopus, gradually releasing the unbearable stench of putrefaction as they were being dragged into the light.

"Doctor, I'm losing control! It's excruciating...I'm going crazy!"

I knew that if I got into the hallucination it would be the end. I should not have had to follow that instinct that drew me towards it. I should not have allowed myself to be in its control. I could have continued the way I was, an inoffensive invalid, without having to be locked up in an asylum. It was too late now, I was sinking into blackest lunacy, devastating convulsions.

"Doctor, help me!"

My head is bursting! Tottering, toppling...

Tap tap tap tap tap tap tap taptaptaptaptap...

Tap tap tap tap... The noise is there, so close! It is the

only thing which is not a part of the madness and which is outside the hysteria. I have to find it. I HAVE TO GO TO IT.

I am a baby, a tiny little girl, hardly able to walk. I'm taking a walk in a big forest with Nanny and my papa. "Can I do number one, please?" Nanny has hidden me behind a bush. She had looked for a long time to find the right one. You have to hide to "do number one, please." Squatting, I hold the fold of my *Petit-Bateau* pants against me and look at the jet of liquid coming out of me and burying itself in the ground between my feet, between my nice, freshly polished shoes. It is not without interest. Tap tap tap tap tap tap tap tap tap... a noise at my back. I turn around and see my father standing there. He is holding a funny black thing in front of one of his eyes, a sort of metal animal which has an eye at the end of a tube. That's what's making the noise! I don't want him to see me doing peepee. My father musn't see my backside. I straighten up. My pants make it hard for me to walk. Even so, I go towards my father, and I strike him with all my strength. I hit him as hard as I ean. I want to hurt him. I want to kill him!

Nanny tries to tear me away from my father's legs; I am scratching, slapping, hitting, biting while he continues to defy me with his long round eye. Taptaptaptaptap... I hate this eye, that tube. There is terrible anger in me, an incredible rage.

Finally, my father and Nanny speak to me. They say some words I don't understand, others I do. "Crazy, very naughty, very bad, crazy, no manners! It's wicked, it's shameful! You mustn't hit mama, you mustn't hit papa! It's very wicked, it's shameful! Vengeful, crazy! Very ugly, very naughty, crazy! Shame, shame, shame. Wicked, wicked, wicked, wicked. Crazy, crazy, crazy." In the end I understood that they think what I did is horrible, shocking, terrifying, and, suddenly, I am ashamed of myself.

The noise has stopped.

Silence. Peacefulness. Great peacefulness.

I unmasked the hallucination, exorcised the demons. I was absolutely certain that the hallucination would never return.

Everything was adrift around me...I had come back from very far away.

"Doctor, I understood, it's over. The hallucination was made up of all those things."

"Of course. The session is over now."

When I got up, I felt the perfection of my body for the first time . With ease my muscles set in motion the articulation of my joints. My skin relaxed over them. I was standing tall, taller than the doctor. My breathing was calm and regular. I was taking in the right amount of air. My rib cage protected my heart, which tirelessly pumped my blood. My pelvis was a white basin in which my insides had just the room they ought to have had. What harmony! It didn't hurt, it was simple. My strong legs propelled me towards the door. My arm held my hand towards the doctor. All this was in my power; it worked well. There was nothing to fear.

"Au revoir, Doctor."

"Au revoir, Madame."

My glance met his, and I am certain I saw joy there. We've done such good work together! Haven't we?

He had just helped me give birth to myself. I was just born. I was new!

I left the cul-de-sac. Everything was the same and yet different. A fine drizzle, soft as face powder, fell on my cool, pink cheeks. The old familiar cobblestones caressed the bottoms of my feet through their shoes. The reddish sky of a Paris night stretched above me like the big top of a gigantic circus. I was on my way towards the clamorous street, to a fiesta.

All of a sudden, as I was coming to the end of the cul-de-sac, everything became lighter, gayer, easier. I was flexible again. Suddenly, my shoulders had dropped, freeing my neck and the nape of my neck, which had been hunched for so many years that I had forgotten the feel of the wind in my hair at the back of my head. What was behind me was as little to be feared as what lay ahead of me!

I had only one goal in mind: to find my mother and to question her.

"Do you remember something which happened to me when I was little: I hit my father because he was filming me while I was going peepee?"

"It happened. I wasn't there, but I saw the film. Your father showed it to me at the time on his projector. Who told you about that?"

"No one. I remembered it. Was I punished?"

"Without a doubt. Perhaps you didn't get your goodnight kiss or perhaps you got a little spanking. A little punishment for a very little girl. You were a real savage when you were small."

"How old was I?"

"That's easy enough to remember. It was the first summer you spent in France. Your father was just getting out of the sanatorium. He wanted to get to know you. He was your father, after all.... You were between fifteen and eighteen months old."

She looked at me strangely. I thought I saw in her eyes

154

astonishment of a sort, regret even, a bouquet of faded flowers which hadn't yet lost their perfume. It was at this time that she must have begun to love me as I was—so unlike what she would have wanted me to be.

It was too late, I no longer had any need for her love.

# Chapter IX

The dead end had become the road to paradise, the route of my triumphal march, the channel for my energy, and the river of my joy. It would not have surprised me if this atrophied arm of the city had transformed itself into a fantastic parade ground. The little doctor would have come out through his iron gate entangled in the boughs. He would have had on his usual clothes, but, in addition, he would have had on his head a brilliant top hat with sequins and in his hand a long horse whip of gilded muslin.

Step right up, ladies and gentlemen! Come right up here! Don't be afraid, the show is free! Fear nothing, open your doors and windows, ladies and gentlemen! Come and see something you have never seen before! Ladies and gentlemen, open your eyes and your ears, gaze upon the only spectacle of its kind in the world!

Rattle of drums! Fanfare of trumpets! Boom, boom,

boom! Listen, brave people, listen to the story of the sweating woman who sweats no longer, the trembling woman who stopped trembling, the bleeding woman who stopped bleeding; her palpitations are all gone. Step right up, step right up! Spread her legs, feel her pulse, open up her skull. Don't hesitate! Go on, I beg of you, please, go on, do it, you won't find a thing. It's all gone!

And now, see for yourselves, ladies and gentlemen! This woman you have seen going back and forth in front of your houses for so many years, doubled over like a fetus, this shadow hugging your walls, this poor beggar who stopped shaking with fear in your doorways, this unfortunate who had been pursued by terror, her ankles twisting on your broken sidewalks. Well, look at what that crazy woman has become!

Leaping forward like a young buck, I would have made my dazzling entrance at the end of the cul-de-sac. Beautiful! Beautiful enough to take your breath away! Beautiful enough for *Playboy* or for a stocking ad, LEGS, slender. A long neck, long arms and legs, long-waisted too! Here I am in the best of health, with appealingly delicate ankles, knees, hips, shoulders, elbows and wrists. Look at me! See how powerful I am, but with something refined in the corners of my mouth and eyes, in the shape of my nose and in the way my neck is formed. Bursting with youth, caught up in the electricity of the astonished crowd, I am here. Arms outstretched and slightly raised, beautiful blond hair spreading against the sky like an embroidered fan. Gay, happy! I am in my wedding dress made by Marinette, the dressmaker in the family, who watched me being born, who with her fairy fingers made my clothes for I don't know how long, always demanding twenty endless fittings.

Next I would proceed with long, catlike steps, like this, gently, slowly. The cul-de-sac would be covered by a lawn, cut close and smelling of new-mown grass. I would see all my favorite trees: palm trees, pomegranates, thorn-apple, and orange. All the flowers and the animals I love. All the perfumes. And the sound of the sea in fine weather, and the wind urging on the little waves with regularity like the weaver's shuttle, calmly, laboriously, deftly weaving the fabric of the beach!

The doctor would have raised his whip, the soft braided lash of which would have licked the reins, and forward! Hazardous somersault, hazardous double somersault, hazardous triple somersault, splits, cartwheel, headstand, hup! Hup! Pirouette here, somersault there! Again hup! Hup! Hup! *Jeté battu, pas de chat, chasse croisé, pirouette*. And keep moving. Another headstand! I made my body do whatever I wanted it to and it obeyed me; it took me where it seemed good to be. It was no longer that great pile of flesh beside me, oozing everywhere, quivering, the inescapable and disgusting shelter of my panic-stricken mind.

What a triumph! Everyone applauded. The public crowned us with flowers!

But it didn't happen like that. The little doctor continued to sit in his armchair, stiff, correct, mute, almost cruel, now and then ironical in his behavior. And I, like a well-trained dog, would gratefully bring him my finds. Just as in the old days when I would bring my mother pebbles, hoping that in her hands they would become jewels. My mother rejected my imaginary treasures, but the little doctor, for his part, listened to my recitations without flinching, very attentively, helping me to understand on my own the precise value of what I was telling him.

I discovered my health, my body, my power over it, the privilege of moving about freely. I experienced great joy from it.

I discovered the night. I never tired of letting it carry me off at the end of each day. The lights in public places...it was Christmastime. The comfort and luxury of stores without customers, lit up inside, exhibiting their treasures to the curious: evening dresses, fur coats, champagne, foie gras, jewels, toys, orchids. Glistening winter sidewalks. The alternating zones of light and shadow in the streets. Night people. The warmth of friends in the cold. Drinks. Men. The intoxication of entering a place, barely looking at the crowd, yet having designs on this one or that one. The conquest. The game of conquering and being conquered.

Discovering hotel rooms, bachelor flats, studio apartments. Did the men know who was sharing their bed for a few brief moments? Not one of them ever figured out that what counted for me was to do everything forbidden until then. Nothing more. And to do it with a voraciousness which was extreme. Wasn't I "living the life"? How easy it all was! Afterwards, I would slip away by myself; that was the best time of all. I discovered solitude and the sunrise on a street I didn't know, the transgression filling my body, darkness everywhere, and still I was fearless. It was four or five in the morning. I had scarcely an hour or two to sleep before the children woke up, yet I knew I wouldn't be tired and that tomorrow would bring the same pleasure.

Discovering makeup, perfume, dresses, black underwear, necklaces, earrings. In the restaurants I stuffed myself with anything and everything, and yet I got thinner and thinner. The weight that had attached itself to me like a ball and chain dissolved without my doing anything.

During these weeks, or months even, I no longer remember, I was forever drunk with joy, health, alcohol, good food, the night, and caresses I'd never known before. I spent days amusing myself with that extraordinary toy: my own body. Everything surprised and pleased me: the way my fingers moved, the way my feet carried me along, the way my eyes opened and shut, the way my voice emerged from my throat, the way I modulated it, the way everything functioned so well. It was me. I was alive.

I took a secret pleasure in summoning the blood, the fear, the tube with the eye, the sweat. I made them come before me one after the other: they remained outside. I scrutinized them. I manipulated them, first with fear, then boldly; they wouldn't come in.

I would have wanted it to go on for a long time, never having amused myself in this way. I had never known what it meant to be carefree. All my life I had been weighed down, tormented, even in the games of my childhood. I had never really played hide and seek, tag, hopscotch, or jacks. My mother's eye, which I confused with the eye of God (and unconsciously with the eye of the movie camera), was always there, looking at me, assessing the way I moved, the way I thought even, never letting anything slip by unnoticed.

"Father, I have sinned in thought, word, and deed, and by...omission." That was the worst of all! For I could sin without knowing it. Sins were like germs. They were everywhere. They could not be seen. They could be caught at any point, whether I wanted them or not.

First came the sin, then guilt, followed by the Thing. I had always lived obsessed, pursued, spied upon, guilty, until the day I discovered the meaning of my hallucination.

With delight and an enormous hunger I then let myself give in to the illusion of freedom and health.

But cunningly the Thing returned by fits and starts. Until, one night it leapt on top of me, shaking me like a plum tree, agitating my brain, which knocked against the doubtful sheets, in the sweat of the beard which was on its own sprouting on the face of the man asleep beside me, the thirty-four-year-old madwoman with three children in the vanity of that shabby bachelor pad. I ran into the street and saw garbage cans overflowing, winos sleeping on the sidewalks, scrawny cats running from me, the workers and the whores out there at dawn, human misery! Putrefaction was everywhere! Everything was rotten! My brand new body was rotting.

My high life vanished into thin air. I was finished.

I was nothing but a puppet, a marionette, a robot, a doll!

What sense was there in my being healthy? What was my body good for? Nothing!

The storm was violent. It tore away everything. The Thing's new weapon was more terrifying than what came before. More terrifying than the blood, more terrifying than death, more terrifying than the heart pumping with all its might. The new weapon was anxiety, pure, direct, dry, simple, unmediated, without any protection, naked. An anxiety without perspiration, trembling, tachycardia, the anxiety did not any longer generate in me an impulse to run or to curl up inside myself. I wasn't sick any longer.

I was just a stupid, aging woman of no importance whose life made no sense. I was nothing. Nothing, to the point of dizziness, nothing, to the point of howling even to death.

To die. To die and finish it. I wanted to die, I wanted its mystery. I wanted it because it was something else, something incomprehensible for mankind, something unimaginable. I wanted only the unimaginable and the inhuman. I wanted to dissolve into a charged particle, to disintegrate into circular pulsation, to be annihilated. Nothingness.

Why didn't I kill myself during this period? Because of my children? I couldn't bequeath them the corpse of a nut who would have weighed as heavily on their lives as my mother had weighed on mine. I didn't want to have them enter the circus of the Thing. Was it really because of them I didn't kill myself? I don't know.

I would go to the dead end and insult the little doctor. I would fling in his face everything I heard about psychoanalysis: that it makes people even crazier, or sexually obsessed, or destroys the personality.

I summoned to the rescue the vocabulary of psychoanalysis, words he had asked me to put aside when the sessions began. I juggled with the libido, the ego, schizophrenia, the Oedipus complex, repression, the psychotic, the neurotic, paranoia, and fantasy, keeping transference till last. Because it made me feel bad handing myself over so completely, confiding in him, loving him to such a point!

Freud was the puppeteer! They were his thick strings operating the little doctor. He was the priest of psychoanalysis, that religion in which a certain pompous, vainglorious, and malevolent intellectual elite reveled.

"Yes, you malevolent species of monkey! A religion

which further alienates mental patients. What are you doing for the mental patient murmuring in your living rooms, on your television, in your magazines with their enormous circulations. You species of defrocked priest! I know perfectly well that you went through a teaching analysis, like all the rest of you clowns. What did you get out of it? Did you learn the rituals in the Mass? You know how to get people on the couch, how to speak, how the other is behind you listening, how everything is slyly managed in a hushed and secret atmosphere. What could you possibly have found to talk about during your teaching analysis? Well? Some vexation must have been the cause of your little rat's tail?

"It's not enough to say you know about mental illness! It's a horrible illness! What it means is living in a viscous fluid made up of what is on the outside and what is on the inside, the living and the dead, the shrill and the dull, the light and the heavy, the stifling and the impalpable from here and from there. What it means is being handed over to the horrifying Thing, forever changing, joined to the patient, enthralling him, pulling, cutting, growing, weighing, dragging, never leaving you alone, occupying all space and time, frightening you, making you sweat, paralyzing you, making you flee. It is the incomprehensible and the void! But a void which is full, a dense void! Do you even understand what I mean, you miserable prick?"

I couldn't take any more. Leaving these sessions, I would go out and get drunk, dead drunk. When a woman uses the expression "dead drunk," it seems vulgar and coarse. For a man it is less vulgar; it sounds strong and sad. A woman gets tight, she becomes intoxicated, at worst she drinks. I refuse to use these hypocritical circumlocutions. I got dead drunk, I was destroying myself,

I was running away from myself, I despised myself.

I no longer had any hold on myself. I was nobody. I had no desires, no will, no likes, no dislikes. I had been fashioned to resemble as closely as possible a human model which I had not chosen and which did not suit me. Day after day since my birth, I had been made up: my gestures, my attitudes, my vocabulary. My needs were repressed, my desires, my impetus, they had been dammed up, painted over, disguised and imprisoned. After having removed my brain, having gutted my skull, they had stuffed it full of acceptable thoughts which suited me like an apron on a cow. And when it was verified that the graft had taken, that I no longer needed anyone to control the waves which welled up from the depths of my being, I was let go. I could live freely.

Now that, in the dead end of the cul-de-sac, I had made an inventory of the mess and was recalling precisely the details of the scrupulous brainwashing to which I had been subjected, and thanks to which I had become more or less worthy of my mother, my family, and my class; now that I knew, that I discovered the trickery by which these agonies had been inflicted and endured to the very end in the name of love, honor, beauty, and the good, what was left to me? The void. Who was I? No one. Where could I go? Nowhere. There was no more of beauty, love, or the good than there had ever been, nor, for the same reasons, was there any more of evil, hate, shame, or ugliness.

In deciphering the hallucination I had believed that I was putting myself in the world, I had really believed I was being born. Now it seemed to me that by putting out the eye at the end of the tube I had aborted my self. That eye was not only my mother's eye, and the eye of God, and of society, it was my own eye as well. Everything I was, was destroyed, and in its place was zero, this beginning and end, this point from which everything vacillates between the more or the less, the zone of living death and of dead life. Could one be zero and thirty-four years old at the same time? I was a genuine monster. The most frightening thing was not in having been there, but in knowing that I was there and in knowing it with the cold conviction and clarity which psychoanalysis provides. I was a giant paralyzed by a mere strip of flypaper, or a fly imprisoned in a gigantic trap. Grotesque, ridiculous, stupid.

Hey! Look at the madwoman! Hey! Look at the madwoman!

The worst of it was that everyone from my background had submitted to the very same fate. Why, then, was I the only one to have reacted at once so well and so badly to the training? Was it because my mind was really sick, or because I was particularly weak and inconsistent? This was the only alternative conceivable to me, and it was an abyss and a hell.

I continued to go to the cul-de-sac. I would lie down, and now I would no longer say anything. I had nothing more to say. The doctor and I knew each other so well, a few words sufficed to fill him in on what had happened since the last session. Then silence. A heavy, dismal silence. Sometimes I even went to sleep on the couch, thus escaping from an absurd and derisive reality.

The emptiness. The emptiness. The same landscape as that of my adolescence: a gray, somber desert under a colorless and cloudy sky. What was the point of continuing to take myself there? It was always the same.

Why did I persist in going to the cul-de-sac? The couch. Eyes open, looking at the grasscloth that covered the walls, that gray, colorless flatness, smooth and fuzzy at the same time. Eyes opening on my agonizing desert, which was both hazy and clear.

One gloomy day in my childhood I had run into my father in some flat, smooth place where nothing was growing. I was six or seven years old. He had brought me a present: a cube of red velvet with a gold satin ribbon around it. Magnificent! Such wrapping could only contain a very beautiful present. I was still bothered by my father's doubtful presence, the tenderness and high spirits which were a part of his love for me. He was laughing, his eyes were sparkling. "Open it, see what's inside." I would have preferred to open the box when he wasn't there, but he insisted. "Open it, open it. I want to watch."

Then, slowly, I pulled on one of the ends of the gold knot. Almost brutally the box opened by itself, releasing a little devil bobbing at the end of a string, sticking out its tongue, eyes protruding from sockets, grimacing. It was very ugly, very stupid; it frightened me. What deception! I started to cry from the very depths of my shame. Betrayed!

My little devil of an adult was the doctor. I had been doing myself the favor of going three times a week to see a little devil who deceived me and made me an object of ridicule. The expense was enormous. The cost of the sessions swallowed up almost all the money I earned. Once the rent, gas, electricity and the children's school cafeteria fees were paid, I had five francs a day for the rest. It was hard. But such poverty went with my desert of anxiety. Once the children were taken care of, what would I have done with more money? I was lost in inconsistency. I was a disheveled nebula revolving around an undefinable center. Until then, the center of my life had consciously or unconsciously been my mother. She had been consumed by the analysis as though by an acid. Nothing was left of her. But I didn't know how to do anything but revolve around my mother and her principles, fantasies, passions, and her sorrows. Even if certain parts of my being unfurled in long ribbons floating wavelike in the distance, apparently free, they were in fact firmly attached to the vortex, which was the now unseeing eye of my mother.

In Serato, a particularly dry and arid region of Brazil, a few rare trees trained in the shape of bushes grow. When one tries to uproot them, one discovers their roots are stronger and thicker the deeper they go in the ground. If one persists in digging them up, one finds they communicate with neighboring bushes and that they converge in one thick stem that descends even farther while thickening, making its way finally as an enormous single trunk which bores into the earth like a sharp instrument. One understands that it is in fact an enormous tree which has buried itself twenty or thirty yards below the surface in order to find water.

I was those bushes. But, deprived of the trunk which drew the water from the depths, I was going to die.

# Chapter X

I didn't know why I still came to the cul-de-sac. Moreover, I was missing sessions. Either I forgot them completely, or I was mistaken about the hour or the day. I made my way to the door where there was a little ritual involving the ringing of the bell. First you had to open a glass door, which in turn opened directly onto the garden, and inside it, against the door jamb, was the button. All you had to do was to push it in order to ring the bell in the doctor's office. Only the initiated knew about it. And in that way, he was the only one I ever saw. If I arrived precisely on time, he would have me enter his office directly. And I was able to imagine that he had stayed there waiting for me since the last session. Yet it was enough to arrive five minutes early or late to encounter the outlines of a figure, or rather its shadow. Either the "patient before," head hunched between the shoulders, embarrassed, caught out, hidden, and furtive. Or the members of the household, whom over the years I had identified as the father, the mother, and the sister. I am not certain that that is who they really were.

It often happened in that period that I would climb the narrow flight of steps, open the first glass door, push the button inside, and wait. Soon I would hear the door to the office opening, the three steps taken by the doctor crossing the hall, and then I would see him appear in the half-open entryway. His eyes were flat, cold, direct, rounded in feigned surprise, his small body very straight, his voice a little hoarse and dry, however.

"You have made a mistake; I am not expecting you today." (Or else, "This is not the right time; I was expecting you earlier.")

Before I had time to make my excuses he'd already disappeared, leaving me in front of the closed door, that is to say, facing myself. Frustrated and guilty. Guilty, because I knew what a shock it was to hear that bell in the middle of a session, even when one was saying nothing. To see the doctor rise and leave was intolerable.

During this interminable period he had from time to time made several brief remarks which were slowly germinating in me.

That the forgotten session had to be paid for. To think that I, who didn't have a sou, for three quarters of an hour of silence had to shell out a fortune: forty francs.

That the silence had a meaning. Holding my tongue did not mean I had nothing to say. It meant either that I was hiding something, or that I was confronting an obstacle I was afraid to surmount. If I wanted to get beyond it, I had, therefore, either to speak of what I wanted to hide, or struggle to define the invisible obstacle that was stopping me; the only way to arrive at this point was to say absolutely everything that came to mind, and nothing did.

That the least important symptom had a meaning—for example, during this period of total silence, if I breathed a sigh, even a very little one, the doctor would say, "Yes?... Yes?..." as if to make me understand that there was perhaps an opening there, at the precise moment when I had uttered the sigh. I had to try to recover what was in my mind at that instant. Likewise, if I altered my position (because I could lie low like a hunting dog, my face to the wall, without moving a muscle during the entire session), I would hear his "Yes?... Yes?..."

My attitude differed very little in the world from the way it was at the doctor's. I tried to control myself with my children so that when we were together, just the four of us, we spoke, we played, we did the homework for the following day. I tried to do my work (I edited advertising copy at home, thanks to which I was able to pay for my sessions and feed my children). The rest of the time I was silent. I was unable to communicate with anyone. I would curl up on my bed and stay there for hours, thinking of nothing in particular, wallowing in a sort of indifferent and pointless stew from which fear occasionally pulled me out, making me sit up, agitated, my breathing accelerated. Impossible to say of what I was afraid. Sometimes I'd fall asleep fully clothed. I would open my eyes. It was dawn. It was all the same to me. The fact that there were days and nights had no importance whatsoever.

Forgetting is the most complicated of locks, but it is only a lock  It is not an eraser or a sword, it does not efface, nor does it kill; it imprisons. I know now that the mind picks up everything, files it, classifies it, and keeps it all. It all has meaning: even what I think I have not seen, heard, or felt, even what I think I haven't understood, even the minds of others. Every event, no matter how minuscule, no matter how ordinary (as, for example, stretching in the morning when yawning) is catalogued, labeled, and locked away in oblivion, but marked in consciousness by a signal which is often microscopic: a scented sprig, a flash of color, a blinking light, a fragment of sensation, a shattering word. And less even than that: a rustling, an echo. And still less, even: a nothing that is nevertheless something.

It's sufficient to pay attention to these signals. Each of them guards a path at the end of which is a bolted door behind which, intact, is a memory. Not cold and lifeless as in death, but, on the contrary, alive, truly alive, with not only its own light, smells, movements, words and colors, but also its own sensations, emotions, feelings, thoughts, and two antennae, two possible recordings of what came before and after.

In plunging into an investigation of the unconscious, as I did for seven years in order to heal myself, first of all I understood the system of signals, then I found the secret for opening most of the doors, and finally, I discovered the doors which I thought were impossible to open, and in front of which I stood, desperately marking time. The anxiety came then from my certainty that there was no longer a way to make the march backward in time. The situation was irreversible: impossible to abandon or forget, a door that was difficult to open, behind which was to be found a remedy for appeasing and taking care of my sick mind.

And if I didn't get there? And if the whole thing was only my suggestibility? And if I was in the hands of a charlatan? And if I went back to those good pills that put me to sleep? And if I just dropped the whole thing?

The resistance which the mind offers to opening these doors is formidable. My own resistance was amazingly powerful. It was guarding, back in there, something which had wounded me, which had done me great harm, which had stolen my identity and shattered my life. It resisted my going back there, it didn't want me to suffer again that forgotten injury. It enlisted death on its side, in order to better guard the door. Death with its putrefactions, its stinking fluids, its decomposing flesh, its whitened skeleton from which dangled the meat crawling with worms. It posted its horrors in front of it, everything which I then considered to be horrors: spectacles to make me run away, visions to make me vomit, something dangerous in the extreme. But there was most of the time an empty space before the door: an empty space crawling with invisible things, a fascinating void which made me dizzy, a void which was terrifying.

It was almost without my being aware of it that the first door opened of itself.

One night I had a dream I hadn't had for a long time, but which I had had repeatedly almost every night when I was growing up.

I was in a pleasant place which was sometimes open ground, or sometimes planted with sea pines. The ground was soft, sandy even, but firm nonetheless.

Into the peace and sweetness of the setting came a horseman, who was himself quite in harmony with the scene. His horse went along at a little trot, very slowly, measured. The horseman guided the horse into a rectangular ring which he demarcated precisely by making a number of perfectly identical turns, the horse placing its hooves in the prints it had left on the earlier rounds. The man might be either a medieval knight in armor (in this case he held a splendid banner and the horse was richly caparisoned), or a modern-day horseman wearing tweeds and fine linen (a small silk scarf, smelling deliciously of a subtle mixture of *couscous*, leather, and droppings). Never once did he look at me. I found him terribly seductive, and I knew that he was aware of me.

At a given moment he increased the tempo of the trot or, more precisely, the movements of the horse had become more profound, more strongly marked, as in the exercises of *haute école*; the effect was to make the rider rock backward and forward regularly. At the same time as the cadence became more marked, the horseman made a smaller and smaller circuit, until he was turning around and around in the center of the rectangle. I didn't see his eyes, I did not meet his glance, and yet I guessed that it would have been easy to jump on behind him, and that he would not have been displeased if I had. But the more he turned, the more the ground became pasty, a sort of bechamel or mayonnaise in which I would sink and get bogged down, and which paralyzed my movements, making them painful. In the end I could not extricate myself from this thick, soft glue smothering me.

I would wake up with a start, breathless, covered with perspiration. I detested this dream, which turned into a nightmare and made my heart beat almost to the breaking point. I was incapable of identifying the rider, who was faceless for me, as I had never caught his eye. Moreover, I could understand nothing about this vision, which left me with a feeling of terror, and whose memory I tried to suppress.

Reliving this dream on the couch at the end of the dead-end street, defining each of its elements as exactly as I could, it came to me that I was describing two worlds.

One, which I knew well, from my own background, was the world of my mother: harmless, pleasant, a little dull, a little sad, wise, conventional, harmonious, and flat. The other, which I didn't know but which, unconsciously, I desired at the time of the dream, was the world of adventure, the world of men and sex (for the horseman attracted me enormously), the world of the street. Whether to go or to stay. I was bogged down in the effort of trying to resolve a problem which could never be resolved by a little girl.

My mother was the melancholy harmony of the countryside. I had no need to feel her eye upon me for it to impose her discipline on myself. Her eye was already in me. I saw with her eyes. I had no vision of my own, or, at any rate, even at the age of seven or eight (when I started to dream about the horseman), I was capable of struggling unconsciously against the conflict within me at the risk of being paralyzed or suffocated.

For his part, the horseman did not look at me; he left me alone. In speaking about him, I began to understand what I truly loved and desired when I was a child. I also understood why I didn't like to be watched when I was making love, and why, when my illness became more severe, I could feel pleasure only if I imagined I was coupling with an animal, most especially a dog. This fantasy disgusted me more than anything about myself and I was ashamed even to speak of it.

I began to speak of it and the fantasy became more distant from me, as had the hallucination. It was simple enough: the dog couldn't judge me and would leave me alone. The look of a dog could neither humiliate nor hurt me.

Each time I opened one of the dreaded doors, I realized

that the mechanism of the lock was not as complicated as I had believed, and that, where I dreaded to discover terror, torture, and horror, I discovered the little girl in all her moods: unhappy, infatuated, and terrified. I was afraid of finding something which could frighten a thirty-four-year-old woman who had seen men killing each other in the streets, who had felt, in bearing children, her insides being torn apart, who knew about napalm, torture, and the concentration camps. But what I discovered was a child's fear. Behind the door was the little girl terrorized because a big cockroach had disappeared into a hole in the wall just above her head, or a little girl terribly disturbed because a gentleman was filming her while she was doing peepee, or a little girl paralyzed by a horseman visiting her at night, or a little girl frightened by a paper spigot. I relived the moments with her, I became her, I felt her fear. When she disappeared I would wake up and begin to clear the newly conquered terrain. My space became increasingly enlarged. I was getting better.

During the first part of the analysis I had won health and the freedom of my body. Now, slowly, I was going to begin to discover my self.

It was a painful process at the outset because I distrusted myself. I was afraid of encountering a person whose faults and vices I would not have known how to contain. I had to make numerous inroads into the unconscious in order to convince myself that it was wild and free, yet incapable of malice. Good and evil were the province of my conscience and were for me to invent in my own time.

The treatment terminated when I felt capable of taking responsiblity for my thoughts and actions, whatever they might be. This took me four more years.

# Chapter XI

It had taken the first four years of analysis, such a great number of sessions, to begin to understand that I was in the process of being psychoanalyzed. Until then I had handed myself over to the treatment as if it were a form of witchcraft, a sort of magic trick to give me refuge from the psychiatric hospital. I had progressed well, but I could not convince myself that mere words were going to definitively drive away my disorder, this sickness which was so profound, this devastating disorder, this ongoing fear in me.... From one minute to the next, I expected everything to begin again: the blood, the anxiety, the sweat, and the tremors. I was so astonished to see the respite continue that I did not understand I had changed profoundly. I was less and less at the mercy of others.

The dead end became the laboratory and, at the same time, the castle of the locked doors. The little doctor was my safety net and the witness of my journeys into the unconscious. My trail was ablaze with landmarks as familiar to the doctor as to myself. I could no longer lose my way.

I first relived moments which served as a shield against the Thing, as though I wanted to prove to him and to myself that I had not always been sick, that there existed in me a hidden embryo which I could rediscover and, beginning there, I could expand and flower. I tried to define how and why I had become a mental patient.

In so doing, I uncovered my mother's dangerous personality and saw again the scenes I am about to describe in the sudden bursting forth of life itself. I was once again totally the child.

We used to spend part of our summer vacations in a house by the sea called the Salamander. It was white with blue shutters. A central hall gave access to eight bedrooms and, at the end of it, a big living room, open to the Mediterranean. At the other end of the hall was a courtyard planted with zinnias and convolvulus, and surrounding it, the kitchen, the servants' quarters, wash house, scullery, and garage. A little universe, quite complete, open only to the sky and the sea, closed in on the entire family gathered there.

I spent my days in a bathing suit, running among the rocks and on the sand, playing in the water. Nanny had her eye on me from the beach, where she stayed for hours on end gossiping and knitting with nursemaids from the neighboring villas, which were occupied by friends or relations.

Although meals at the Salamander, complete with gazpachos, salads, sherbets, fried fish, and shellfish, were delicious, I was not allowed to have any. Children were not allowed to eat at the table with grown-ups until the age of ten. Theirs was a special diet in the Anglo-American style, consisting of cereals, chopped meat, fruits, and vegetables, cooked or raw. Very healthy. So I had my meals before the adults. Nanny was nearby, observing my behavior and my chewing. For my mother used to say in her pedantic way, "Chew. *Por l'amor de Dios*, chew!" So Nanny repeated it: "Chew. *Por l'amor de Dios*, chew!"

One evening at the Salamander, I had sat down at my place at the end of the table, which was already set for the grown-ups' dinner.

Benaouda had closed the shutters, making faces at me from every window. This was our evening game. The dining room side of the living room was lit by an Arab chandelier, which I thought magnificent because it looked like a Christmas tree. It was made of copper stars one on top of another, whose numerous long arms supported little cups of colored glass—blue, red, yellow, and green. In these cups (once oil lamps) burned bulbs which sent out multicolored light into that corner of the vast room.

The living room side remained in shadow. The youngest of my uncles, who was only about ten years older than I was, that is to say, he was about fifteen, sat, feeling bored, in a big rattan armchair. His right leg was extended in a cradle splint: he suffered from a discharge of synovial fluid. My mother had explained to me that synovial fluid was like the oil which Kader put on the chain and pedals of my bicycle. So after a fall, my young uncle had lost the fluid that kept his knee lubricated. In order to get it back, he had to stay put.... He loved me very much and was always giving me compliments on my curls, my freckles, my skinned knees, and my dresses. I too loved him very much. He was neither an adult nor a child, and yet he had the extraordinary superiority of being my uncle, my mother's brother. It would sometimes happen that I was so tired out from my days by the sea in the sun and the sand that I would fall asleep at the table in the middle of my dinner. When my uncle was well he would take me in his arms and carry me up to my room. I felt his tenderness just before falling altogether asleep.

So it was that on that evening I was protected: Nanny beside me, my uncle facing me on the other side of the table, chandelier in the shape of a star above my head, and the sea in repose outside, heaving great sighs. It was then that Messaouda served me a full bowl of vegetable soup, which I detested. Particularly the strings of the leeks, for which I felt an absolute repulsion. I was incapable of swallowing them. This was a visceral reaction which I could not overcome. I clenched my teeth and refused to lift the spoon to my mouth. To help me, Nanny put the spoon to my teeth. I swallowed the broth, which went down easily, but allowed in not a single particle of vegetables, above all, not the leeks.

That was when my mother came in, beautiful, perfumed, her hair flat against the scalp. She understood the situation in a single glance.

"She has to eat her soup."

"Madame, there is no possible way to get her to swallow the vegetables."

"Let me do it."

She took Nanny's place, spoon in hand.

"Aren't you ashamed to be made to eat like a baby!"

There was nothing to be done; my disgust was too strong, and it was impossible to unlock my jaws. Provoked, my mother got up out of the chair.

"Keep at it. She won't go to bed until she's finished what

there is in her bowl, and she won't get anything else."

Then she left, and I remained with my soup in front of me, quite sure that I wouldn't eat it, in spite of the pain I might be causing my mother by acting this way.

Several minutes later there was a crunching of the gravel in front of the house. Someone was out there. Then a pebble knocked against the shutter nearest me. I opened my mouth and swallowed the vegetables. My uncle and Nanny didn't say a word. After a time a second pebble, another spoonful swallowed like castor oil. A third, a fourth, a fifth spoonful, as I clung to the table to fight off my nausea. It was then that my uncle, who did not appear to be distressed, said: "You'd do better to eat all your soup, because I have a feeling that the old clothes man is around somewhere, and if you're not good he is going to steal you away."

The old clothes man was a man who bought old clothes in the better sections and went to sell them elsewhere. He walked slowly through the streets, giving forth at regular intervals a piercing cry, "Old...clo! Oo...ths...!" He inspired in me genuine terror because he wore, hanging by their tails from his belt, the remains of dried rats, which made a sort of girdle around his hips. I would hide when I heard his cry, and my mother threatened, if I wasn't good, to give me to the old clothes man.

But the old clothes man didn't come by the Salamander on his rounds. It couldn't be him. Even so, I swallowed the spoonfuls of soup which Nanny held before my lips.

Suddenly, in the silence of the large room, in the night when time was standing still from the surprise, I heard very close to me: "Old...clo! Oo...ths!"

He was there! My bowl wasn't finished! He was going to take me away! Horror swept through me; a great shuddering took hold of me, gripping my stomach and, as if I was vomiting up my very heart, the soup I had swallowed came back up from my mouth in a geyser. I was seized by spasms, I vomited water, air, nothing. Nanny held my forehead, and — surprisingly — my uncle was laughing.

My mother came in again. In a fraction of a second she saw the beautiful tablecloth spattered with vomit. Her face tightened: I had, once again, disappointed her. I understood her stratagem: she had pretended to be the old clothes man to force me to eat my soup. It hadn't gone the way she thought it would. There was in her expression as well as her voice an hysterical exasperation. "She's going to eat all her soup all the same! One of these days this child will stop her fits once and for all. I won't move from here. We're not going to have dinner until she's finished."

Then, all by myself, I ate the vomit of my soup, and I did so not to please her, but because I felt in her something dangerous, sick, something stronger than she was and stronger than I was, something even more horrible than the old clothes man.

Alerted by the noisy outbursts, the entire family laughed at this episode. Among themselves, they went over every detail. In the end they said about my mother, "She's stern but just." I couldn't get these words into my head. I didn't understand what it meant, I rejected it.

Unless I was sick I was unable to get my mother's affection and attention. I returned from school feverish, my eyes burning, I was shivering. On the way home Nanny had already made her pronouncement, "You are not well." Hardly in the door, my mother was alerted and my room was transformed into a sickroom. My mother spread a sort of heavy embroidered altar cloth on the dresser on which she set down the remedies: the thermometer, the silver spoons on saucers, and, on a throne above all the paraphernalia, a little flowered porcelain basin, the base of which made a grotto in which burned a votive candle keeping hot the vervain tea, which I adored.

"You have to drink a lot when you have a fever."

My mother came towards the bed, bent over me and felt rather than kissed my forehead and temples. This she did carefully with her lips and cheek, first on one side of my face and then the other, with many little swoops, while holding my chin firmly in her hands. These quick, precise, gentle touches filled me to the brim with happiness and love.

"You've got quite a fever. Let's see, open your mouth."

That's where the trouble always lay. She made use of one of the spoons on the dresser as a tongue depresser, using a little flashlight to look in my throat.

"A real tonsillitis with white specks. You'll be down for a week!"

She did her best to explain to me that I was sick because I was careless, disobedient, imprudent, etc., but that didn't keep me from being the most contented little girl in the world. I knew that she would zealously take good care of me for a week. With a sore throat and my body already aching, I let myself fall on my bed which had just been remade with cool sheets, so cool that contact with them made me shiver as I snuggled down in them. I was as soft and fragile as a dead-ripe fruit.

Not only did she nurse me; she stayed there beside me, silent, absorbed in a book or needlework. The days passed quickly in her presence, and when night fell my whole room would begin to sway gently because of the quivering flame of the night-light which made the vervain tea give out a delicious perfume. The exaggerated shadows of the furniture and objects formed a warm, enchanted retreat in which my mother's raised voice put me to sleep, rocked me. In her soft, full, and rather low voice she intoned: "The little fellow's mother told him one morning, 'At fifteen you'll be as tall as our bread hutch. In town you could make a good apprentice, but to farm the land you are much too small, my friend, you are much too small, oh yes!'" There followed the story of Grégoire, the little Breton rebel, up until his death in the middle of the bullets whistling: "But one of them gets him right between his eyes, his soul escapes through the hole, and Grégoire is in paradise." This atrocious ending and the couplet following, with Jesus opening "his pink cloak" to watch over the child and hide him, was devastating to me. She sang with particular attention to the passages which were poetic or dramatic. There were also the "Little handkerchiefs of Cholet" and many other songs, sad and pretty, which have stuck in my brain and will always be with me. For me they will continue to be important because they are heavy with the scented nights, and love.

Her hands were so cool, so light, capable in the extreme, and made for nursing. No one could give an injection or change a dressing like my mother. Hands like birds, sometimes like cats. Hands which seemed to multiply as they moved quickly and skillfully, tucking me in, feeling my forehead one more time.

"Now you are going to sleep, my darling little girl."

She spoke to me as I had heard her speak to her child in the tomb at the cemetery. Her voice and her hands caressing me.

I did have her love then. How beautiful and how simple

it was. I fell asleep blissfully, burning with fever.

The best was to come. In the morning, my throat was not so sore. I could swallow more easily. The thermometer showed my temperature was down. There was impatience growing inside me. I wanted to get up and move about.

"You must not get out of bed. You are still far from cured."

To keep me quiet she made me sit up in bed, plumped the pillows behind me and began to read. She was reading from the fables of La Fontaine and then there were the poems which she read, later, with so much expression. It was always the same books. I knew exactly where they were placed on the shelves in the library. There was one which I waited for with a mixture of impatience and horror. It was a collection of poems by Jehan Rictus about the poor and the miserable in Paris. She particularly relished a story called "The Old Woman's Tale." When she announced this one it gave me goose bumps. It was the story of a boy from the Paris slums who took to crime and ended up on the scaffold. The criminal's mother, kneeling on the nameless earth in that section of a Paris cemetery set aside for the condemned, let out a dirge which dragged on for several pages. My mother assumed her voice in the story. In this transformation, it was as if my mother had put on the mask of a whore or a pauper, her body disguised by poverty. This gave birth to an extreme curiosity in me. To tell the truth, at that instant my mother was at once fascinating and disgusting to me. Where had she gone to dredge up an old crone, so astonishing for a woman who was in her own life so dignifed and proud, brought up correctly, so puritanical? It was because the text was written in Parisian slang that my mother would let her lips droop in feeble abandon when pronouncing such words as "Ménilmuche," "Montmertre," also certain other words having to do with murder and violence. I didn't understand their meaning very well, but I knew these expressions were lower-class. She did, however, provide me with a commentary on the text, and then I understood that the poor woman in the story was crying because they had just buried her son in that plot of ground reserved for the condemned. She didn't know exactly where, since the grave of a person just guillotined would not have been marked by any cross, not even a marker. In her crying through the character in the story, I saw again the little boy who would have been my brother, pink, plump, on whose tummy she loved to press her lips and go "prrrt," making him laugh. She was feeling his tender lips sucking her nipple. She was looking at his blond curls. It was the same head which in the story had been cut off and buried, separate from the body.

This story was one of my mother's showcase pieces, and when she read it, it was not unusual to see the household servants come in and listen. In our family, it was said of my mother: "She's a true artist."

Sometimes she had me on my knees so that I could look at the Gustave Doré illustrations in Dante's "Inferno," which she had had bound in snakeskin, or at her grandmother's catechism, replete with fat, ecstatic angels and grimacing devils....

Then the recovery. And life once again took on its familiar qualities. From the instant I stopped being physically weak she would get up and go away. She returned to the sick and the destitute. Leaving me with the precious memory of her attentiveness, her being there, and the impression that I was too little to understand her songs, her pictures, and her stories. I had the vague feeling that there was something wrong. Perhaps she wasn't normal.

In Switzerland we lived in the Edelweiss: a large two-story wooden chalet with a big open porch all around it, onto which the ground-floor rooms opened. Surrounding the house, the Swiss countryside which all white colonials dream about: a meadow of cool green grass studded with ravishing little flowers, a forest of pine trees in the distance and farther still, the Alps.

"Breathe deep, fill your lungs: you're here to build up your health."

We were living there with the best friend of my mother and her two sons, who were the same age as me. Three children between six and seven years of age entrusted to an ecclesiastical tutor for their school work. Our freer Mediterranean spirits were too much for the Abbé de Grandmont; to keep us quiet he would tell us about the life of Saint Guy de Fontgalant, a young man recently beatified, whose special peculiarity was to seek and find the lost objects of those who prayed to him; "Saint Guy de Fontgalant, help me to find my handkerchief," and you'd find your handkerchief.

This was in 1936.

Our schoolroom, located on the second floor of the chalet, appeared to be suspended between the sky and the snow-covered mountain tops.

One morning we heard a cry, a shriek really, a powerful voice giving the alarm. In one second we were at the top of the stairs, leaning over the polished railing. Everyone in the house had done as much, so that lower down I could see the shoulders and backs of necks bent over in the direction of the entrance hall. In the center of the huge stairwell my mother lifted up her agitated face, her features drawn back as if by claws, her eyes even greener than usual, wide with terror.

"The communists took power! It's just been announced over the radio!"

The communists? What does that mean? Are they Germans who are going to nail us to the doors of barns the way they did in the Great War? Why is Mother so scared?

The household was seized by panic. In twenty-four hours our bags were packed, the chalet locked up, and we were on our way back to Algeria at top speed.

"We'll take the night express; that way we'll cross France without seeing a thing."

And it is true that in the morning we were already in Marseille, the Mediterranean, the port, and the big steamer at the dock. What a relief! We were the first to board. I had the impression of having had a narrow escape. Apparently the communists were not to be found at the seashore, for everything appeared calm. We were fortunate in still another way: we were living in Algeria and not in France. I did not ask any questions and did my best to be good. For in moments of extreme tension, my mother had a quick hand, and if I so much as looked at her the wrong way, she knew how to use it, slaps which really stung, leaving the mark of her five fingers on the face or the backside. Nanny also walked softly, and everyone else with her.

All the same, once on board the atmosphere became easier. There were flowers in my mother's cabin. Who had sent them?

My mother was speaking to Nanny. "I was able to get a telegram to the house in time to warn them. According to the captain it seems everything is all right over there... no trouble yet."

Then we went out on deck. By now many people were out on the wharf. A gentleman in a white suit (one of those suits that used to be worn by Frenchmen on their way to the colonies), white shoes, a panama hat, a red necktie, and a red carnation in his buttonhole was walking at quite a pace on our deck in the middle of a group of men who listened to him solemnly.

A loudspeaker announced that all those who were going ashore should do so. We were ready to get underway.

The man was left alone and came over very near us to lean on the railing. The crowd on the dock and even on the terrace of the shipping company opposite us had grown much larger. The man was signalling to some people on the other side. Incomprehensible cries could be heard here and there in the commotion. I could feel my mother was nervous. The atmosphere was electric.

And suddenly the man, who had appeared to be very well bred, raised his right arm, fist closed, and the entire crowd opposite, after a loud "Ah!" did the same. A forest of fists above their heads. My mother took a rather severe tone of voice while speaking to Nanny.

"I suspected as much a moment ago. He is surely one of the leaders of their party.... Apparently they are not as poor as all that, since they travel first class, and, moreover, wear an alpaca suit to address those in the marketplace, as it were."

I was bold enough to ask: "Who is it?"

"A communist!"

"And those people?"

"Communists, workers. Stop bothering me with your questions."

Workers! Communists! Her tone of voice seemed to indicate the two were the same. I didn't understand. The communists seemed to be dangerous people, and yet my mother was always saying, "We must be polite to the workers, they are poor unfortunate people." Or else, "There are some workers' children who have nothing to put on their plates, not a toy to play with. You should be thinking of them when you're wasteful."

So great was my perplexity that at the risk of getting into trouble I questioned her once again. "What do they want?"

"Our money, our houses, our clothes."

"Why?"

"Because they don't like us."

"Because we haven't been polite enough to them?"

My mother shrugged her shoulders. I exasperated her. I'd better hold my tongue and ask Nanny to explain later on.

Then the siren issued the signal for the departure. Sailors busied themselves on the ship and on shore, casting off the moorings. And when the ship had visibly started to go away from the wharf, the crowd in one enormous voice sang a song which was grand, impressive, and very beautiful, though to me it was unknown. "It is the final conflict, let us unite, and tomorrow...." My mother was pale; she spoke in fits and starts.

"We must stay here and maintain our dignity. We must not let them think we are afraid of them.... You must stand straighter than ever. Don't be frightened, it's only a masquerade."

She pushed me in front of her. I stood straight, almost at attention, as if paralyzed, while the communists' song washed over me. I don't know what made me think that my gray flannel coat came from l'Enfant Roi, that my tam o' shanter came from Old England, that my shoes came from somewhere I couldn't remember, and my linen socks from the Grande Maison de Blanc. I was very correct, very well behaved, in order to represent the dignity of my family. For once things went well, although I was always so untidy, as my mother used to say.

The man in white who was near us had heard my mother's words and saw her gesture, and he too began to sing, raising his fist even higher, "Arise, ye prisoners of starvation, arise, ye wretched of the earth...."

What end? Our end? Our death? My mother was so very pale now, stiff, her face hard almost. I had never participated in so grandiose and dramatic an occasion. The eyes of the crowd never left the man with the red carnation. I had never seen comparable expressions, determined, ready for anything, dangerous.

I who loved running around the deck on such trips never set a foot out of the cabin on that trip.

Some time later we were at the Salamander. I no longer thought about the communists, although they were the principal topic of conversation in my family, who, when I went to say goodnight in the living room, were juggling with the names of politicians, reading newspapers and magazines, or glued to the speaker of the radio.

For me the communists were an ambiguous subject which I did not even try to elucidate. I had been forever told that we should love one another, share with the poor, etc. But when the poor demanded in other ways than by begging in the streets, we couldn't give to them. Why? It was a mystery.

One of my uncles skidded into the courtyard of the Salamander during the dinner hour. He slammed the car door and rushed into the house, running all the way to my grandmother's, where, gasping for air, he announced, "The Reds are getting ready to make a raid on the villas along the beach! Alert the neighbors!"

The Reds? The red carnation, the red necktie! The communists! Here we go again. So they were going to put me in my good dress and push me in front of them when they sang their grand and terrifying song. No! I didn't feel capable of it.

But instead, it turned out to be the same as it was in Switzerland: the uproar, the decks cleared for action, the house upside down. My mother had taken command. She began by organizing our defensive position: iron bars on the windows and doors, all bolts shut, all padlocks padlocked, and, for extra security, once the servants were loaded with provisions in baskets and locked in with us, she had them push heavy furniture in front of the doorways which were most exposed.

I was more than afraid, I was horrified. I was shivering all over. In order not to have me in the way of all the goings and comings and the moving of furniture, they had sent me to bed where I imagined communists cutting off my hands, disemboweling me....

Hours went by. I was cowering in my bed all through the night, trying to predict the approach of the communists, who had already fallen by now. I had understood that my family had decided to play bridge calmly, and my grandmother had even said to Lola in the hall, "Serve the champagne, it may be the last of it. Better to profit while we can, and do open some for the kitchen, my dear!" which doubly increased my shivering. I thought they were much more courageous than me. Nanny, making a hasty visit to my room, deposited the fat chamber pot behind the door, which was an indication that I must not move from there in any circumstances.

A great big June bug, incapable of escaping, circled in the fan around the light. Sometimes the creature was blown into the ceiling, and the shock was so great that it was knocked onto the floor, where it stayed for a moment, wriggling its thin legs in order to right itself for flight. Before finding again the light in the center of the room, it darted low, flying, sometimes landing, stopping its incessant buzzing to undertake the fumbling progressions of the blind. About eighteen inches above my head there was a deep round hole in the wall, the purpose of which I did not know. All of a sudden I thought I could not stand for the June bug to crawl in there. That is, however, what it did. At that moment I was paralyzed with fear, transfixed on my bed, incapable of making any movement. The June bug was clinging to the edge of the opening. It was going to fall on me and scratch my face, put out my eyes. It was then I began to shriek. My uncle was the first to arrive. I remember that he took me in his arms and prevented my mother from slapping me. I had given them quite a scare with my screaming.

"At a time like this! You chose the right day! At your age, to be afraid of a June bug. Clearly the child isn't normal."

They drove the insect away, and I fell asleep. I never heard the communists. But the following day, in leaving the house to go to the beach, I saw that they had been there: on our door and on the doors of the neighbors, there was a large design, a kind of cross with broken arms, painted with thick strokes of a brush which had been dipped in tar, some of it dripping down, here and there, in thick black streaks, drying now in the sun. No one told me it was the communists who had done it, but I knew it. I had learned that the signs were called gammadions and I understood from the silence in my family that they were degrading. I don't know why, but for several days I felt profound shame living in a house thus designated, the more so since, in spite of a hasty job of redecoration, the marks, because they were so thick, were coming through the new paint like scars. I had the impression that my family was also ashamed that it wasn't perfect.

Every year, on the feast of All Saints, I accompanied my mother to the cemetery.

Before the war, we went there in the car and Kader carried the flowers and the packages. Later, it took us more than an hour and several changes of streetcars in order to make our way to this precipitous overhang above the Mediterranean, where, far from the beaches of the bay and because of the sun's abrupt descent into the sea, it was already vast, somber, and mysterious. This spot could be seen from everywhere through the black trunks and foliage of the cypresses which bordered the walks. Pungent odor of trees. Insipid scent of chrysanthemums. Smell of the sea. Smell of the dead. Mineral smell of all these slabs nearly level with the ground, assaulting the mountain to the very top with its basilica consecrated to Our Lady of Africa: a virgin with delicate features smeared with black shoe polish, like the negresses in a carnival, dressed in a gold cape, stiff, hieratical, carrying her baby on her folded arm. In spite of the explosion of crosses above the tombs, in spite of the bell towers above the chapels, everything was crushed between the immense sky and the enormous sea, which met in the distance.

In this spot, which would have forced whoever was

there to think of annihilation and of the stupidity of our own kind, there was a little sea breeze which felt good and which provoked in me a desire to dance, to love. I felt gay and alive, particularly on the feast days of All Souls and All Saints, when an abundance of flowers and well-dressed women visitors was in evidence. All this, in the magical light of an autumn bathed in sunshine, that season of resurrection after the torrid summer.

We were clambering up to "our" tomb at a point which was part hillside, part cliff, staggering with armfuls of flowers and cleaning utensils which rattled together in a metal bucket to the tempo of our ascent.

Along the way my mother pointed out the other tombs and showed me which ones were beautiful and which were not. She often stopped and emphasized the vulgarity which had led to the erection of the various funeral monuments we found along the way. Thus I soon learned that porcelain cherubs with fat behinds, artificial flowers, marble books whose false pages were encrusted with color photos of deceased males with pomaded hair and deceased females fully made up, all that, which I found magnificent, was only good enough for *nouveaux riches* grocers. On the other hand, the opulent simplicity of a gravestone of costly marble and the cross without ornaments were in good taste. The old tombs of those who had died in the conquest had a strong attraction for her, as did the graves of the poor. Little mounds of earth covered in crabgrass, with a mustard jar containing one or two celluloid flowers stuck in the earth as though it were the cadaver's decomposed navel — that merited a stop and a prayer. From our supplies she would take several pretty flowers, arranging them here and there on the unfortunate's necropolis. Before the field where these wretched tombs were, she would say, "They are better off here than anywhere else." This translated as: It is better to be dead than poor. Hence the deep fears that shook me when I heard some member of my family say, referring to a major expenditure, "If this goes on we'll have to go and beg in the streets."

If she was capable of bittersweet or sometimes even harsh reflections on the living and the dead, it was the dead who were always the object of her affectionate interest. There was a complicity between my mother and decay, a taste for death which she did not try to hide: her room was lined with photographs of dead people, photographed sometimes even on their deathbeds. When she laid flowers on the graves of the poor, she did it kindly; as when she gave me a candy or smoothed back a lock of hair which had slipped onto my face.

Having reached our tomb—which was the simplest in the entire cemetery, a large slab of rare marble, light in color, without a cross, without anything, bearing only a name in the upper left-hand corner, the name of her little girl, and two dates: her birth and her death (between the two there had been eleven months of life)—she would kneel down, run her hand over the stone, for her a caress, and cry. She spoke to her, "I am going to make you a beautiful tomb, darling, it will be the most beautiful one of all. I have brought you the most beautiful flowers from Mme. Philippars, the most beautiful in all of Algiers. My little darling, my tiny girl, my love, my poor child."

My work consisted in going back and forth with my pail to fetch the water. Bordering the path was the columbarium: a long, high wall divided into units of little pigeonholes, each with its shelf for placing a jar of flowers or an *ex voto* in front of the compartment for the urn. I knew that they put in there the bones of those who were not to receive care in perpetuity. I had understood very well that it was the poor under the mounds of earth covered in crabgrass, filed away after a few years in those drawers. Alive, they had been swarming in the slums; dead, they were swarming in the columbarium. For the others, it was no different: in life they had large country houses, in death they had tombs all to themselves, each family properly separated from its neighbors. It all made sense.

People were in line with their containers. The faucet ran slowly, now in spurts, now in dribbles. If you turned it to make it go faster, it played a trick on you. First the water would form a lovely transparent bubble which would swell, expand, and inflate. Then, with sudden powerful belches, it burst into the form of a parasol and then a sunburst, spraying the people, who yelled out and then frantically retreated. The guard, having been summoned, arrived panting and said the faucet mustn't be touched, and that for the last time he would adjust it. Then, like a bullfighter placing his banderillas, his hands at the end of his arms, his arms at the end of his shoulders, his body doubled over to protect his stomach, on tiptoe to get the greatest possible extension, he would reduce the flow of the faucet until it started to spit again. People took their place in the line. It was long. The more the morning wore on, the more the cypresses, warmed by the sun, infused the atmosphere with their strong smell.

When I got back, my arm sore with the weight of the pail, I saw my mother working on the stone with pumice, polishing it, brushing it, washing it, her lovely hands reddened by the effort. There was sweat on her brow.

"You've been away such a long time!"

"But there's a line at the tap."

"It's the same thing every year."

"Do you want me to pour the water now?"

"Yes, and then go back and get some more."

I would take the pail with one hand on the lip and the other on the bottom, and fling its contents onto the tombstone. In the air and sun, this made at first a liquid iridescent fan, which in crashing down on the marble swept away the debris, the dust, and the scrapings with the suppleness and the power of the waves breaking against the pier in the port on days of heavy weather. Finally, the water ran off into the gutters hollowed out for that purpose on the lower level of the slab. The stone, already pumiced in some areas, was dazzling.

She resumed her task, and I went back in search of water.

While I was away I knew that she continued talking to her child and weeping. In the beginning, a long time ago, it seemed that she came here every day. Now, sixteen or seventeen years had gone by since the death of her little daughter. It wasn't the same. She no longer needed to come as often because, little by little, her dead baby had again begun to grow inside her and would live there forever. She would be carrying her until she died. I imagined that they would be borne to infinity together, one cradling the other, drifting happily, frolicking to the music of the spheres amidst the perfume of the ethereal fields of freesias, where pink donkeys, golden butterflies, and plush giraffes would also be frolicking. They would laugh, they would sleep, satiated on the love they would give each other constantly.

At the cemetery, her child was nothing more than a big white marble slab. In the middle of her discourses to the stone, she would embrace it with extreme tenderness. At those moments I would have loved to be the stone, and, by extension, to be dead. Then maybe she would love me as much as she did this little girl I had never known, and whom, it would seem, I resembled so little. I saw myself stretched out among the flowers, ravishing, inert, dead, and her covering me with kisses.

When, because of the sun, which had reached its zenith, the stone had become blindingly white and purified, she would begin to arrange the flowers impeccably. She knew all there was to know about their flexibility or stiffness, their colors and shapes, the very essence of flowers. She would form a large insane cross, beautiful, disheveled or distinct, which rambled. A cross is simple and in its appearance always the same; it is the intersection of two straight lines, usually at right angles. It is also the cathedral at Chartres. My mother erected botanical cathedrals on her daughter's tomb.

I saw her do it and understood that she worked until she achieved a composition at once delicate and strong which would be the precise expression of her love, her pain, her tenderness, her heart swollen with her loss.

It was said of her, in the family, "She is a martyr."

All the stories rose to the surface, each one set in order according to its relation to others. Still more surfaced because of those which were more or less ancient, more or less lengthy in the telling; sudden flashes or the longer takes, spreading out over time.

This little girl who was slowly coming back to life on the doctor's couch was different from the little girl I had kept to myself as a memory during my illness (that is to say, roughly, from my mother's account of her attempted abortion until my psychoanalysis); the one was obedient, devout in the love of her mother, constantly on the look-out for her own defects and faults in order to correct them by thrusting them away without a thought for her own welfare, letting herself be guided in every circumstance. The other little girl, on the contrary, had quite an eye! An eye which could see with clarity and harshness even her mother and her surroundings. She could see her mother making her eat her own vomit of soup, her mother in-dulging herself in the vulgarity of Jehan Rictus's story of the old woman and her grief for her son, her mother shrieking at the bottom of the stairwell in the chalet in Switzerland, her mother who was pushing the furniture in front of the doors with an unsuspected fury and power, her mother embracing the stone in the cemetery, her mother exhibiting herself before her own tiny little girl, as she might have before a captive audience. An eye which was above all sensitive to the Thing, an eye which the Thing had overthrown, an eye which had seen the Thing in her mother.

Not everyone is sensitive to the Thing. The Thing can only be recognized as madness or genius. But, between these two extremes, is it imagination or illusion, fits of hysterics or floral arranging, witch doctor or doctor, sor-cerer or priest, actress or maniac? Hard to know. I knew it (even if I was unaware of this knowledge): I didn't trust my mother. She tried to kill me off; she failed to deliver the blow. She mustn't have another chance. I was an arbitrary and confused person who did not accept going any which way. What can even a willful child do in the face of an imperious, seductive, secretly crazy adult who is, furthermore, her own mother? Hide as much as possi-ble her falcon's feathers, transforming herself into a dove in order to preserve her true nature. I had played the game so early and so long that I had finally forgotten my appetite for competition, for victory and freedom. I believed I was a dutiful daughter and I was a rebel. I had been one from birth. I existed!

I didn't yet understand completely the meaning of my discovery. I only knew that I possessed a character all my own and that it wasn't an easy one. I also understood why my training had been so cruel and so intensive. There was in me an independence, a pride, a curiosity, a sense of justice and of pleasure which didn't square with the role which fell to me in the society of my family. To stifle it all, or not to let it show any more than was convenient or necessary, I had to work at it continually. The job had been done. The only part which had remained intact was my sense of the Thing. I always knew deep down that my mother was ill and, at the center of the big ball of my love for her, there was a hard core made up of fear of her and of contempt tempered by pride.

Now that I knew some of my faults that protected me better than my virtues, I was capable of approaching her as I had never done before. I was no longer afraid of getting hurt; they were my armor. I saw her struggling in her anguish. I saw her gross and odious belly, an added burden, a shame to be carried around with her today and tomorrow, her whole life. I saw her as she was when I was born, in her youth. She was twenty-eight then, her strawberry blond hair, her green eyes, her beautiful hands, the passion in her heart, her need for love, magnificent and vast as the sky, her gifts, her charm, her intelligence, and this cursed embryo swollen inside her which brought her back to a reality she detested—this young woman who had spoiled her life and squandered her birthright. Because in the matter of divorce her religion made her intransigent: not to have the love of a man, not to have his strong arms to comfort and caress her, or his moist skin next to hers, not to have his sweet lips to ease the fire which burned inside her. Not ever! Further, a sense of class made it prohibitive to earn a living or develop her mind beyond the acceptable limits for women. She might have been a brilliant surgeon or an inspired architect.... Forbidden! Then at least let her make something exceptional of this daughter she had brought into the world, this daughter who was so different from the other, the first, the marvelous one, the one who had died. This child, the pink-cheeked postulant must—since she had not known how to die in order to please her mother— become what the mother had been unable to become: a saint, a heroine, someone different from the others. Like the fairies who lay down gifts in the cradle of infant princes, my mother had granted me madness and death at my birth. How many times during my childhood had she helped me out of a difficulty so that I might do her will! Each time I had refused the outstretched hand, even though it would have lifted me onto the shore of her love. I wanted to love her, but in my own way. I refused to enter the alienating or macabre meanderings she proposed to me. Every time I had seen her make her gesture I had taken refuge in imbecility, docility, or the sort of whining which exasperated her and earned me her sarcasm: "You are a lowly martyr," or else, "You are the martyr of number twenty-four!" (We lived at number twenty-four on our street.) That is to say, a ridiculous martyr! When I really disappointed her she would call me by my surname, my father's name, thus letting me know that I did not have the same blood, that I was nothing. I refused to

I was standing right next to her. She held my hand. She told me about the enormous distances separating us from these lights, some of which had already gone out even though we continued to see their reflection, so long was the path the light had to travel from there to us. She spoke of the moon, the sun, the earth, that fantastic pavanne that was danced by all the heavenly bodies, and us with them. This scared me a little and I pressed up against her, in her warmth and her perfume. But I felt that her exaltation was in accord with the majesty of the subject. It was a good fear, a fear that ought to be exalting. To me, this great universe to which I had the good fortune to belong was beautiful.

We got on so well in these moments. Why had I forgotten them?

Is it because of these moments that throughout my life, and even today, my thoughts have always led me to my condition — a particle in the universe? Is it because of the harmony of these far-off nights that I accept my existence only to the extent that I feel it to be a cosmic one? It is because of the accord that then existed between her and me that I am happy only when I feel that I am participating in a greater whole?

# Chapter XII

The first encounter with my real shortcomings gave me an assurance I had never had, enhancing my virtues, which I was also discovering and which interested me less. My virtues did not allow me to progress until stimulated by my shortcomings. They took precedence over sin, that infamous mark designating the wicked, the evil and the damned. My shortcomings were dynamic. I felt deeply that as I learned about them they became useful tools for the construction of my life. It had ceased to be a matter of pushing them aside or passing over them in silence, still less of being ashamed of them, but rather of mastering them and in case of need, making use of them. My shortcomings were in some way virtues.

Now I came to the cul-de-sac as in the past I had gone to the university to learn. I wanted to know everything.

I had conquered such strong resistances that I was no longer afraid to find that I was face to face with myself.

204

The anxiety attacks had completely disappeared. I could (and I still can) feel the physical symptoms of anxiety (perspiration, accelerated heartbeat, cold extremities), but there was no longer any fear. These symptoms now served to unearth new keys: my heart is beating! Why? When did it start? What was the provocation? What word struck me, what color, what smell, what atmosphere, what idea, what noise? I would regain my composure and I would save the episode to be analyzed by the doctor when I was incapable of doing it all by myself.

It often happened that I would be floundering, unable to get back to the origin of my malaise, only to find comfort in the knowledge that it did have an origin. On the couch with my eyes closed, I would try to disentangle the knotted threads. I no longer got excited as I used to, I no longer sought refuge in silence or insults, whose meaning I now understood, and about which, consequently, I knew that they were as eloquent as calm words, though more tiring. I looked for relaxation, peace and freedom. I was in the dead-end street in order to be completely cured. I let the images come, and the ideas; one image led to another and I tried to express them without sorting them through, without choosing what was flattering, intelligent, pretty or funny rather than mediocre, base, ugly, or stupid. It was difficult for we were a perspicacious and exacting audience, a kind of tribunal for my shadow theater. Some slipped through and disappeared like sand between the fingers. We felt them very near, ready to appear, and yet, the second we thought we had grasped them, they had vanished into the unconscious which they frequented. My words had betrayed us. I had to begin again the exacting work in which I was both actress and spectator, and in which the doctor was at once spectator and director: just by asking, "And that? What does that make you think of?" he could transform everything, provided I said what the "that" in fact was.

It was in the same way that I discovered my greatest shortcoming, the one that gives life to my finest qualities, the one which occasionally gives me real power and which makes of me the person I truly am.

For a long time I would cry about nothing without really knowing why, finding even that the tears were often inappropriate or in certain moments excessive. It's true that I had taken great pleasure in rediscovering the tears I had been deprived of for so long. I felt their warmth as a benefit. They were necessary, like all the warm fluids the body needs to appease its suffering or its desire. I remember with pleasure every time when, during childbirth, the sac of waters burst, thus allowing the amniotic fluid to flow over my buttocks, my thighs, my pelvis—a respite, a pleasure, a siesta before the great spasms of delivery.

But there was not only the simple pleasure of crying, released with the tears. I felt that there was something more. What? Simply the habit I had formed as a child of seeking refuge in sniveling? The consolation of looking upon myself a victim? I was no longer a child, no longer a victim. What then? The comfort of assigning all my setbacks to the ingratitude of others: nobody loves me, everything always happens to me? This wasn't true. I didn't know how to find the solution to this problem. I didn't know why I shed too many tears. I would even cry at the doctor's because the telephone rang during a session, or because he told me it was over while I was still in the middle of my divagations. I had a big lump in my throat and I swallowed the warm tears to bathe my face like a delicious bittersweet balm. Sometimes even sobs were shaking my shoulders, my rib cage, my entire skeleton.

When I had begun to enter the world, to think of myself as an independent person and an individual, I had experienced a need to have a car to go farther, faster. I was in a hurry to make up for lost time, to see everything, to know everything. So for a few hundred francs I had purchased an old jalopy. I felt good at the wheel, at once capable and protected. She had become my best friend. I wept with her, I sang with her, I had conversations with her as I drove. She made my life more expansive and less fatiguing. I lived in the suburbs, and thanks to my old bus I no longer had to wait on icy railway platforms or worry about the last subway. I often spoke to the doctor about my rapport with this car, about the affection which linked me to it. Finally, I was driving instead of being driven!

One day, before going to the dead-end street, I had stopped my rusty, battered old jalopy in a clearly marked no-parking area. Only an errand to do, a package to pick up, I wouldn't be there for more than two minutes. It should be said that my car constituted a tolerable expenditure in my budget only so long as I had no repairs to make or fines to pay. So I took good care of it and tried to avoid any infraction.

I run, I pick up the package at full speed, I come back and see a policeman calmly writing out a parking ticket. I go up to him, my heart in my mouth. "It was for my job. I've not been here five minutes."

"License and registration, please."

I hand him my papers, and at the same time start to cry like a baby. A crying jag, sobs, gulps, impossible to stop myself. The policeman gives me back my papers with the look of someone who refuses to be taken in. I bawl even harder.

"Will you pay the fine now or later?"

"Later."

"OK, move on! That'll help you learn not to leave your car just anywhere."

I get to the doctor's in a deplorable state. I stretch out on the couch, my face swollen with tears, sucking down mucus, because, of course, I forgot to bring a handkerchief, my throat painfully irritated, hard as a rock.

I start to tell my little story—the no parking area, the street to be crossed, the package to pick up, just a few seconds, and yet there is a policeman already there with his book of parking tickets. I complain of being broke,... of always being the scapegoat... of being unable to get people to love me, of not having a good personality,... of not being attractive physically. My mother was always saying to me, "You are as ugly as a louse." "Your eyes are like the holes in a blanket." "Your posture is bad, your feet are too big, fortunately you have pretty ears...."

My throat constricts and makes me suffer more. I have the impression that I can no longer swallow my saliva, it's difficult to breathe. I'm choking... I'm two or three years old, I am in the playroom of my childhood with my brother. It's winter, there's a wood fire burning in the hearth. My dolls are arranged according to size on shelves that run all the way around the room. Everybody gives me dolls for Christmas and birthdays. It's the nicest gift for a little girl. I have them in all sizes and colors, blondes, brunettes, redheads, some with blue eyes and some with brown eyes. I never play with them. I don't like their stupid eyes, their fake hair, their hands which don't open and close, their feet without toes, their chubbiness. I prefer boys' games and toys.

Near the fireplace, in a cradle decked with organdy, sleeps one of my dolls I hate the most. Actually, it is a boy doll, that is, he is like the girls except for not having long, curly hair and not wearing a dress. His name is Philip. It's always Mama who names the dolls when they're given to me. I do not understand why we have to give children's names to these objects, why we have to say, "Her name is going to be Delphine, or Catherine, or Peter, or James."

A few days ago I gave Philip to my brother, officially, in front of Nanny. The doll is now his. That way I got rid of it, and at the same time, I've gotten in the good graces of my brother, who is five years older than I, and who is always tormenting me. He scares me, he pinches me, he makes fun of me, and at night he wakes me up to go with him to the toilet—he is afraid to go make peepee in the dark. But he threatens to pull out all my hair, slap me, and call the old clothes man, if I say he is afraid of the dark. And then he is loved by my mother. Under the pretext that he is very thin, she coddles him, she is anxious about his health, all the time, as well as his moods.

Of all my toys, the one I like the best is a plush monkey on roller skates. He has a funny face, hazel eyes, a long tail with a loop in it which moves when I pull him behind me. He is soft to pat.

Suddenly my brother gets bored, he wants to take a Ping-Pong paddle away from me. It belongs to him. I don't want to give it back. Then he grabs my monkey by the tail and, swinging it like a windmill, throws it right into the fire. Almost immediately there is a smell of burning wool coming from the fireplace. My monkey is burning!

A veritable whirlwind of fury shakes me like a tree, an earthquake takes hold of me. I am filled with a murderous rage. I am powerless before my brother's size and strength, so I fling myself upon the boy doll, yank it from its cradle, and start to stamp on it as hard as I can. What I want to do above all is to destroy its head, crush its face so that nothing remains of it. I am in a frenzy to smash it, destroy it, kill it.

My mother arrives and slaps me twice without holding back; I start to yell, to stamp my feet in rage. My mother slaps me again. This excites me further, I become enraged, I want to bite, rip, break. I hear my mother tell Nanny: "Put her under the shower, it is the only thing that will calm her down."

I do not believe they're going to put me under the shower. Even when they grab me and march me to the bathroom I do not believe they're going to really do it. I yell even louder, I jump up and down, I struggle, I want my monkey. I experience my powerlessness to fight them like a genuine torture. It isn't fair, I haven't done anything, I don't deserve such treatment. It's my brother's fault, I want to hurt him, to get revenge.

The stream of cold water hits me full in the face, it takes my breath away. My mother holds my head; Nanny pushes me forward while holding my arms behind my back; my brother looks on from the end of the bathtub. I feel this situation as intolerable, unthinkable. It has to stop. I understand that the three of them are too strong for me, and that there is only one thing to do to stop the water which is pouring into my mouth, my nose, and down my neck, and that is to stop it and calm down.

I make an enormous effort to put a stop to the anger flowing through the pores of my skin, my hair, my fingers, my whole being. A colossal power is rising up in me to check my rage — the will; to the rescue comes the will to dissemble. All my forces mobilize to seize hold of my violence, seal it off, and bury it. To succeed I must concentrate so hard it hurts me. I hurt all over, especially my throat, through which nothing more should get out.

I am in the middle of the bath now, soaking. The shower is off. All three of them are silently looking at me. I know that I will never again find myself in such a situation. My throat is being squeezed as though in a vise. What is left over from the suppression of my sobbing forces me to breathe in irregular gasps. Tears burst forth quietly and soothe my face, burning with fury.

On the couch in the cul-de-sac my tears have subsided. Stupefied, I had rediscovered my violence.

I, who had preached non violence and never given so much as a cuff to my children, nor responded to injustice or to any arbitrary authority with anything but silence or tears; I was, in reality, steeped in violence. I was violence incarnate!

A little while ago, with the policeman there, I would have smashed his face in gladly when it was clear to me that he was going to give me a ticket, no matter what I did. My throat became constricted, then it hardened into a painful lump. Tears began to flow, so that the pain became tolerable. I had driven back my rage when I didn't even know that it was in me.

This sudden revelation of my violence is, I think, the most important single moment in my psychoanalysis. In this new light everything became more coherent. I was sure that this force, rumbling constantly inside me like a storm which had been suppressed, muzzled and chained up, was the greatest source of nourishment for the Thing.

Once more, I marveled at the beautiful, complicated organization of the human mind. The encounter with my violence had happened at the right time. I could not have tolerated it before, I would not have been capable of taking it on. How was it that at the time when the hallucination revealed itself to me, I had not stopped to consider that the little girl whom I still saw as a little angel had reacted to one aggression by another aggression? And yet, she had hit her father as much as she could before having been shamed into stopping. The lesson had been insufficient, several months later they had to have recourse to the shower. This time the punishment had been sufficiently severe to padlock the violence for thirty-five years!

During my adolescence there had been a resurgence of the violence in me on several occasions. But I did not know it as such. I believed I was prey to attacks of nerves which I had felt rising up in my throat. Then I would shut myself in someplace, and, alone and ashamed, I would tear my clothes or break an object. Only once my mother had surprised me as I was throwing a silver vase against the wall. She had laughed, then she said to me: "When you marry I'll give your husband this vase, so that he can see what a fine character his wife has!" Another time I had grabbed a heavy curb-chain and struck such a blow against my bedroom wall that the links were imprinted in the plaster, and then like a boomerang the chain had rebounded against my hand, probably breaking a bone. For months I had dragged my painful hand about, never telling a soul, hiding the swelling as though it were a mark of shame.

Afterward, only calm and sweet misery.

My unconscious had prepared the way. In the time between when the hallucination had been accounted for

212

and the revelation of my violence, I had come to know a person who was me and who was not an angel. I had had the opportunity to become used to my pride, my taste for independence and authority, my egocentricity. I had understood that these character traits could be defects as well as virtues, according to how I manipulated them. They were like wild horses pulling my carriage. It was up to me to drive them properly. That didn't scare me. I felt I could control them.

The violence came to me as a splendid if dangerous gift, a formidable weapon encrusted in gold and mother-of-pearl, which I was going to have to wield with great caution. I longed to put it to the test. I knew that I wanted to use it to build and not to destroy.

With the awareness of my violence there came at the same time an awareness of my vitality, gaiety, and generosity.

I was almost complete.

# Chapter XIII

As I worked in the cul-de-sac on becoming more stable, my life on the outside also took on new meaning and form. Increasingly, I became able to talk with others and to listen to them. I was able to attend meetings and to go on my own from one place to another....

As the children were no longer my only contact with reality, I became less burdensome to them. I was a better mother, I understood them better. It was then that the four of us constructed a series of well-traveled bridges linking each of them to me.

In spite of efforts to distance them from it, I knew that my illness had affected them, had wounded them even. As the treatment continued, I became increasingly suspicious of the traditional role of the mother. Instead, I became the observer, and tried to look on at them without intervening, or, more importantly, without filling their lives with prohibitions. Their only fixed point, their only security was my presence by their side. I was constantly at their disposal. I felt (and I still feel) responsible for having brought them into the world. Yet I was in the process of learning that, above all, I must not feel responsible for them as individuals. They were not me, and I was not them. I had to get to know them, as they had gotten to know me. The activity was consuming. I had the impression of having lost time in relation to them. The oldest was almost ten.

At night and very early in the morning, I wrote. I had a little notebook, and I would write in it. When the notebook was full, I began another. During the day I hid them under my mattress. When I shut myself into my room in the evening I retrieved them with the joy that might have been reserved for a handsome new lover.

It happened simply, easily. I didn't think I was writing, even. With pencil and paper, I let my mind wander. Not like on the couch in the cul-de-sac. The divagations in the notebooks were made up of the elements of my life which were arranged according to my fancy: going where I pleased, living out moments I had only imagined. I was not in the yoke of truth, as in analysis. I was conscious of being more free than I had been.

One day at the typewriter, I began to transcribe the notebooks onto sheets of paper. I don't know why.

I had found a job (writing advertising copy) thanks to my university degrees. It's true that I could write proper sentences and knew grammar well, having taught it for a number of years before becoming seriously ill. That's what writing was for me: to put correctly into words in accordance with the strict rules of grammar references and information that had been given to me. In this area improvement consisted in expanding vocabulary in so far as it was possible, and learning Grevisse almost by heart. I was attached to this book, whose old-fashioned title, *Good Usage*, seemed to me to guarantee the seriousness and suitability of my passion for it. In the same way I loved saying that I read *Les Petites Filles modèles* when I was little. In Grevisse there are many doors open to freedom and fantasy, many little go-ahead signs, signs of collusion even for those who do not wish to be confirmed in the orthodoxy of a dead language and a tightly corseted grammar. I felt that these evasions were, nevertheless, not for me, but were reserved for writers. I had too much respect for books to imagine I could write one. Books like *Madame Bovary*, Plato's *Dialogues*, the works of Sartre and Julien Gracq, certain of the Americans and Russians, had burned like a bonfire in the night of my adolescence and later when I was a university student. As I came to the last page of a book, having read it passionately, I was left with the feeling of being torn apart. I had wanted to remain within the pages. There I had found a refuge.

Writing itself seemed to be an act of which I was unworthy. It had never occurred to me to think of myself as a writer. Never, ever. Never from my right hand armed with a pen had there issued forth any poem, review, journal entry or short story.

What were these typographic symbols I filled my pages with? I didn't know, and I didn't try to find out. In submitting to the process, I felt satisfaction.

That year Christmas brought Jean-Pierre back from America. For the children it was a time of celebration. I had done what I could to make their father part of our lives despite his not being there. If his work called him away he was no different from sailors, traveling salesmen or explorers; we were home port. Nothing abnormal should be understood about his not being there. Every day I spoke of him to them, of what his reaction would have been to every event in our life. I told them stories about their father as others tell about the cowboys and Indians. I had a repertoire of stories from his childhood and adolescence, from the province where he was born: the North, the mines, and the miners, the fine drizzling rain and the soot. "Mama, tell us about when Papa said that... when he went there... when the little grandfather came down into the mines... when Papa repaired his motorcycle...." etc. In this way he had become the most important character in our family. All the more important since when he did visit us it was never for more than a few days, and then he was there for the children. He had all the patience, curiosity, indulgence, and inventiveness imaginable. The children worshipped him, and that was as it should be. Not for anything in the world would I have wanted them to suffer as I did a childhood without a father.

For the two of us, it was different. The visits were troubling. The illness had opened up a trench, about which neither of us spoke. It nevertheless seemed impossible to cover over. The misunderstanding went all the deeper because he believed it to be partly responsible for my sickness, which made him feel guilty and at the same time defeated. This feeling was confirmed by my inability to say what I was going through and what had caused the suffering; I had a tendency to accuse him of making me lead a terrible life. In fact, the bursting forth of the Thing, its invasion of everything, coincided with the marriage. The Thing was fed by pregnancies, months of nursing, and the constant fatigue of a young woman with three children, a job, a house and a husband. In my state of mind I couldn't see farther than the end of my nose, and when I took a look at my past, I concluded that I had been sick ever since I had been living with Jean-Pierre, and that he was the one who made me sick. But these reflections were experienced separately, we did not communicate, we evolved apart from one another. The couple we were represented a defeat. We had had to fight a battle together, even if it wasn't apparent we had lost. Our children were an abundant enough source of interest and love so that for the few days we were together we looked like a happy couple.

I was very afraid of divorce, very afraid of following in my mother's footsteps, and of leading the children where she had taken me. It seemed to me that divorce would have created a dramatic separation. As it was, the thousands of miles between us were lived through without any drama. I never did have the impression of raising the children alone even if I was alone in having only my solitary presence beside them.

Jean-Pierre had talked of divorce only once. A long time ago, when I had begun to bleed abnormally. Some months later I surrendered totally to the Thing.

It happened in Portugal, where we were both teaching at the French lycée. My third child had just been born. I have no memory of people's faces, no memory of the apartments where we lived. I was already in the universe of my madness. I lived like an automaton in a sort of blurred nightmare from which inexplicable crises of terror would rouse me. Fear of nothing, fear of everything. A pill would make me fall back into my lethargy, into my fog. I struggled to appear normal. I went to the lycée, I taught my classes, I came back, I took care of my children, the house. I didn't speak. Things were neither pleasant nor unpleasant, easy nor difficult. Time no longer existed. I didn't live the life I appeared to be living. I was inside myself, confronting the incomprehensible and the absurd. Only the poignant impression that I was at a great distance from myself and from others was coming through to me. It made me think of those rockets which are sent to the moon at dizzying speed which, however, take off slowly, awkwardly, almost hesitantly, as if their leaving were a tearing away. I felt that I was being torn away and that at a given moment I was going to be shot out of the world at an insane speed. I did all I could to stay within the bounds of reality for the others, and the constant effort exhausted me.

It was in order to be like everyone else that I had decided to organize a big party in honor of my daughters, the newborn, and the little one who was about to turn two. I had invited any number of children for ice cream and cake, and had asked parents and friends coming to pick them up to stay for a drink. I had invited all our friends and supporters, everyone. The event of the season, as it were, as if I were trying to stave off disaster by upping the ante. In showing myself to be the model young wife and mother, worthy of my own mother, I was going to make everything perfect: the silver would be polished, the linens would be starched, the sweet smell of pastry would be coming from the kitchen, there would be flowers everywhere, and the house would be aglow from all the polishing. Jean-Pierre and I would receive our guests surrounded by our children. I would be exorcised. Such a party demanded days of hard work; I had flung myself into the enterprise as if it were an assault.

It was perfect. I had on a rose silk dress, the buffet (entirely homemade) was delicious. There was just the right touch of understated luxury. It was a tour de force. The feat accomplished, I was one of those marvelous little women who heroically give themselves over to the task of perpetuating the traditions of their class.

When I closed the door on the last guest, I collapsed. I couldn't do any more, not in my entire life had I put myself through such an ordeal! I had had to call upon everything I had ever learned to stand up to it, and to see to the needs of my guests, all the while smiling. For Jean-Pierre hadn't come, and his absence had insidiously poisoned the atmosphere. He had left for the lycée that morning, and I had not seen him since. At first, the guests had asked where he was, and I had responded with assurance that he was going to be there any minute. Then the questions were no longer asked and the guests had left earlier than expected.

The spectacle of the chaos confronting me in the aftermath of the party was a reflection of my own mind: I had wanted to extricate myself from disorder, and I found that, on the contrary, I was in even greater disorder.

It was late when Jean-Pierre got back. I heard him open the door, climb the stairs, and head straight for our room. The house was large. He might have slept in another room and avoided the encounter. I would not have gone looking for him. Instead, he was there, standing at the foot of the bed. He was looking at me. He saw that I had been crying. He held his tongue and examined my body huddled under the sheet. Was he imagining the blood which even then had led us to consult every doctor in town? I saw in his eyes the exasperation and contempt reserved for someone beyond the pale.

"I'm fed up with you being sick all the time, you never stop crying."

"You forget I had a party...."

"Some party! A bunch of cretins all dressed up in their Sunday best!"

"The Ambassador said the house was very beautiful, the children were lovely.... He was suprised not to see you...."

"The hell with the Ambassador! You understand? The hell with him. I want a divorce. I want to drop everything. I am fed up. I'm not capable of making you happy, you're not capable of making me happy. I'm young and I don't want to bury myself with you. I want to get out. I want a divorce."

"No, not a divorce!"

He frightened me. He was normally so deliberate, so calm and reasonable. I felt he couldn't take any more, and that he was determined to end it. For my part, I could not abide separation. I had almost stopped being a wife to him, and he was not my friend; still I could not divorce him. Something very strong was urging me to hang on to him.

I sensed this inexplicable glow coming from him. Someone had moved him. He sat down on the bed in the lamplight, not saying a word. On the deeply tanned skin of his arms I saw the white traces of sea water when it dries. Salt crystals clinging to his lashes formed a faint corona around his beautiful light hazel eyes.

"You spent the day at the beach?"

"Yes."

"In the dunes?"

"Yes."

"With a woman?"

"Yes...with a woman who's alive, a woman who loves me."

I felt the stirring of a jealousy I had never known and showed him my grief. I felt my eyes, even as he was looking into them, becoming lakes of pain.

He believed it was the idea of the other woman that wounded me. But he was mistaken. What really killed me was to imagine his pleasure, walking into the waves, swimming out, letting the sun dry him, feeling the sand under his foot. I was the one who had taught him about the sea, the beach, the warm wind, the freedom of the body surrendering to the water, allowing it to hold him. He came from a cold country where the ocean is for sport. I was from a warmer country where the ocean is voluptuous.

The image of Jean-Pierre in the waves shattered me. It showed me better than any thing else the vast difference between the others and myself: I could no longer swim or run on the wet sand. I was an invalid, who could no longer be left alone with the children.

The vision of his body glistening as he came out of the water forced me to confront my own neglected, heavy, shapeless, body, breasts swollen with milk.

"No, not divorce."

We were not divorced but he accepted a position very far away.

He knew I was in analysis, he saw that I was getting better, he was glad. But when he was there, it was difficult for me to talk to him. So many years of living apart! So many deceptions, secrets, events unshared! Impossible to find the way again, simply.

However, this time on the morning after his arrival, I said: "You know I have been writing at night for quite a while."

"What are you writing?"

"I don't know. It comes to pages and pages."

"You want me to read them?"

"If you want.... I don't know why I'm telling you about it."

"Let's see."

I went to get my pages from under the mattress.

"Why do you hide them?"

"I don't know. I don't really hide them."

"Give them to me."

I was living in the suburbs in a small apartment house with pretensions to being a private residence. My bedroom was a cube of white concrete furnished with shelves on which were piled books and files, on the floor a mattress. The window looked out on a tree and the sky which allowed me to see the seasons go by. I looked on at the subtleties and hesitations of European nature with curiosity. Autumn starting to show its face in mid-August, spring beginning to work the claw-like branches in mid-February. Where I come from, the seasons took only a few days to come into their own, exploding.

The house was quiet, the children were playing outside. Jean-Pierre had settled down on his side of the bed to read my pages, he had folded his pillow against the wall and pulled the sheet up over his back. I was beside him, planning to doze off.

The fact of being on on my back with my eyes closed, as though I were at the doctor's, made me think about the pages in another way...I shouldn't have handed them over....An embarrassing memory surfaced, buzzing around in my brain, without my being able to point to exactly what was annoying me.

A few months before, I had been given the job of writing a publicity handout for a dairy cooperative. At the office I had run into the manager of this cooperative, who, in front of the whole editorial team, had said: "The best thing would be for you to come and tour the plant. That will tell you more than the information I gave you."

Everyone agreed that it really was the best solution, and I had been obliged to accept it. They didn't understand what it meant to me. They didn't know what a labyrinth I was living in. This was the time when with enormous difficulty, having begun to look at my faults, I had begun to talk to the doctor again. Fear was still plaguing me at times. But the plant was located in a big suburb north of Paris. By myself, could I get through this section of poverty and despair where vast modern complexes rose into the sky? Furthermore, I had an absolute aversion to the smell and the taste and the look of milk. I couldn't say so, nor could I tell them that the Thing threatened to grab hold of me and make me run, and sweat, and gasp for air. All the same, I could not refuse. My job was central to my equilibrium. Without it, how could I have lived and paid the doctor?

I went there and it went well. I was so happy to have conquered my fear that in my enthusiasm I had drafted a text in which I compared the plant, which was built in the form of a U, to a person, a sort of magician swallowing up tanker trucks and miraculously transforming them into little pots of yoghurt, buttermilk, caramels, and bottles of milk.... Never had I exhibited such imagination in my work.... Could I afford to do this? Before taking my draft to the front office, I showed it to the editor I considered the most capable and interesting. "I have done a piece for the dairy cooperative. I would like to know if it is any good. Would it bother you to take a look at it?" He read it carefully, and then turned to me with a look of mockery. "So, Madame is doing a Jean Cau now?"

"Jean Cau? Who is that?"

"A jerk who thinks, or thinks he thinks."

"In other words, you don't think this is so great."

"Oh, well... but your piece is good, just the same. Turn it in, they'll take it."

Some time later I learned that Jean Cau had been given the Prix Goncourt, and that same evening when I got back, I started to transform my notebooks into typescripts.

At times, I believed Jean-Pierre had fallen asleep, he was so still, but, no, he would turn a page. I wanted to know where he was, but I was afraid to move. I continued to pretend to be asleep.

Yes, that was how it happened. It was from the day I learned that Jean Cau was a writer that I had begun to give form to the scribblings in my notebooks. I was identifying with a writer? I was taken for a writer? Not me. It wasn't possible. Even a bad one? What an idea! Once again the analysis was going to my head. I was getting so much better that I believed I could do anything.

The apartment was overheated in winter, impossible to keep the covers on. There we were lying on the mattress under a white sheet, Jean-Pierre on his side to read more comfortably, and I resting on my back longing for sleep. At first I had spent a long time looking at the tree shaking its bare branches against the gray and white sky. Then I had closed my eyes, which had allowed me to feel the silence and immobility of our bodies. From time to time the sound of paper which he put down to take another: rustlings, nothing else in the room.

If it interested him at all, he would have said so, he would have made some comment. Jean-Pierre was a silent man, very discreet. I knew he didn't like an exhibition of any sort. But after all!... No, if he was so silent it must mean he doesen't like it.... Never mind. It doesn't really matter.

I open my eyes and see the sheet stretching from the top of my toes to my chin, sloping down in the middle touching my stomach. It beats. The sheet is beating, it barely moves, but it moves regularly and quickly. It beats to the rhythm of my heart.... It matters that Jean-Pierre is reading these pages.... I understand that they are important, that they bear witness to a fundamental turn of my mind.... They are even the most important thing I have ever done in my life.

I should have thought of it before; I should have stopped to consider that I was writing, that I was telling a story if only to the paper; I should have spoken about it to the doctor. And yet I ought to begin to know that one doesn't do things by chance, particularly that sort of thing.... To have handed over these pages to Jean-Pierre, who analyzed what he read so intelligently, with intuition, who (with his doctorate in literature) had such a profound knowledge, almost a lover's knowledge of our language! This was madness! It was as if I was burning up what I had written, at the very moment I was becoming aware of how important it was to me.

Jean-Pierre had gotten into the habit of speaking to me as if I were an invalid, a fragile aging child who could not withstand shocks, who could not be spoken to frankly. In order to soften his thoughts, he would use words which would wound me more than the negative criticism he would normally use. He didn't know what I had become, I hadn't told him, I had seen him so little.... Now, with these pages in which I had come to discover the absurd pretension, I was losing my last chance for a reconciliation. They were going to confuse everything. He would not understand, he would not believe me.

He was stirring a little. He took a long time to turn towards me. I didn't dare look at him, I was still pretending to sleep. Finally I turned to him. His eyes filled with tears! Crying, Jean-Pierre, but why? Was it that he didn't want to hurt me? He was sorry for me?

He was looking at me intensely. There was tenderness, surprise and also some reserve, the way one looks at someone one doesn't know. Then he reached out his hand and gently touched my shoulder.

"It's good, it's amazing, it's a book. It's even a fine book that you're writing."

Two indecent and precious tears had escaped and rolled down his cheeks.

Beautiful eyes, beautiful tears! Beautiful blues, greens, and golds! Finally. Finally.

Happiness. It exists! I knew it, I'd always known it. Happiness, straightforward, simple and complete. Happiness, for which I had reserved an important place at the center of my being, had suddenly, after so many years, made itself known to me. More than thirty years had gone by waiting for it.

He'd come close to me again. He'd slid his other arm around the hollow of my neck furtively. He was caressing me.

"How you've changed. You intimidate me. Who are you?"

I was too moved, I couldn't find the words to speak. I was telling him with my eyes, which were as dark as his were light, that I wanted to love and be loved, that I wanted to laugh and to create, that I had become a new person.

He was holding me against him. He was kissing my eyelids, my forehead, the corners of my nose, the corners of my mouth, the rims of my ears. I could feel his flat stomach, his muscular legs.

"Listen, I don't know what's got into me, I'm in love with the woman who wrote these pages."

Come, let's look at each other, don't take your eyes off me. We're going to enter the waves. I know a stretch of white sand where you can't get hurt, where you can just let yourself go. Remember, my sweet, my beauty—the sea is kind if you do not fear her. She only wants to lick you, caress you, rock you, carry you, let her have her way and she'll please you even more. If not, she'll make you afraid.

Catch the foam. Do you feel underfoot the sand sliding with the wave? Slide with it! Now let the current take you back. Do a somersault! Dive! Let the water knead you, massage you.

Once we're past the waves you'll swim way out. Don't take your eyes off me, I beg of you.

"There are passages here which bowl me over, they're so beautiful, and I don't know who wrote them. And yet it was you."

Hush, don't speak, the sea doesn't like it when you don't pay attention to her. Swim. Stretch your arms and

228

up and churn the water, regularly, slowly, without restraint. Do you feel that you are turning into a dolphin? Do you feel the water's long caress dissolving your body?

When you get tired you'll turn over on your back, we'll go to sleep in the sea, closing our eyes so the sun won't burn them. We'll live a moment that way in the red transparency of our eyelids, carried by the water like a wet nurse with soft, cool breasts.

Then, arching our backs, we'll dive towards the bottom to the seaweed, whose long, slippery fingers will caress our bellies and thighs, our faces, our chests and our backs, until we're out of breath.

Then we'll come up slowly towards the flat, mercurial surface. From our arms and legs and from our lips bubbles of joy will come to the surface in clusters faster than we will to tell the rocks, the beach and the sky of our coming.

From that day on Jean-Pierre and I began to form a unit. We fed on our differences. We confronted our lives, never criticizing them, sharing the best parts. Each time we met we were loaded down with anomalous plunder, from which together we would make out a detailed inventory. The rejoining of our separate worlds offered incalculable treasure, a delicious feast from which we could never get enough.

So these first pages of mine had at least the merit of having given birth to the first of our conversations in which we weighed and measured everything, in which we told our desires, and what was in the way of them, and our dreams. At the beginning these conversations were fed only by the discoveries I made thanks to the analysis. My evolution was so spectacular that Jean-Pierre was fascinated by it. Little by little he began to change. The discoveries we make separately never cease to be grist to the mill which is massive and solid, a mill which turns fast.

When I finished my first manuscript I took it to a publisher who had been recommended to me. Six days later I signed my first contract with a very courteous gentleman whose name was very well known and closely linked to the world of books. He spoke to me very seriously about my manuscript and its qualities. I couldn't get over it. I couldn't believe my ears. I was afraid to look at him. If only he had known he was addressing a madwoman! I couldn't help thinking of her. I imagined her as she was not so very long ago, naked, sitting in her blood, doubled over, crouching in the darkened bathroom between the bidet and the bathtub, trembling, sweating, terrorized, incapable of living.

It was me who pulled you out of there, my friend. I was the one!

It was in the nature of a miracle, out of a fairy tale, magic. My life was completely transformed. Not only had I discovered a way to express myself, but on my own I had found a road which took me away from my family and my background, allowing me to build my own universe.

# Chapter XIV

Those who had known the madwoman had forgotten her, even Jean-Pierre had forgotten her. The book had swept the poor woman away as though she had no more weight than a leaf in autumn. The doctor and I were alone in knowing that she was still there in a corner of my cranium. From time to time she stirred incomprehensibly, making my head hunch between my shoulders, my fists clench, strong-smelling sweat ooze from my armpits. What was going on with her? What was it that continued to wake her up? Where did the uneasiness and the sluggishness in me come from?

I was going only two times a week to the cul-de-sac. One beautiful morning I'd felt capable of staying away for four long days without going back. The doctor and I had decided between us that I would come less often.

My first book sold well. I had the book to thank for the articles and news stories the papers were asking me to write. I did investigative reporting for a magazine.

The people with whom I worked considered me solid and capable, and, in effect, I was solid and capable. I didn't have to make allowances for my new equilibrium. The supports provided by the analysis were perfect and in total accord. I was at ease with myself and my life. I was able to manage all that I had come to understand of my character. As anticipated, my violence played tricks on me, forcing me to live through some wild and woolly sessions. As in a rodeo, I was riding a bucking bronco sweeping me away in mad gallops. As soon as I felt the tension in my throat, I would think, "There it is. No chance of forcing it down and starting to cry. No, let it come, hang on." It was dangerous, the bitch, capable of driving me to murder, to destruction. Let it bleed, let it burst, let it rip. I felt myself becoming livid, I wanted to fight it with my bare hands, to strangle it, tear its guts out. In order to channel my violence, I had to learn respect for others, all others, whoever they were, even for myself. I was becoming responsible.

Yet I knew that the psychoanalysis wasn't terminated. Something was undefined in my geography, I drew a blank on a section of the map of myself, an unknown territory hidden from view. I was aware that it was because I went to see the doctor two times a week that my equilibrium remained in balance. And yet in the dead end, nothing was happening, again there was the vagueness, the great, flat, gray desert extending beyond my closed eyelids and the impression that I would never get to the end of it.

I began to dream a lot. As with joy, I rediscovered tears, I rediscovered dreams. During the illness I didn't dream, didn't have even the memory of a dream, not even the impression of having dreamed. My sleep was an inviolable black cube, a blind screen on which the analysis had begun by projecting ancient dreams. The dream of the horseman, and then another dream, also of the same period, in which I was bouncing higher and higher, first with delight and then with horror. Unable to stop it, I could feel each rebound ineluctably adding to the distance between the earth and me....

I had been an inert sleeper, I was becoming an active sleeper. I brought as many dreams as could be carried to the dead-end street. I had figured out all of them, or almost all, but I loved to display for the benefit of the doctor how well I could function. What seemed normal to others was extraordinary for me, and only the doctor could appreciate the enormous value I found in each new day. When I lay down on the couch I was reminded of the Arab peddlers who would set up shop in the marketplace of my childhood. Squatting down, each would take from the folds of his robes a cloth bundle, which he would open and spread out in front of him; a big square handkerchief holding a few rusty pins and needles, nails that needed straightening, bits of wire, some worn screws, some nuts and bolts that didn't match, and bits of lead pipe. With practiced gestures, the man would make little piles of bits of old metal, then he would roll a cigarette and settle down to wait peacefully in the lacy and wavering shade of a eucalyptus or the dense shade of a plane tree. He knew that during the day customers would detach themselves from clusters of chattering buyers swarming in the dust and the sun, and come towards him, perhaps discovering in the hollow of his dirty handkerchief "the" screw, "the" bolt, the missing piece that would serve to repair or rebuild an old tool, a precious object which without it would have been lost. And to make his happiness complete, two or three bent needles or a blunt safety pin might also be contained therein. In spite of appearances, the peddler knew that his handkerchief contained marvels and that is why he was so calm.

As soon as I lay down on the couch, I spread out the variegated materials of my dreams for the doctor. I'd compose little word sets and images, which I arranged according to whether they were associated with the "dog" or the "tube," the "Frigidaire," etc. Key words which the doctor and I had separated out from my usual vocabulary, and which in their conciseness served to designate a vast area of my life. The explanations of my dreams couldn't make sense, therefore, to anyone but the two of us. Thus, "tube" was associated with my mother's attempted abortion, "dog" with my fear of being judged and abandoned, "Frigidaire" with confusion, the unconscious, etc. We understood each other very well, and that was essential.

Throughout my analysis (and even today), I have never ceased to marvel at the admirable work brought about in the transaction between consciousness and the unconscious. The unconscious going into the deepest strata of life to find riches which were all mine, depositing them on the one bank of my sleep; and consciousness on the other bank, inspecting the find from afar, evaluating it, leaving it behind to be presented or rejecting it, in this manner sometimes causing an eruption in my reality, a truth easy to understand, simple, clear, but which had not appeared to me before, not until I had been ready to accept it.

At the end of this period, when I had learned to analyze my dreaming, I had a dream I could not interpret which I felt was going to hasten the advance of my analysis.

234

In the greater part of the dream, I was reliving an actual incident. I was at Lourmarin, in Provence, where I was spending a few days with my best friends, André and his wife Barbara. I was twenty-one, they were a little older. The relationship among us was the best that can exist between human beings, having in it admiration, warmth, gaiety, affection, and respect. He was a painter, and the work that came from his hands pleased me, overwhelmed me even. Watching him work, I had learned the beauty of what is neither orthodox nor classical. From my mother and my teachers, I had earlier learned the splendor of the masterpieces of our culture. Modern painting was not a part of it. "Picasso is a madman, and his admirers are snobs." End of sentence. Secretly I believed that the country to which André, through his work, had given me access, was magnificent. I was learning the importance of composition, mass and materials, above all. I had seen him in the streets or in the fields pick up bits of wood, paper, or metal, pebbles, cherry stones, string, corks, closely guarding such scraps which for me were merely garbage. He used them to decorate his studio or incorporated them into paintings. Barbara, his wife, would cry out in admiration when he brought in his finds. She was a Slav, and rolled her r's: "André, how beootiful!" She call in her children to admire them too. Under my very eyes the trash would turn into treasure. It *was* treasure. But when I had left their home it turned back into trash. On my own I was not capable of abandoning "good taste" or conformity which set the tone for people of my background.

I had come to join them again at Lourmarin under the impression that to vacation in their company was a considerable mark of my independence from family, a bold act. We slept in tents, we hadn't a penny. We were bohemians! One day André suggested that we go out for a ride, the purpose of which was to see a dovecote he had discovered in the hill country of Luberon. I climbed onto the back of his rusty old motorcycle (as I would have liked to mount the steed of my dream horseman), and we took off.

On a motorcycle one has the impression of going fast, even when one is going slowly. One cleaves the air as a battleship divides the ocean. In Provence, when the sun turns the mountains red in summer, the air is filled with the odor of vegetation and the shrilling of the cicadas. We surged forward at full speed, as if we were in an airy jungle, brushing against the lianas of the thyme and geranium, with the noise of our exhaust frightening away parrots of rosemary, shaking the grasshopper orchids. How I loved this country!

At the end of our ride, we came to a barren-looking hill, and at the top almost completely hidden in a great thicket of fig trees and brambles was the ruin we had come to see. Crushing underfoot the clumps of dry earth, we clambered up to the very top. André didn't speak. He was not the sort to be holding forth. Rather, he expressed himself with his eyes and his hands. But I felt that like me he was moved by these surroundings: a cavalcade of the white hillocks of the region, the gray flight of the crickets, the blue of the sky disappearing now in the end of daylight. The little clouds becoming rose-colored in the sunset.

The ruin was a very high tower, a cylinder made of stone without an opening, save for a small door at its base, in front of which we were standing. André, who knew the way, quickly found the entrance and was the first to enter the tower. He held the door open, and, while attempting to extract the pine needles sticking to my blue jeans, I saw on the earth floor of the tower, lit from above, an enchanting low form of green vegetation marked with a deeper rose and blue like the grasses growing at the feet of the Angel of the Annunciation in the Botticelli painting. Such prettiness was the more astounding in the arid, stern beauty that surrounded me still. While continuing to extract the wretched pine needles, I understood, "It was the bird droppings which must have fertilized the soil in here."

I went in finally, and the beauty of the place took hold of me. It was as if I had been put under a spell. The tower had no roof, it proceeded from the ground to the sky, cutting an almost perfect circle. The walls were pierced by deep niches of blue and yellow porcelain, one row blue, one row yellow, in staggered rows of fives, in which the birds nested. The delicacy of the plants on the ground, the infinite depth of the sky overhead and in between, the perfect regularity of the mysterious blue and dazzling yellow niches. To be a part of the Whole, to be complete. To know satisfaction, silence, because the essential has been expressed.

Somewhere in Provence, I don't know where, I could find it again. The dovecote, where I experienced all of this, exists.

In my dream I relived every detail, every particularity of place, feeling, emotion, and above all the sense I had had of doing something in secret beyond the law of my mother where I profited from a freedom which was total if precarious. In some way I knew even while dreaming that it was an extraordinary moment in time.

There I was in the tower of my dream, dazzled by its

simple force, by the peace in there and the beauty. In my dream, André had disappeared and, as it often happens in dreams, this disappearance was, while unexplained, without significance. My being alone was not dramatic, on the contrary. Suddenly, water had begun to break out at an angle against the walls, isolating me at the vortex of a whirlpool. Somehow I was not soaked by it or dirtied. The water was spinning rapidly before it disappeared below inexplicably. The water was clear and bright, and through its beautiful transparency I could still see the blue and yellow pigeonholes, and the birds who were so peaceful in their niches. The spectacle was magnificent. I felt good there. I had the sense of being complete, the distress I felt in my life had vanished into thin air.

All at once I understood that this splendid water carried along glittering oblong objects. I saw that the objects were finely worked silver cases, each one more beautiful than the next, all different and yet united by their form: they were round though more or less elongated, like sausages you get by rolling modeling clay between your hands. Then I knew, with a certainty that came to me from I don't know where, that these long silver boxes contained excrement, turds, whose contours they followed perfectly. I was, in fact, right in the middle of a magnificent toilet bowl. This all seemed perfectly normal and pleasant. I was not at all shocked by either the pleasure I found in such a place, or by the fact that such precious and beautiful containers could hold such base matter.

I woke up full of joy and satisfaction; I had dreamed the dream.

Yet in the cul-de-sac, on the couch, I had such difficulty putting into words the silver cases and what was in them, swirling past me.

238

Words! I had stumbled against them when I was at my sickest, I found them now that I was almost cured. "Fibromatous" had made me tremble, curl up in a corner of the bathroom. Today, to introduce "turd" into an account I wanted to be happy and beautiful, which was happy and beautiful, I needed to mobilize all my energy and overcome a profound distress, a resistance from the unfathomable depths.

For several weeks at the doctor's, I had taken on the task of analyzing words to discover their importance and their variety. I was confronting myself in a subtle conflict in which consciousness and the unconscious were apparently not in question, since I and the words were both on the surface and clearly visible. When I thought "table" and wished to express the thought, I said "table." But when I thought "turd" it was hard for me to say the word "turd," I tried to hide it or substitute another word for it. Why was the word unacceptable? What was this new censorship?

I understood that words could be allies or enemies but that, either way, they were strangers to me. They were tools fashioned long ago and at my disposal in order to communicate with others. The doctor and I had put together a small, ten-word vocabulary, which, for the two of us, encompassed my whole life. Man had invented millions of words, all of them as important as those we were using in the cul-de-sac, and which expressed the universe in its totality. I had never thought of this, never understood that any exchange of words was a precious event. It represented a choice. Words were boxes, they contained material which was alive.

Words could be inoffensive vehicles, multicolored bumper cars colliding with one another in ordinary life, causing sparks to spray that did no harm.

Words could be vibrating particles, constantly animating existence, or cells swallowing each other like phagocytes or gluttonous corpuscles leaguing together to devour microbes and repulse foreign invasions.

Words could be wounds or the scars from old wounds, they could resemble a rotten tooth in a smile of pleasure.

Words could also be giants, solid boulders going deep down into the earth, thanks to which one can get across the rapids.

Words could become monsters, finally, the SS of the unconscious, driving back the thought of the living into the prisons of oblivion.

Each word which was difficult to pronounce, in fact, concealed a domain I refused to enter. Each word which was pleasurable to pronounce, on the other hand, pointed the way to a domain that suited me. Thus, it was obvious I longed for harmony and found excrement rejectable. How was it, in the dream, that harmony and excrement could go so well together?

Then I understood there was an entire area of the body which I had never accepted and which somehow, never belonged to me. The zone between my legs could be only expressed in shameful words, and had never been the object of my conscious thought. No word contained my anus (since this term was only acceptable in a scientific or medical context, it constituted a sickness in itself). Any word that I pronounced that contained my anus would immediately have brought down upon me scandal and filth, and, above all, the confusion in my own mind. As for what passed through there, I could only bring myself to say the "number two" of my childhood.

I was an invalid and it was while I was laughing that I made the discovery. I was made to think of circus clowns who slap their great shoes on the sawdust, seemingly unaware of a little red bulb which lights up their rear ends as they say with an exaggerated and pretentious mimicry: "I'm sooooo smart!" Making the children laugh. They are grotesque, because they appear to ignore what is happening at the base of their spines.

I rediscovered laughter. Poking fun at myself was delicious. I'd lived until the age of thirty-six with an opening in my body with the horrible name "anus." I had no ass! What a farce! I understood better why I had never liked Rabelais. Deep down, I had a front and that was all, I was flat like the queen in a pack of cards. A queen with a big bosom, broad hips, a crown on her head, a rose in her hand, hieratic and no behind!

The happiness of laughter! The beauty in the laughter of my children. Jean-Pierre's breaking out into laughter: "The less mad you are, the more mad you are!" The laughter in the street, my own laughter! What it meant in terms of peace, well-being, confidence, tenderness!

Every time I took a big step forward in the analysis I took several weeks to manipulate my discoveries and admire them. I measured the immensity of the ground I'd covered and it made me giddy. Had I ever really laughed before? Had I ever weighed my words? Had I ever suspected their importance? I had written books with words which were objects. I had arranged them in an order I considered coherent, suitable and aesthetically right. I had not seen that they contained material which was alive. I had arranged them on the page in the same way that I arranged the objects and the furniture I couldn't get rid of and therefore brought with me wherever I moved.

When we moved on to still another teaching position, I couldn't begin to live again until the precious packing cases had arrived. Opening them in front of the children, as my mother had done before me, I taught them the dead words designating a dead history, a dead family, dead thought, dead beauty. I'd show them Minerva's head in the hallmarks of the silver, the rose on the pewter, the pearls on the Louis XVI furniture, the embroidery on the linens, the bindings of the books and the gilt-edge pages, an ancestor's portrait, a great-grandmother's lorgnette, an old aunt's dance program, an aged cousin's rosewood sewing table ... relics. Packing cases like coffins and corpses I exhumed from the excelsior for my children to live with, as I had done before them. I made the crystal shine for my children and then I'd make it ring: "When glass sounds like that, it's crystal." That's crystal: expensive glass giving off a particular sound, indicating value, the preciousness of an object.

All these words designated the value of things, but not the life in them. The hierarchy of values had been established long ago and was transmitted from generation to generation: a succession of words which functioned as my skeleton and brain. They contained the value of objects, people, feelings, thoughts, countries, races and religions. The entire universe was definitively labeled, sorted and classified. By all means, don't reason or reflect, or call into question these values, since it would be a waste of time as it was impossible to end up with any other categories. Bourgeois values were alone in embodying the good, the beautiful and the intelligent, to such a point that I didn't even know that they were called bourgeois values. For me, quite simply they were the only values.

That did not involve either my asshole or my defecations, any more than the lungs of the man whose breath had fashioned the ravishing crystal vase. Or the little bruised feet of the great-aunt who waltzed on and on, never stopping, so that her program would be full and get handed down with veneration and admiration even: "She was a grande dame, a beautiful and virtuous society woman." Or the seamstress' eyes, destroyed by doing initials and lace on the baptismal linens, tablecloths for wedding receptions, and shrouds. Or the lacerated wombs of the women who generation after generation gave birth to humanity.

Such things didn't exist if one didn't have the right to say their names. All that had no value save as objects of laughter, that is to say, scornful mockery and disdain. And if they had to be arranged on the scale of values (though there was no place for them), the worn-out lungs of the glass blower, the great-aunt's swollen feet, the seamstress' eyes which were destroyed, the lacerated wombs of women and my asshole, such things were in the lowest ranks along with the other objects of pity, commiseration, or charity, about whom one made amusing remarks or vulgar, derisive comments, because they signified the minimal, the negligible, the poor, the small, the wretched, the ridiculous, the empty, dirty, or meaningless.

I was a red queen in a castle of cards. It was enough to say the word "shit" free of shame and disgust before what was contained in the word, for the castle to fall down!

# Chapter XV

And so it was that thanks to the beautiful dream of the dovecote, I came to understand that everything is important, even excrement, and even the castle of cards in whose dungeon I had been living for so long. Sadly, I realized that my mother was in that dungeon too. While I felt distress for her, I also knew with certainty that it was too late for my mother and that there was nothing I could do to get her out of it. I could not explain to her what I was in the process of learning, the knowledge was still too new and incomplete. I had been in an extremely dangerous situation from which I had to extricate myself and my children. The bus was full, there was no room for my mother beside me.

Ever since her arrival in France, she'd begun to fall apart. Her body was worn out and misshapen. Her face had about it a look of sadness and fatigue. Indeed, there was an angry flame in the green of her eyes although nothing she ever said in words revealed the source of it. She had walled herself off in her bedroom, leaving it only when she had to, dragging her feet, maintaining a growing inaccessiblity in her expressionless face. It might have been said about her that she was abandoning the struggle, renouncing it, letting go, having finally understood that she had allowed herself to become an object of ridicule in her world, forever the butt of jokes in her family.

I am certain that she saw clearly the stupidity of her involvement with the Church which had never really offered her love, not in France where pretension and self-interest reigned, not in her beloved Algeria either, from which she had been ejected along with the others, as a profiteer. Duped. Deceived. Mistaken unto death. I am sure she knew, in secret, all of this, and that in the middle of her universe, ravaged and destroyed, there remained only me with new energy emerging. This she could watch happening with her own eyes as she tried clumsily to hang on to me.

But in spite of this distress which she inspired in me, I could not check the repugnance I felt for her body, and I avoided being in her presence. It bothered me. I thought I should have been able to overcome it in myself, not to draw closer to her, but to be free of her. Free of all that she had been for me. This distaste kept us intimately connected and I did not know how to get rid of it.

I was going only once a week to the cul-de-sac, and soon enough the sessions would occur at even greater intervals.

I had become strong, responsible and solid, a woman who could be depended on. At an age when others believe their lives are coming to an end, my own life had barely begun. Enthusiasm and passion were stirring in me. I had uncovered an unsuspected vitality, and an enormous capacity for work. I loved the world of books. After my discovery of words, I had stopped writing for myself. I took time off, I was no longer able to write in the same way. Then, with no less interest, I busied myself with other people's books. I learned about paper, pasteboard, ink, glue, typesetting and typography.

The beauty of the printed word. A world withdrawn and inspired, a silent world. Twenty-six capitals, twenty-six lowercase letters, ten numerals, and the punctuation marks. Little galaxy perfect and harmonious. Words, containers full of life, are in themselves contained when written down in the letters, which are containers. Each typeface has a style all its own, which it communicates to the word it designates and to the material within the word. Every people invent a typeface which resembles them. The Germans have alphabets which are heavy and powerful, alphabets made for strong texts, rigorous analyses and dangerous aberrations. The English have letters which are both precise and extravagant, made for a carefully calculated freedom. The Americans have new technocratic alphabets, made and thought out by robots. Latins have ravishing typefaces made for subtlety, love and tears. Living in that world was an enchantment. Yes, it was true. Everything had become important and interesting.

I never talked about my analysis, because I understood the subject was an irritation to people. "Those stories of yours are a lot of nonsense. The people who are really crazy should be looked after in asylums. As for the rest, it's a mixture of aging housewives, homosexuals and the disoriented." Then there were the endless quantities of personal histories which would begin: "I was psychoanalyzed. And it just about finished me off. So don't tell me about it. It took me five years to get over it!" Later I'd learn they'd seen a doctor for two months, or six months, or even two years. Some man with whom they'd talked about their life, who listened, gave advice, and made them swallow some new form of medication which would soothe them. In brief, they'd not been in analysis, or if they had, they'd given up at the moment it had become difficult, when nothing was happening for weeks or months. When, having told what they knew, they found themselves confronting the unknown, they put up a blank wall which obscured the horizon, that infinite desert, the other side of which apparently one could never reach.

I learned that one could only speak of psychoanalysis in terms of a defeat. My recovery and my energy were shocking to them. "You weren't sick, you had the vapors. They make us puke with their fake problems. Those are just female problems, none of it is really serious." But I knew mental illness wasn't restricted to women. Over the years in the cul-de-sac I had crossed paths with men. No less than women! Their heads pulled down into overcoats or jackets. Their eyes unseeing, their faces full of fear!

I understood that the people all around me lived in their castles of cards and that for the most part they were not conscious of it. All of them brothers! And I had believed myself alone, abnormal, monstrous!

Without the blood, the sweat, the trembling, the oppression in my lungs, the fog which shrouded my eyes and ears, would I have had the courage to go deeper and deeper into analysis? I don't think so. If I hadn't had the occasion to sink into the illness perhaps I wouldn't have had the energy to go to the very end of the confrontation with myself.

I had the sense of being privileged.

It was therefore with the feeling of belonging to an elite, a sort of secret society, that I went to the cul-de-sac from then on. It bothered me when I met the eyes of the hardware dealer on the corner or those of the people who lived on the dead-end street. I knew when they saw me heading for the iron gate they were thinking, "Hey, that's the crazy woman who comes on Tuesdays," with a sort of mockery mingled with pity and even fear. I felt like telling them, "No, I'm not crazy, and I never was. Or if I'm crazy, so are you!"

To make them understand and to help those who lived in the hell where I also lived, I promised myself that I would some day write an account of my analysis, and turn it into a novel in which I would tell of the healing of a woman as like me as if she were my own sister. I would begin with her birth, her slow reentry into the world, the happy arrival into night and day, her "joie de vivre" and her wonder before the universe to which she belongs. For analysis can't be written down. It would take thousands of pages, many of them repetitious, in order to express the interminability of nothingness, the emptiness, the vagueness, the slowness, the deadness, the essential and the perfectly simple. And then, in this immense monotony, several strokes of lightning, those luminous seconds during which the entire truth appears, of which one takes in only a fraction, believing one has taken it all in. Then, again, thousands of pages more of the flat, the inexpressible, the material in gestation, the gestation of thought which is as yet unformed, and finally the inestimable. Once more the radiant splendor of the truth. And so it goes. Enormous book bloated with blank pages, on which there would be nothing and everything. Fantastic volume composed of all the paper in the world and all the ink and all the words, letters and diagrams.

But in order to create such a novel, my analysis had to be terminated and I had to feel entirely capable of living outside the cul-de-sac. But this was not yet possible, for my rapport with my mother continued to be poor. There was that nausea she provoked in me, which totally unnerved me.

I dreamed. My nights were animated by my library of films of the forgotten. I would wake up relaxed and clearheaded. I felt within me the quiet strength which was going to make every hour of my day alive with interest. I had found a baroque consistency, illogical yet sound, which fit me like a glove. This unity of my being, this cohesion of nights and days permitted me to move out towards other people, to meet them, to know them, often to understand them, sometimes even to love and be loved by them. I was happy, I had confidence in myself, I knew that I would go the whole way.

Two nightmares allowed me to complete the analysis.

In the first dream, I returned home to Algiers, to an apartment I had never seen. Nor did I recognize the building, a nineteenth-century structure of the kind to be found in all large towns on the Mediterranean, whether in Piraeus, Naples, Nice, Barcelona, or Algiers. A middle-class stone structure with beautiful proportions, four or five stories high, with venetian blinds drawn, shutters partly open, an entry supported by two ugly caryatids, and a very dark stairwell lined with ceramic tiles which repeated a green motif against a white background all the way up to the roof. A sort of enormous well which had been constructed in order to give coolness to the surrounding apartments. In my childhood, I vaguely remembered having spent time in a similar building.

I was going home, therefore. As soon as the door closed, my mother came towards me. She was coming out of a room on the left off the front hall in which there were some other women. Her face was the face of the good old days, she had on her tragic mask: "Come with us, we have to hide you. Three partisans just came into the apartment."

Three partisans didn't frighten me. I was for Algerian independence, my mother knew it perfectly well and I couldn't understand why she was so frightened. If I were out there in the street, I would have been a woman to shoot down. In a revolution there isn't the time to make such fine distinctions, but it wasn't the same in here: I could speak, explain my position, they would quickly realize that I was decent, that I wasn't their enemy, that I wasn't trying to deceive them, that I truly understood their cause.

In spite of my mother's opposition, I began to go towards the room where they were. I saw three men in there speaking softly in an atmosphere of conspiracy. This apart, there was nothing special about them. They weren't frightening or ugly or excited. They had no weapons.

But I was unable to make contact with them. My mother and the other women were dragging me back. I was linked incomprehensibly to their group. And yet I was not their prisoner; it was fate which absurdly attached me to them, which, moreover, I didn't even question. It was the way things were.

Little by little I retreated, and found myself shut up in the room with the other women. Mediterraneans, dressed in black, muttering prayers, fingering rosaries, crossing themselves, whispering "aie, aie, aie," "madre mia!" "my God, the poor thing," and I, in the midst of them, "santa madonna," "mater dolorosa, ora pro nobis."

Their fear had become my fear; like them, I was sweating, I was trembling. I was appealing to Divine Providence. We were huddling together, young and old, adolescents, children, matrons, prostitutes and old maids, all of us with fear in our bellies and terrible stories in our heads, stories of women raped and disemboweled.

After a while, the situation became intolerable. I couldn't go on in passive submission to them. I had to do something. There must be a way to save ourselves. I decided to try to get out and warn the neighbors on the floor below, who I knew had a telephone.

I could hear no sound through the door, nothing from the rest of the apartment, nothing to indicate that the partisans were nearby. They must still be off plotting in their own corner. I decided to leave. The front hall was empty and dark. It was all right. But I was barely on the landing when I discovered the partisans had found out about my escape and were after me. I began to run down the steps of the enormous staircase. The partisans were behind me. I heard them coming after me on the stairs. I couldn't seem to make it past the first flight of stairs. As I reached the landing of the floor below, one of the men grabbed me from behind, throwing one of his arms around my neck. Thanks to the speed of my flight and to sheer willpower, I was able to drag him almost as far as our neighbor's closed door. But before I could get there, I fell backwards; the partisan was almost strangling me. I could see the tips of my shoes inches from the door. I wanted to try to drag myself still closer, so I could kick the door. They would have to come out then, they would have to save me. I couldn't do it, the man was paralyzing me. I felt his breath against my neck, and I heard him panting from the chase. At that moment, with his free hand he pulled a knife on me, a sort of penknife with a tiny blade, which he brought close to my neck. He was going to cut my throat with it, it was horrible. And while I was feeling that it was over for me, I was also thinking, "That's a harmless weapon, he couldn't hurt me with that knife." But that did not make me any calmer, and I woke up with a start, covered with sweat, completely destroyed.

To recall images in a dream, as one looks at a film, and to hear one's own voice recounting this dream, is equivalent to living through two completely different moments, and yet they come out of the same event. So I listened with astonishment to my own account of the beginning of the dream; I applied myself to describing in every detail the house and the stairwell, with its Arabian ceramic tiles. If it had been a film, it would have been over in a few seconds, while my words were so long in coming. Why?

Then I remembered a stairwell from my childhood just like the one in my nightmare. It was at the beginning of the war, I was ten years old, and my mother had decided several days before that I could go to school by myself. That was the time when I was dizzily discovering the streets, knocking against the fig trees on the Rue Michelet because I didn't know how to walk by myself. I was used to being led, to having my hand held, I didn't know how to look where I was going.

At the door of the school, I discovered that a man had followed me, without my having been aware of it. I had never even imagined such a man could exist. I remember it was summertime. I had on a linen dress with big blue and white stripes which made a pattern of big chevrons. It was very pretty. It looked very well on me and often I looked at my reflection in the mirrors of shop windows to see how it looked. I felt cool and alert in the heat because of it.

The man slipped in behind me when I went into the apartment house, and caught up with me on the stairway. Stairway laid in white ceramic tiles with a green motif. As soon as I became aware of him, I was so afraid, inexplicably afraid. He was a gentleman of about forty, dressed very correctly in a coat of a light color, a kind of raincoat. He had a common face with blue eyes and sickly blond hair, nothing unusual. Yet he horrified me. He began to speak to me, he asked my name, giving me a knowing artificial smile. He was breathing heavily. I did not understand the way he looked at me. He was panting like an ox. My voice stuck in my throat even though I wanted to tell him to leave me alone. He pretended to help me carry my schoolbag, just to rub against me. This I understood very well. I elbowed him. Then he came right up to me, so that I was trapped against the railing. I couldn't go up any farther. With disgusting gestures, he began to caress my torso, looking for the breasts I didn't have and the high, firm, muscular behind that growing children possess. I couldn't stand it. Panting still more violently and gasping for breath, he began to feel around in his pants for his fly. I made a leap, and clutching my schoolbag like a rifle, I took the stairs four at a time. Surprised at my departure, the man lost ground and then, recovering himself, began to quickly climb too. But now, he was insulting me, "Little bitch, little whore, I'm going to get inside you." I was quivering with fright. Three long flights to climb.... The doorbell was high up, I had to put down my schoolbag and stand on tiptoe to get at it. I didn't have the time. I flung myself against the door and banged with my feet and my fists as hard as I could. But the man had come up behind me, and while I was throwing all my energy into banging on the door, I felt his disgusting hand pull down my underpants, and his fingers between my buttocks, writhing there, in that sacred, shameful, precious dirty unmentionable place, of which one never spoke. The sound of footsteps in the front hall. "Little whore, I'm going to put it inside." Oh God, he's going to kill me, save me! The man would not stop, he was tearing my skin off, hurting me with his finger, never letting go of me until the last minute. When the door opened, the bastard was racing down the stairs. He was already far away. And I, in Nanny's arms, was relieved by a terrible fit of hysterics.

I hadn't forgotten the episode, but I had forgotten the details. My nightmare brought them it back, and with it, the disgust, the nausea, which this man had provoked, and the intense fear of this finger digging into me. A finger which, after all, was only a finger, not a weapon....

I was on the couch, agitated by the words coming out of my mouth, possessed by an intense excitement within, but apparently calm, almost asleep like a cat watching a bird. I felt that I was on the right track: the stranger's finger, the partisan's pocket knife. They couldn't kill me. And yet I had been terrorized by the death they could have inflicted. What death?

I had to go further still. The road was in front of me, the direction was indicated: fear of a particular death, the death which a man inflicts upon a woman. An ancient fear revived in me by the nightmare. Fear felt by my mother in the dream and perhaps by the other women as well.

Until that day, in spite of the analysis of the dream, I was not conscious of being afraid of men. I was floundering on the doctor's couch, I hesitated to take this tack, it wasn't my problem. Naturally I had been afraid of the man on the stairs, but never since then had any man ever frightened me, on the contrary. From them had come the only tenderness and love that I had ever known. I had no fear of the penis.

The knife... the finger... my fear... my mother's fear... the other women's fear... fear of death which wasn't merely physical? But what death?

Where to begin? My mother, who was there in my dream, like the doorway to the words, represented the other women. She was the only one who addressed me in words. My mother... men... myself... my mother... my mother.

She had gotten a divorce when she was twenty-eight, and in order to be able to continue to receive the sacraments, had taken the vow of chastity. I do not believe she ever broke this vow. She was beautiful, intelligent, passionate, inaccessible and... she attracted men. I'd felt it throughout childhood. I detested anyone who came near her. I didn't know it, but I was jealous, I thought that men were going to lead her astray from the right path, the one which was leading to paradise....

At the farm, off the big living room, which was more than sixty feet long, was an old veranda which had been enclosed. Consequently, my room with its two windows opened on one side to the garden, and on the other to the big living room, for the original openings had not been walled up. They were used to display books and objects.

Nights when I couldn't sleep because of the heat and my bad thoughts, I would sometimes hear beautiful music—my mother's music. I would get up, and on tiptoe go and hide in the alcove formed by the window, which was closed by curtains on my side and cluttered with knick-knacks and curios on the livingroom side. I was spying on my mother. She was alone, pacing the long room. So that each time she went by I could see clearly the expression on her face and it dealt me a blow to the heart. Her features were relaxed. Her eyes, almost closed, her mouth partly open, let out intense pleasure and satisfaction. I found her indecent.

The plush wool carpets swallowed up the sound of her footsteps. Only the music could be heard coming from a phonograph which resembled an English church. When a record was over she'd put on another. I loved them all. It was jazz. I didn't understand the connection between my mother and those rhythms. It was music which came from the belly, the loins, the thighs, a whole area of the body which my mother couldn't and shouldn't know. To me it seemed I had surprised her *in flagrante delicto*. Why I couldn't say. Two songs in particular, "Tea for Two" and "Night and Day"... "Day and Night." I knew the words by heart... The words! The voice of the black singer like the harsh meowing of a cat! I was thrown by it. Where were the men in my mother's life?...

"Would you like Roland to be your father?"
"..."

It was summer at the Salamander. Roland, that dashing officer, a widower, the one she referred to, was there every day in his uniform and boots, the skin of his face shiny as a well-shaved bacon rind. I detested him. I didn't want him for a father and I didn't want him for my mother's man, under any circumstances. It seemed to me that he was bad for her. I felt that she wasn't happy. The anxiety and agitation which had taken hold of her since Roland had entered our lives troubled me. And yet she was as lively as if she were deeply in love.

On the beach I would often go off from the group of children and nannies and play behind the beach umbrellas in whose shade my mother and her women friends would be gossiping. In this way I could listen to them without being seen. There was no question of whether or not she and Roland would marry. It was horrible, my throat was so constricted I thought I was going to suffocate. She spoke about what they would be wearing, about the ceremony, the reception. The wedding was going to be in October after the vacation. She was asking my opinion when it was already arranged. I began to whine continually. "The child's nervous, I wonder what is going on with her."

Fortunately, we were leaving for Europe. Once there I would never again see the man my grandmother called "the handsome officer," with his gloves the color of fresh butter, his cane and his conceit. He used to pat me on the cheek perfunctorily to say hello. I knew that I didn't interest him. To say nothing of his dead wife who left him two babies my mother doted on, slightly blond ghosts whom I detested. Finally, I took the boat alone with my mother. No more Roland to come between us.

We had to spend a night at the hotel in Port-Vendres before taking the train to Paris. Why such a complicated itinerary? At the hotel a bellhop in a red uniform, with a hat on his head like a red and gold candy box, took our bags and showed the way to our rooms. A staircase with steep risers and a carpet in the middle held down by brass rods. The bellboy goes winding up ahead of my mother, I bring up the rear. Potted palms at the edge of the bannister. I look up, and on the landing, framing the red carpet, two shiny boots. Roland! He was here! That is why she brought only me! That is why she'd changed steamship lines! My throat contracted, a storm began to brew in me. No, not him, I didn't want him here! I began to complain of not feeling well, I had a stomachache, I vomited. I don't know why my mother put me on a chamber pot right in the middle of the room, in front of him! It was intolerable!

I screamed louder than ever.

"I'm going to call a doctor. Roland, I must ask you to leave. It would not be proper for you to be here."

"And I was looking forward to such a beautiful evening!"

"What do you expect, my friend, that's the way it is with children."

It seemed to me that she took even better care of me than usual that night. She appeared to be relieved, easier, she hummed in the bathroom. The following morning we left, and I never saw Roland again.

Later, I was eight or nine, another gentleman became a frequent visitor. Older, with gray hair slicked down, a signet ring on his finger and the beginning of a paunch, he was a Parisian and a fop: Gäel de Puizan. Half man-about-town, half businessman.

Same scenario: "Perhaps Gäel will be your father one day, if you'd like that."

This gentleman had succeeded in making himself more insistent. He must have talked her into meeting him away from the family. Once more she took just me with her, not telling me the real reason for the excursion. We walked along a French country road. She held my hand. She smelled good, she had taken particular care with her appearance and mine.

I was old enough to understand exactly what was

wrong now and why she'd become so nervous when she saw a car coming towards her from a distance, slowing down, stopping beside us. Gäel was driving, he was alone. I will never forget the way in which he looked at me. Ah! If only he could have gotten rid of me! He understood what my being there meant, and I understood that I was being used as a screen between my mother and her lovers.

There, on the couch, I figured out that the religion of my mother got all the blame; that it was not the only thing in the way of her responding to these men to whom she was surely attracted. She was afraid of something else. The fear was in the nightmare.

I had begun to think, as never before, of what it meant to be a woman. I thought of our bodies, mine, my mother's, the others'. All the same, all having holes in them. I belonged to that gigantic horde of penetrable beings, delivered to the invaders. Nothing protects my hole, no eyelid, or mouth, or nostril, or grating, or labyrinth or sphincter. It hides in the hollow of soft flesh which does not obey my will, and is naturally incapable of defending it. Not even a word to protect it. In our vocabulary, the words which designate this particular part of the female body are ugly, vulgar, dirty, coarse, grotesque or technical.

Never had I thought of the protection embodied in the hymen, of the vacuum created when that delicate membrane surrendered, while bleeding, under the rough answers of men, leaving the passageway hereafter vulnerable to anything... the finger, the penknife. Could this be the origin of the essential fear as old as humanity, unconsciously submitted to and forgotten? A fear which women alone could feel and transmit instinctively, which would be their secret? A fear which would be attributed to violent penetration by men, but which would in fact be much more deep-running and profound. A fear invented by women and taught to them by other women. Fear of vulnerability, of an absolute inability to shut ourselves off completely. What woman can oppose a man who really wants to from penetrating her and depositing in her his alien seed?

When something happens during a session, it happens fast. At most a few minutes had gone by from the instant the dream motif suggested a motif in reality, to the question: why be afraid of that which cannot harm, to the vision of a woman having an opening, a way in?

Why not have chosen to analyze the caryatids of the building in my dream, or the shutters rather than the stairwell? Why focus on the penknife rather than on the partisan, or on the women in black, etc.? Why select certain details and not others? Because it was there I felt the weight of the unconscious. Only in the dream was the little pocketknife an enigma to me, and in telling about it at the doctor's, only the emphasis on the description of the stairwell surprised me. My unconscious was signaling me at precisely these two points, the one in the dream and the other while awake. I had gotten in the habit of hovering. By now, I knew exactly when the unconscious manifested its presence and when I'd come in contact with it.

I was lying down; the doctor was silent, as usual. I'd made another discovery. But the discovery was perplexing in a new way. I felt the strangeness of it within the context of psychoanalysis. It was not shut in with the little doctor that I would make use of it. I had to go off on my own.

It was seven years since I'd come here. Seven years just to be! Seven years to find myself! Seven years which had slipped by in slow motion. First I became healthy; then, little by little, my character emerged in all its individuality. I had become a person. Then, thanks to my anus, I understood that everything was important, and that what had been called dirty, small, shameful and wretched was quite different in reality. That it was the scale of values used by my social class which had thrown a veil of hypocrisy over people and things, to show to better advantage what was clean, great, brilliant and rich. Now I had discovered my vagina, and I knew that henceforth, as with my anus, we were going to live together, in the same way as I lived with the hair on my head, the toes on my feet, the skin on my back and all the parts of my body. I lived with my own violence, deceit, sensuality, authority, capriciousness, courage and high spirits. Harmoniously, without shame, distaste and discrimination.

I was sure that it would be outside the dead end that I would discover the true meaning of my discovery. I said goodbye to the little doctor that day, knowing that soon I would no longer be coming back.

It was, outside in the streets and in the stores, at the office and in the house, that I understood what it meant to be a woman was to have a vagina. Until then I had never questioned the notion of femininity, that specific quality of being human having to do with breasts, long hair, wearing makeup and other provocative and adorable qualities which are spoken of little or not at all. Certain creatures who live out their lives in pastel shades, pinks above all, pale blues, whites, mauves, pale yellow and moss green and whose role on earth is to be the servant of the lord, the diversion of the fighting man and the mother. Dressed, scented, embellished like a shrine, fragile, precious, delicate, illogical, bird-brained, available, the hole is always open, always ready to receive and to give.

It wasn't true! I knew what it was to be a woman. I was one of them. I knew what it meant to wake up in the morning before the others, to get breakfast, to listen to the children, who all want to talk at the same time. Ironing at daybreak, mending in the early morning, homework at dawn. Then the empty house and an hour of working frantically to do the bare minimum, sorting dirty laundry, sprinkling the clean laundry, preparing the vegetables for the day's meals, scrubbing toilets. Bathing, doing your hair, putting on your makeup, fixing yourself up, if not you'll have a guilty conscience: "A woman should always be clean and nice to look at." Taking the youngest to nursery school or kindergarten. Don't forget the shopping basket for doing the errands, later. Go to work. The only work that counts, the work you're paid for, without which there would be black misery. Come back for lunch. The older children eat at the cafeteria, the youngest one is home. She has to be given affection, to feel the warm presence of her mother. The older ones will look after her in the evening. Provided they don't get into mischief, play with matches, cross the street without looking. Out again shopping. Orders from superiors received and carried out as fast as possible, as best you can. Errands in the evening. Not a penny in your pocket. It doesn't matter. Use your ingenuity to put together a meal that is appetizing and good: "A good meal drives away unhappiness." The shopping baskets which are heavy on your arms. The fatigue which begins to gnaw at your head and your back. It doesn't matter: "A woman must pay with pain for the happiness of bringing children into the world." Home again. Listen to them all. Prepare the dinner. Hang up the wash. Bathe the children, supervise their homework. Put

262

the soup on the table. Fry the apple fritters while they're finishing their noodles. Tired legs. Brain heavy with sleep. The dishes. See as a reproach the fingerprints on the walls and doors, the windows which need to be cleaned, the knitting isn't getting anywhere: "You've made your bed, now you can lie in it, my daughter. A dirty woman, a dirty house." I'll do it on Sunday, I'll do it on Sunday. The following day it begins again: move the furniture, down on your knees to scrub the floor, carry the baskets to the market, pick up the kids, keep counting the small change without which you can't buy anything. Look at the beautiful dress in the shop window, costing more than you earn in a month.... And keep giving out kisses when all you want is to sleep, to rest. Have a guilty conscience because of it, play the game, regret not getting anything out of it, fear another pregnancy. Fight off bad, selfish thoughts: "You should be as much a wife as mother if you want a good husband." How many days before my period? Didn't I make a mistake in my calculations, was he paying attention? How many days to the end of the month? Will I have enough money? Am I going to manage? My God, a child crying! It's the baby. Just so she isn't sick. I've taken too many sick days this year, what with the oldest having measles and the others getting the flu. I'm going to wind up in trouble. Start up from sleep, get up in the night. Night in the apartment made of concrete, crying in the distance from other people's children having nightmares, flushing toilets of neighbors coming back late, the drunk on the third floor yelling at his wife. To sleep. To sleep.

That's what it means to have a vagina. That's what it's like to be a woman and serve a man, loving the children until you grow old and they take you away to a home or a hospital where the nurse will treat you with a certain indulgence as though you were a child or senile: "We'll be just fine here, isn't that right, dear!"

It's true that in the life of an old woman, there is often the rainbow of her children's laughter, the dream of an old love and sometimes even the warm afterglow of tenderness. But most of all she's learned the red of her blood, the black of her fatigue, the shit brown and pus yellow of diapers and underpants worn by her babies and her man. And then the gray weariness and the beige of resignation.

Consciousness of my specific femininity led me to discover a thing or two! The castle of cards which I had been poking fun at not so long ago, which I thought I'd extricated myself from in emitting (rather clumsily) such words as "shit" and "crap," that very castle which I believed demolished, was still standing, its foundations intact! It is only now that I understand that I had never really read a newspaper or listened to the news. I'd looked upon the Algerian war as a sentimental matter, a sad story of a family worthy of the Greeks. And why was that? Because I had no role to play in the society where I was born and had gone crazy. No role, that is, other than to produce sons to carry on wars and found governments, and daughters who, in their turn, would produce sons. Thirty-seven years of absolute submission. Thirty-seven years of accepting the inequality and the injustice, without flinching, without even being aware of it!

It was frightening! Where to begin? Was I doing it all over again?

A pit. A bottomless pit. The need to resume more regular sessions. Again a wave of anger against the little doctor.

264

"I got out of the yoke of bourgeois thinking, only to get back into another yoke, analysis. It's the same thing: a system that imprisons people, and in which you are one of the overseers."

"At least you're aware of it."

He was right, the cretin. If I didn't want to go there, all I had to do was not go. All these stories of justice and injustice, equality and inequality, when it was up to me to make the rules for myself. Could I be the woman I was? No. To stop fighting now meant to accept going back there between the bidet and the bathtub, to curl up like the fetus inside her, to hand myself over once and for all to the Thing. Not for anything in the world!

What to do? How to begin?

What agitation, what isolation, what awkwardness, what confusion!

Another nightmare came to my rescue.

I was on the beach with Jean-Pierre and our best friends, André and Barbara again, and Henri and Yvette, another couple whose integrity would never tolerate any compromise. Henri was the one who could make us laugh. We could not help but like him because of his honest fussing over trifles and his intransigence. He had been driven out of Algeria by the OAS.

So there we were, the six of us, on a magnificent Atlantic beach, broad and glowing (a beach very much like the one Jean-Pierre had once taken the other woman to), with big breakers striking against the shore. The weather was superb, the sea was high but not dangerous, the sun made the white foam sparkle on the crest of the waves. We were amusing ourselves by jumping, diving into water alive and swirling, covered with light foam, which dissolved irregularly into lacy fragments. I love the sea. I love to submerge myself in it, swimming or lolling about in it like a dog in dust.

We would confront the waves, moving towards them, they would tower over us, and only at the last would we dive under. I've known the game since childhood and I was good at it. Better than the others, who shouted, swallowed water, gulping and laughing, or raced out beyond the reach of some huge breaker rising up like a wall before collapsing on us.

Suddenly, a splendid wave, higher than the others, lifted me up, flipped me in a somersault, rolled me in a profusion of bubbles and backwater and finally abandoned me a little brutally, way up the beach near dry sand. I was lying there, dazed, transported, trying to catch my breath. I felt the delight of the sand sliding underneath me, pulled in by the receding wave, which created a veritable bathtub under my back and pelvis. It was then that I realized with horror that an immense snake was coiling itself around my thigh, its head raised high between my legs. It was a magnificent snake with glints of blue and green. It was merely raising its head, it wasn't attacking me. Nonetheless it terrified me and with my two hands I tried in vain to push it away. It was stiff and powerful, and nothing I could do would dislodge it. Friends had gathered around me laughing.

"It's a harmless snake. Don't be afraid. He's more frightened than you are."

The snake had disappeared the way it had come, without hurting me. But I still was upset and uneasy. Back at the house, I told my story to the old servant working in the garden.

"You don't have to be afraid of those snakes. There are plenty of them all over the countryside, they will never attack you. They're not even poisonous."

Even so, I couldn't calm myself; I lay down on a bed with a somber enough blue-green velvet spread. I was lying on my side, my head resting on my hand (the same position as Jean-Pierre's when he was reading my first pages), and in my dream I was analyzing my fear. The snake: fear of the penis. No reason to be afraid of the snake: no reason to be afraid of the penis. Moreover, I wasn't afraid. There wasn't any reason to fear.

Suddenly, I saw against my elbow, coiled upon itself, blue-green like the bedspread, a snake like the one on the beach, head held high, mouth open. This time, it wasn't between my thighs, but very close to my head. That made it even more dangerous. One stroke of its forked tongue at my temple, and I'm dead. Panic, terror! The snake so near, its gaping mouth and quivering tongue darting in and out. Fear paralyzes me, prevents me from escaping. I am terrorized, endlessly incapable of moving. And yet all of a sudden, with a swift motion, my arm shoots out, I catch the snake by the neck just under its mouth, and squeeze. At the same time I stand up. The snake is struggling at arm's length, its tail lashing the air. Where to go? What to do? I won't have the strength to keep on squeezing very long. And it isn't choking, it's writhing frantically. The fear is intense. I think that I'll have to pay for my rashness. This time the snake will get its revenge.

I am running to the bathroom. Jean-Pierre is in the tub. Gravely, he watches me come in, me with the snake still at arm's length and panic in my eyes, in my whole being. I go towards him. I am with him in the warm, beneficent water of the bath. He puts his fingers opposite mine on the neck of the snake. He pulls until the throat rips open. He keeps pulling until the snake divides in two beautiful strips, two ribbons of supple bronze. And then calm.

Yes! It was that easy! Not too complicated to understand. This fear which paralyzed me, my mother and the women in black, was not fear of the phallus, the *membrum virile* (the penis), it was fear of male power. To divide this power was sufficient to displace the fear. I was certain that that was the significance of my dream.

And, for my part, if I wanted to play a role in society, I would have to begin by what was within reach, what I knew best: Jean-Pierre, the children, the five of us, a family, a microcosm, the ferment of society.

This was the solution. I was sure of it. There were surely other ways to go about it, but this was the only way for me. Analysis had given me the habit of thinking in a certain way, to go deep into thoughts, each one calling for another, until I got to the simplest, the most direct. And for me it had come from having discovered the word "politics" and a little of what the word contains. Such a perception, at the end of seven years of gestation, allowed me to understand to what extent life had to be lived in relation to organized society. The easiest way to begin was by constructing genuine relationships among the various members of the family.

Such a lot of work! Hypocrisy and lies were everywhere around us. The most ordinary words and gestures were pretenses, disguises, masquerades. And what was happening to the imagination in all that? Amputated! Even the imagination of the children was almost completely effaced to leave room for the ready-made imagination with which they were fitted out at school and in the house. For, in speaking to them as I did, in dressing them as I did, and in having them live as I did, I was imposing my rules, ideas, and tastes on them. I understood I didn't listen easily or well, and that, as a consequence, I didn't really know them. Thanks to the children, I had begun again to learn how to walk, speak, write, read, laugh, love, play.

I was inspired. The days went by so quickly!

Such pandemonium! All doors opened, all the ropes were let out. WHAT HAPPINESS!

That did it, the castle of cards really collapsed.

# Chapter XVI

During this last year of my analysis, my mother was living through her final agony.

I never suspected it.

On the rough draft of my manuscript I made a slip of the pen: I wrote, "my mother was living through her final analysis" instead of "my mother was living through her final agony." It was clearly not an accident that I confused these two words. For I think that a well-conducted analysis must lead to the death and the birth of the subject in question, securing his own freedom and truth. There is an inestimable distance between the person I was and the person I have become, so that it is no longer even possible to compare the two women. And this distance between them only increases, for the analysis never comes to an end, it becomes a way of life. The madwoman and I, however, are but one and the same person, we resemble each other, we love each other, we live together happily.

Thus in her sixties, when my mother found herself propelled out of her universe, and when her entire life was called into question because of the war in Algeria, she chose to die. The upheaval was too profound, she did not herself feel capable of taking it on. It was too late. It is my belief that everything collapsed for her when she unconsciously analyzed the content of the word "paternalism." She often said with irritation, "it works better to be paternalistic than nothing at all, like those giving us lessons today. The Arabs knew I was taking care of them forty years ago. Those who call us paternalists cannot say as much." She understood very well that in this terrible word was the condemnation to be found of what had been her reason for living, her excuse, her justification: Christian charity. When she defended herself it was as if she was crying out for forgiveness.

When my mother and grandmother had come to France to live, we occupied two apartments with a common living room, in the suburbs.

My psychoanalysis had begun more than a year before, but I was still so sick, so fast asleep in my cocoon, that I willingly accepted our being together again, I was even delighted by the presence of my mother. She would help me look after the children and do the housework. Let alone the fact that my grandmother could be counted on to help out at the end of the month.

At the start of treatment the doctor had cautioned me, "It is my duty to warn you that psychoanalysis involves the risk of upsetting your life completely." And I had thought, what could possibly upset my life? Perhaps I would get a divorce because it was at the beginning of my marriage that the Thing had taken root in me. So what, then, I'll get a divorce. It would work out. This apart, I didn't see what else in my life could be changed....

Two or three years passed in this quasitotal cohabitation. Two or three years during which I was beginning to have some awareness of coming into the world. Two or three years during which I expressed my secret hatred for my mother, in the cul-de-sac, a sentiment which, until then, I had kept hidden like an imperfection. Right away, my relations with her changed direction. Now that the analysis was making me stronger, wiser and more responsible, I began to discover the fragility of my mother and her innocence. I saw too that in some respects she was also a victim. She, whose relations with me were of no great significance, merely the stereotypical relations of a mother whose daughter is over thirty, and who is herself officially a "mother of a large family" entitling her to the thirty percent reduction on train tickets, also felt the change. And yet we didn't speak of it. She never spoke save to tell me about the failed abortion. And as for me, I had long ago given up trying to communicate with her. I have no doubt that if I had wanted to be reunited with her, at that time I could have been. In the calm which follows combat, in the disenchantment and the lassitude of a battle which is lost, in the sullen grayness of France, this detested fatherland to which she had sacrificed her beloved son, she was a prey to such chaotic feelings it was a propitious moment for a reconciliation. But I no longer wanted it. All I did was ascertain her weakness and her ignorance. I found her pathetic, I didn't have the time to concern myself with her, I had too much to do to save myself from the Thing.

The Thing was our only link now. Having passed it on to me, she knew it well. In the worst of my illness she saw it shining like a jewel and she approached me with respect and maybe even with love. My tremors, my sweat, my blood, my stubborn silence did not discourage her. She interested herself in it, as never before. And when it became clear that the Thing was losing ground, her confusion became even greater. Not only had Algeria gotten away from her, but the craziness too and her sick child, her abnormal baby, her tortured fetus. With considerable though unforeseen effort, at that time, she changed her attitude and tried to hook up with me like a railroad car. I wouldn't let her do it. Why did she make such an effort? Was it some instinct for self-preservation? Self-interest? Love? I will never know.

My grandmother died. She alone had been able to make living with my mother tolerable. Any confrontation with my mother could only be deadly without the humor, youth, curiosity and wisdom of my grandmother. One of us had to be the loser. If my grandmother had died a few years earlier, that is to say, before the start of the analysis, I think I would have been the one to give way.

The situation dragged on for some time. I was no longer able to endure the influence of my mother on the children, but did not dare either speak of it or abandon her, knowing what dire straits she was in. At the time, I tried to get her to parlay her medical qualifications into getting paid for the care she offered instead of doing it for free. Her resistance was incredible; it was as if I had asked her to prostitute herself. She really wanted to continue to look after the poor, to bathe them, sit up with them all night, act as midwife, comfort them, but not for the money. To give up the benevolence she had practiced all of her life would be so shameful and so scandalous. "In our family that just isn't done." As my mother said herself, she would rather beg. To accept payment for the care she provided would be depriving herself of her last prerogative as well as her final talisman. So it was out of the question.

How could someone so intelligent be so stupid? By what aberration and what fear could she follow rules which were so stupid? The rich must give to the poor in order to please God; their charity is the incense that rises up to paradise, sweetly perfuming the divine beard! Those who have the power must set an example, guarding their dignity in adversity. To be a master is not a state which is observable but a condition of the soul.

"Listen, you don't have a penny, there's nothing left, all you have is your old-age pension, you know it perfectly well. You're not rich anymore, you're poor. You're even among the poorest of the poor."

"I never was rich, my girl, but I never cared about money, and I'm not about to begin now."

How ridiculous! How obscene! How farcical! In addition to everything else, she was proud of her poverty and made a show of her down-at-heels look, the stained dress, the heavy, run-proof stockings and the moth-eaten sweater. But, lest anyone be deceived, she often played with her queenlike hands, revealing on her right pinkie a tiny signet ring bearing the family coat of arms, on the fourth finger a diamond engagement ring and on her left hand an emerald set in diamonds. The very picture of offended bourgeois dignity! She was so far from being a bourgeoise who ought to have used her hands. She didn't know it.

The break between us came after the discovery of the violence that was in me. The apartment in the suburbs had become unbearable. It was too large, too expensive, too remote and too pretentious. I could no longer live in

274

that concrete cube of hypocrisy and sham. In order to revel in the bourgeois life, one needs thick draperies, high silent rooms and well-kept secrets. What kind of a game were they playing behind their cinder block walls and their indiscreet bays? Abused monkeys, caged turkeys, silly geese, circus donkeys, this is what they had become! These substantial buildings which surrounded me and their gardens with weeping willows and manicured lawns, iron gates, white fences, so calm and untroubled by the cries of well-bred and polite children and sonatas by Chopin, it wasn't for me, they could take it back.

I had made my decision. It was without difficulty or shame that I went to find my mother in her room.

She was on her bed, surrounded by the relics of her dead: photographs, portraits, objects. On her night table was an ashtray full of butts and a glass with something red in it. (I thought it was black currant syrup.)

"I wanted to tell you that I've made a serious decision: we're going to separate. Partly, I don't want to live here anymore, and partly I want to be alone with my children. I want to bring them up my way.... You have all summer to find something else.... I'm the poorest member of the family, there must be someone who could give you more of a welcome than I can."

She didn't say a word. She bowed her head and began to cry softly. I went out, it was over.

I thought only of building my own life, I was absolutely determined. She had understood very well that no blackmail on the grounds of sentiment or health or poverty or age could have made me change my plans. She knew very well what my early years had been, my childhood, my adolescence, her indifference to me and her occasional peevishness. She had nothing to say.

Perhaps she thought at first that I couldn't manage, that I couldn't stand up to it physically, that I would have to appeal to her for help. But things went well for me. Perhaps even the difficulties of my new life hastened the progress of the analysis.

She came upon a haven with one of her friends, whose husband was a helpless invalid. There she found again an atmosphere entirely Algerian, and reasons for devoting herself to this old gentleman who for her was, in some sense, the incarnation of Algeria for the French. I thought this separation had been beneficial for her as well. I saw her from time to time, I telephoned her almost every day in the late morning.

Then the old gentleman died, and she was deeply affected.

As far as I was concerned, all that took place in another universe which I had abandoned, and which was relayed to me only by the few words I exchanged with my mother on the telephone. I no longer felt any curiosity about a world I had abandoned in disgust. I knew enough about it. I had no wish to devote even an hour of my time to it. I had too much to learn, too much to see, too much to do elsewhere. Every morning I opened my eyes with an appetite for life. I thought I had forever finished with the past.

That is why I didn't understand when I heard on the other end of the receiver, early in the morning, the voice of the person my mother was living with.

"Well, that's it... I wanted to tell you: I don't want to keep your mother here in the state she's in.... You'll have to look after her, it isn't up to me to do it ... I've already told your relative, the one who is a doctor. He'll be dropping by here, later this morning. It would be good if you were here. I'm warning you, I won't keep her here another twenty-four hours."

"I'll be there."

I was afraid to ask what was the matter. I'd find out, later. The woman's voice was peremptory, clearly she couldn't do it any longer.

I got there at half-past eleven. My relative was also there listening to my mother's heartbeat with the stethoscope, then taking her blood pressure. How she'd aged in only a few weeks! It was horrible to behold. There was no one behind the eyes in that ravaged face. It was as if the eyes had turned inwards away from anyone or anything which might come in her way now. Her body was no more than a great stinking heap concealed in a squalid pink flannelette nightgown with little blue and white flowers. Her dirty and swollen feet swung in the emptiness.

The relation had seen me enter, but said nothing, he had gone on listening to her heartbeat with a stethoscope. Then he took her blood pressure.

"Blood pressure two hundred and fifty! Do you understand what that means!"

She replied slowly as if she were in pain when she spoke: "I suspected as much, it's my nerves."

"Nerves or no nerves, you've got to go on a strict regimen. To begin with, you can stop smoking. Look at all those butts!"

He looked with disgust at the night table which was covered with ashes and crushed cigarettes.

"Don't give me any more of your excuses, do you understand?"

She shook her head like a dotty old woman, as if to say, "Keep talking, you interest me."

"The only way to get proper care is to go into a hospital. Besides, Paulette doesn't want you with her anymore. You frighten her, and I understand how she feels. Just look at the condition you've got yourself in."

She drew herself up, assumed her empress look, and said, in a tone which permitted no reply, "There is no question of my entering a hospital. I wouldn't stay in one. And besides, it isn't necessary. Since I have to leave here, I wish to go to my daughter's and rest."

I was thunderstruck. No, not at my house! Jean-Pierre had come back to France. We had found a three-room apartment in the XIVth arrondissement, where the five of us were living. We were very comfortable there. We didn't need any more space to have our evening talks and reconstitute our family in our own way. We were happy. There was no room for my mother with me, either physically or in any other way. Above all, not in the condition in which I'd found her. She had brothers and a son, who had bigger houses, "servants," no young children. Why did she want to come to me?

The relative must have felt my shrinking back, my refusal, for he said, "You'd be better off with your son."

"No, I'll go to my daughter. I won't go anywhere else."

I didn't like the scolding way this man spoke to her, as if she were an idiot. From my first look at her earlier on when I had come in there, I had seen that she was in the clutches of the Thing, that, in that great heap of flesh she was engaged in a desperate fight.

"That's all right. You can come home with me, but you can't stay long. It's very cramped, in our place, you know. I don't even have a bed for you, one of the children or Jean-Pierre will have to sleep on the floor."

Her face changed, suddenly, she really looked at me: she was happy to be going with me!

I answered her with my eyes: you cannot live with us, it's out of the question, I cannot concern myself with you. And then I said: "You're sure you don't want to go to my brother? It would be better for you there."

"No, your place."

Again her eyes went blank.

Her bags had to be packed to go immediately. There was rage in my heart.

Four days went by. Since the day of her installation, which was a Sunday, I hadn't seen much of her. She stayed alone all day. In the morning the children left for the lycée and did not come home for lunch. Then Jean-Pierre and I went to work. We didn't get back until evening. I left something in the kitchen for her lunch, but she never touched it. I had told her that there was a church nearby where she could easily hear Mass.

"I don't set foot in church any more. I've stopped believing in that nonsense. Christ is a laughingstock."

I knew from the concierge that no one came to see her during the day. I didn't have a good reputation with that side of the family and in coming to live with us my mother knew what she was doing: she was cutting herself off from them. No one had tried to reach me, either at home in the evening or at my office, to get news of her. I didn't know how to take care of her, I had no time or money. I didn't want her to stay, but it seemed unthinkable to put her in a nursing home, it would have been one more deception, an impermissible cowardice on her part, on my part, on the part of our family. She knew she had to take care of herself. She was only sixty-five. In spite of appearances, she was not old.

During those four days, I saw her prostrate on her unmade bed in the living room. She didn't move, she didn't speak, she looked at her dirty feet. She no longer washed up. Her toilet articles had remained in her suitcase and she had not even gone into the bathroom, I was sure of it. I knew all these symptoms by heart. I knew that with the Thing there were no longer days or nights, that "cleanliness" had no meaning, any more than "sleep," "children," "living room," or anything else. The battle was too fierce, the internal agitation too great, for anything else to exist. One moves through a world apart, disturbing, sinister, sometimes terribly aggressive, always sluggish, mobilizing all one's energy and will. You have to pay attention. Careful!

I couldn't stand to see her like that. It drove me crazy to know the children were alone with her in the late afternoon, from the time they got out of school until we got home. She did not have the same instinct which made me hide myself. On the contrary, she didn't give a damn, she exhibited herself as if she took pleasure in exposing her wounds. I hated her.

I went to the dead-end street to analyze my hatred.

The evening of the fourth day, I had to go to a conference. I went out after dinner feeling like a coward because I was leaving Jean-Pierre alone with her in a house ravaged by her presence.

Won't THEY ever leave me in peace!

When I got home, it was midnight. The conference had been interesting and I was eager to speak of it with Jean-Pierre. The front door opened directly into the living room. As soon as I opened it, at that very moment, the spectacle of my mother shattered me. In a fraction of a second, I was caught up in a brutal and savage storm shattering my head, squandering my mind: in the whirlwind of my former insanity.

She was there, facing me, sitting on her bed as usual. Her nightgown had been pulled up over her stomach, so that I could see her hairless vagina. She had done it where she sat, and her shit was oozing out down to the floor. On the table, beside her, there were two square bottles of rum, one empty, the other half-full, and the large glass beside them was full. She was swaying back and forth in order to rock herself.

The noise I had made coming in had made her raise her head and look at me. She was vile: the bags under her eyes drooped onto her cheeks, her cheeks drooped onto her neck, and her gaping mouth hung down on her chest. She recognized me. She looked at me, she looked at her dirt, then she went to search in the depths of herself, I don't know where, for an expression. I experienced everything she was going through, I knew the effort she was making to find in the confusion of her internal images, the gestures, the signs which might serve to communicate to those on the outside. I saw surprise on her face, at first, but that wasn't what she wanted. Surprise remained while she plunged in again to look some more. She found it finally. Then I saw her face transformed, the folds of her skin changed direction, stretched out. She was smiling!

She started to speak, she rummaged about among the words she could not articulate. Finally, I understood.

"I...had...an...ac...ci...dent."

Her eyes went back and forth from her excrement to me with a mischievous look, and then she put her smile back on her ravaged face.

If I didn't kill her then and there, it's because I will never kill anyone. The analysis was working, even in the paroxysm of anger in which I had plunged, I was able to contain my violence. I was perfectly conscious of the devastating madness which was there throughout my body, beneath the skin, which vibrated like a gong in the rapid rhythm of my beating heart. Without the lengthy practice exercised in the analysis, without those seven years of painstaking work to achieve an understanding of myself, I would have sprung on her, I would have beaten her, I would have knocked down the walls, burst open the ceiling, I would have howled, howled like the frenzied madwoman I would have become.

Instead, I moved in her direction, I took three steps. I thought I had to whip her. Not to do her any harm but to bring her back to the surface, to make her conscious of her condition, to get her to fight it so that she could find the courage on her own, to take herself in hand. If not, she wouldn't come out of it. If she still had an ounce of awareness, she must have expected me to pretend that I hadn't seen anything, neither the shit nor the alcohol. Then, in a firm though calm tone of voice, I said: "My poor mother, you are as drunk as a horse's ass."

I had pronounced these words as though I found it normal for her to have drunk too much, and that she had to get over it.

It had worked, I had gotten to her. I saw a kind of stirring of her body, her features returned to normal, she straightened her back, also, and trying very hard to gain control in order to attempt to clearly articulate her words, for she was very drunk, she lashed out at me, "My child...one does not...speak...like that...to one's...mother."

Then she fell back across her bed. She was already

asleep, snoring gently, when I went over to her. She must have found comfort finally in letting me in on her secret. She thought that I was going to rescue her. She abandoned herself to me.

I ran to our bedroom where Jean-Pierre was working while he waited for me. He had not heard a thing. The living room was separated from the rest of the apartment by a sort of anteroom which had its own door. I threw myself on my bed, I couldn't take any more. What a shock, to have seen her in that condition! I had never looked at anything more horrible and revolting. Jean-Pierre understood that something had happened between my mother and me. He didn't question me at all but began to speak softly to me: "This cannot go on. You'll be sick again. There is no reason for you to have sole responsibility for your mother. For your own good, for the sake of the children and for my sake too, you've got to find a solution immediately, this very night. We can't put it off."

"But I'd be waking THEM up."

"And why should you be the only one to go without sleep?"

I telephoned all her immediate family, her brothers, her son. I explained what was happening and that tomorrow was Thursday and the children would be home from school, and I didn't want them to spend the whole day alone with her in her condition. The relative who was the doctor said: "She'll have to go to a detoxification center."

"Because you knew she was drinking?"

"Of course, Paulette told me. You know she's been drinking since the death of the old gentleman. It was as if she were losing Algeria a second time...and even before, she never had any qualms about putting it away."

"Why did you let it happen?"

"You know, it's an awkward subject... she didn't talk about it. I wasn't going to be the one to speak about it. I couldn't imagine she'd let herself go this far. With her blood pressure, she could die."

"But you're a doctor, you knew she had very high blood pressure."

"Not to this degree, but the heavy concentration of alcohol she's had in the last few days hasn't helped a bit."

"Did she know it? Did she know she might have killed herself?"

"Certainly. Anyone having even the slightest knowledge of medicine knows it. She knew it better than anyone else. She's looked after enough old drunks in her Red Cross dispensaries."

"Something has to be done right away."

He heaved a deep sigh of irritation. "OK.... With this family nothing is easy.... I'll have her hospitalized tomorrow in a specialized facility. I'll take care of it. I'll call you back."

I couldn't erase from my mind the vision of my mother like an old bag lady.

The telephone in the night, strident, hysterical!

"Hello."

"Hello. OK, you have an appointment tomorrow morning... at ten o'clock, with Dr. X, at such-and-such an address. He has to see her before he can hospitalize her, but he can't take her in until day after tomorrow, he doesn't have a free room."

"She's not going to stay here tomorrow."

"That's your problem, you'll have to take care of it, I can't do any more. Ask your brother."

Jean-Pierre came back into the room. He looked grim.

"Did you see her?"

"Yes. She's in bed now. It's all cleaned up. Don't worry, she's all right, she's sleeping peacefully."

"You did that?"

"It was nothing really, she's your mother, you've already seen enough.... And then, she's so far gone. She made me feel sorry for her. To kill yourself with rum... what a thing to do!"

The following day, Jean-Pierre stayed home with me. We'd let my brother know that we'd bring her to his place right after we'd been to the doctor's, and that he'd probably have to take her to the clinic the day after.

I got her things ready. It didn't take long. She hadn't even opened one of her suitcases. She had a very heavy wicker basket, in which I found the empty bottles, carefully wrapped up in such a way as to keep them from making any noise. Where did she expect to get rid of them? She saw that I was busy.

"What are you doing?"

"I'm getting your things ready, we're going to take you to the doctor's, and then to my brother's."

"I want to stay here."

"You can't."

Had she really forgotten the scene of the preceding night, or was it that she didn't want to remember? Nothing in her attitude gave proof of anything having gone on between us. She had revealed herself to me in a very bad light, and I had spoken to her with a brutality hitherto unknown in our relations. She was absent, feeble, without any awareness of what was happening. She was in the depths of despair.

We waited for a long time at the doctor's without speaking. She complained several times, "I'm thirsty, I'm thirsty." We asked for a glass of water. Then she went in. She absolutely insisted that we be present at her interview. The doctor would have preferred to see her alone, and we would have preferred to wait outside, but no, she insisted, so we went in with her. She sat down in front of the desk, and we stayed in the background, behind her, on two chairs.

After a few preliminary questions about her age, her previous medical history, her blood pressure, and the medications she took, etc., the doctor finally asked her to speak about her life.

I was very impressed by the fact that she didn't feel the reprimand in seeing the specialist. For her, medicine was something joyful and strong. She herself was an excellent doctor, her diagnostic skills were very sound and her hands were so very able to examine, to nurse, to comfort. She had a gift for it. She knew it. She was proud of it, and, as soon as she found herself in the presence of a representative of the medical profession, one felt she was in her element. But that day, her mood did not change while she was with the specialist. She had remained exhausted, she had dragged her feet from one room to the other. In the middle of her face, her dry lips were sagging.

When the doctor asked her to tell him about her life, however, she became more animated, she began to speak more quickly and more distinctly. Until then it was a jumble of words coming out of her mouth. She spoke of leaving Algeria. She said she didn't like France, neither had she liked the French nor General de Gaulle. She didn't like the OAS either. No, all that was hateful. What she missed was the Algeria of her own past, the long lines of patients in rags waiting to be taken care of by her, the cakes to thank her and the bouquets of wild tulips.

Then she began to put herself back in time, farther still, telling how it was that she began to take care of people, the rounds in the dispensaries of the casbah every morning, the circuits she made in the health service trucks which plowed through the nomad campgrounds in the interior in order to vaccinate, to dress the wounds, to give the injections, to sound the poor with a stethoscope.

Then she went back, farther and farther to her marriage and her little dead daughter.

Never had I heard her speak so simply on the subject of this man who, at once, shocked and attracted her and of her beloved baby who resembled him. I found it indecent of her to talk this way, whereas the other night when I saw her sitting with her legs spread in the shit, I had not found her indecent. Until that instant, she had been my mother and only my mother, not a person.

I lowered my head. I thought of her name. For me, she had no name, it was: my mother. In this Parisian doctor's office, I met for the first time Solange de Talbiac (a name straight out of an operetta!) called "Soso" by her friends. "Soso" in the sun, "Soso" in the shade of her broad-brimmed hat, tiny pearls of sweat on her lip, superior because her redhead's skin couldn't take the heat. "Soso" in the garden of her parents, with a sheaf of flowers in her arms, "Soso" with unsuspected desire in her belly for the man coming towards her, the handsome Frenchman who smelled of adventure, "Soso" sweet, very young, innocent. "Soso's" green eyes, so beautiful, so pure, so greedy for experience and so ignorant....

The emotion was choking me. I found her so touching, so naive and so despondent: it was too late.

She continued to narrate the illness of her husband and the death of her first child. She was full of the details of their misery coming full circle. She said, "My husband did this," "My husband said that," "My husband went there...." Never did I hear her speak of my father in such terms.

She cried in remembering. Her tears ran down her cheeks as she gradually made these old images which had never faded come alive.

Next she spoke of my brother and of the fear she had had seeing him in his turn infected by tuberculosis. Happily, the B.C.G was already in use. She spoke of the treatment for tuberculosis and of the progress that had been made.

She kept coming back to her son's curvature of the spine....

Not a word about her divorce, not a word about her religion, not a word about me. Her life had stopped with the birth of her son in 1924. She was twenty-three years old. I had no part in her life.

When I left there, I was drained and tired out, as if I had been beaten unmercifully. Jean-Pierre and I held her up between us in the street. She let herself go trustingly in our arms. She was relieved by her long monologue. The doctor had said when she was leaving: "Your depression is not serious, I am confident I can get you out of it in two weeks, three at the most." To me he had said, in the corridor, "The alcohol poisoning isn't too severe. She'll get over it." I didn't share his opinion: to me she was already done for.

We left her at my brother's. Jean-Pierre had made it clear that I was going to leave for the country, that very day even in order to rest, that I couldn't be counted on for several days. Once we were outside, he said to me, "Just tell your office switchboard not to put any calls through.

You are out of reach. Don't think about any of this for the moment. If there's something that has to be done, I'll take care of it."

The following day, it was close to twelve o'clock, a friend came into the office where I worked. He put his hand on my shoulder and, because he didn't know how to go about it, because it wasn't easy to say, he told me clumsily: "Your mother is dead. They've just telephoned to let you know."

My mother dead! The world split apart.

An ambulance was supposed to come and get her at eleven o'clock, to take her to the clinic. When the ambulance driver got there, they went to find her in the room where she had slept. She was on the floor. She had been dead for ten or twelve hours already. She was curled up in a ball. Rigor mortis had fixed the horror on her face and body. They couldn't lay her out in a saintly attitude, or compose her face serenely. She grimaced terribly in pain and in fear. It was unbearable.

My mother dead! The world has gone mad! This is the Apocalypse!

In the street, it was cold but sunny, very sunny.

I will never see THEM again. I am not going to go to the funeral or to the cemetery. I refuse to participate one more time in their masquerade. It's over and done with.

As a farewell, I leave them my mother's grimace of horror before a life that was false from beginning to end, her features, tortured by all the amputations to which she had submitted, this mask worn in the great Punch and Judy show which was her life.

The shock had been very violent. I had to return more frequently to the cul-de-sac.

The upheaval of the first few days following the death of my mother was succeeded by a sense of relief and freedom. As if everything had fallen into place. She was through with it and so was I. She was free and so was I. She was healed, and so was I.

Something wasn't right, however. I didn't feel as free as I said I did.

For several months I was dragged down by the vague impression of not having gotten to the bottom of something and of not having been completely honest with myself. I said to myself that I would have to go to the cemetery, once, at least. At the same time, I thought it a stupid idea. There was nothing at the cemetery. Nothing.

It was plaguing me and it was in my way. So I took the car one morning and went: spring was in the air and it was beautiful in the country just outside of Paris.

I had no difficulty finding the grave. I had come there not so very long ago to bury my grandmother. It was a tiny little cemetery in the country at the foot of a sparsely wooded hill, just at the beginning of a great plain in the region of Brie. It was in the gentle countryside of France which is known as "La Douce" in France. It didn't really go well with my mother. There should have been the dry and stony red earth of her beloved Algeria, complete with olive trees and Barbary fig trees. It wasn't important, in the end, people do not inhabit their corpses. .

I was fixed there in that useless and thankless place. Four sickly thornbushes grew near the iron gate which squeaked shrilly when it was pushed. A crucifix stood erect against the brilliant sky not far from me. It was an old cross from the beginning of the century, which made me think more of Toulouse-Lautrec or Van Gogh than Jesus.

Why had I come there? There wasn't even a name on the tomb.

They must have been doing some masonry down there, for the ground was covered with light-colored sand which was luminous and perfectly dry and which I had an impulse to touch. Then I sat down on the grayish slab — it wasn't as beautiful as the one she had picked out for the grave of her daughter — and I played with the sand. The sand is beautiful. The beach is beautiful. Especially on a day after a storm when the sea throws up great quantities of shells and seaweed of every color and shape.

Do you remember? You took me with you on a treasure hunt. The waves had deposited their meager spoils in lines of garlands festooned on the moist sand. You said I had the eyes of a lynx, that I knew better than anyone how to find the mother-of-pearl shells, cowries, pointed sea snails, ear shells and the pink razor clam shells. You knew the names of them all, just as you knew the names of the stars. Then you would make holes in them, polish them, varnish them, and put them together on brass wire with some cardboard and glue, and then from your hands would come a marvelous bouquet. I spent long summer evenings watching you at work with admiration while the sea heaved steady sighs in the hot night.

So now I imagined myself talking to her the way she used to do with her child in the cemetery at Saint-Eugène. What's come over me! I felt a little ridiculous. Fortunately, there was nobody there to see me! Muttering all alone in that cemetery. I really looked suspicious.

It was a fine day, the sun was warming my back. With my index finger in the sand I went on drawing big snakes, intermingled s's.

Soso, how beautiful you were on the night of the ball,

when you came to my room to show me your dress. I was already in bed. You dazzled me. I have never seen you more beautiful than on that night in your long white dress tied in back at the waist with a huge sash as green as your eyes. You spun around to make the fullness of the skirt flare out. You laughed.

I love you. Yes, that's right, I love you. I came here to declare it to you, once and for all. I am not ashamed to speak of it. It does me good to say it to you and to repeat it! I love you. I love you.

It felt better to say it: three little words strung together and repressed a thousand times over throughout my life. They had accumulated and must have ended up forming an airy ball which rebounded here and there inside my head, cumbersome, in the way and unseizable. It had taken this catastrophic death, the earthquake that she had provoked in me in order for the ball to rise to the surface of consciousness to vanquish the final resistance, the ultimate defense. I had to go far away from the cul-de-sac, to be isolated in view of this flat place, so similar to the one which had offered itself to me so often on the couch but bathed in sunlight this time, to dare to listen to my voice utter these three words: "I" (I, the madwoman, the woman who is not mad, the child, the woman) "You" (my mother, the beauty, the expert, the proud and haughty person, the demented one, the suicide) "love" (attachment, union but also the warmth, the kisses, and again the possible joy, the wish for happiness).

How good it was to finally love her in the light, in the springtime, in the open, after the terrible battle from which we were delivered. Two blind people armed to the teeth, claws exposed, in the arena of our class. What blows she had struck me, what venom I had distilled!

What savagery, what butchery!

If I had not become insane, I would never have emerged. As for my mother, she had forced back her insanity until the end, until the departure from Algeria. It was too late, the gangrene had gone into her marrow. She was afraid to rebel through the words and the gestures of rebellion, she didn't know them, THEY had never taught them to her. She had even left them the possibility of attributing her suicide to a secret vice. I was the only one to whom she had shown her bottle, her circus revolver!

# Chapter XVII

Once more, the cul-de-sac, its little houses pressing one against the other, its broken paving stones, its cracked sidewalks, the gate at the end, the steps into the little garden, the waiting room done in the manner of Henri II, the office, the gargoyle on top of the beam, the couch, the enigmatic little man.

"Doctor, I am going to settle our accounts. I will not be coming here anymore. I feel able to live alone now. I feel strong. My mother transmitted the Thing to me, you have transmitted the analysis, they are in perfect balance, I thank you for it."

"You don't have to thank me, it's you who came here to find what you were looking for. I could not have done anything without you."

"Goodbye, Doctor."

"Goodbye, Madame. I'll be here if you need me. I will be happy to hear how you're doing if you consider it necessary to tell me."

Inviolable little man, so he's going to maintain the role to the end!

The door closes behind me. In front of me, the cul-de-sac, the city, the country and an appetite for life and for building as big as the earth itself.

# Afterword

This beautiful, captivating, deeply moving story speaks for itself. Still, at its end there remain a number of unanswered questions for the layperson and the psychoanalyst alike. That this is so attests to the veracity of what we are told, because this is not a novel of the imagination; this is a tale based on the author's own experience, which brought her as close to utter destruction as any person can come and still live to tell about it. Like many others who have been extremely ill and undergone psychoanalysis to successfully work through their problems, the author seems at the end not to be consciously aware of all that was once involved.

We are not told, for example, why the "Thing" caused the near-continuous flow of menstrual fluid that tortured, incapacitated, disgusted, and shamed her, nor why this symptom stopped as if by magic, although there are no magical cures, as the long period of psychoanalytic treatment she underwent amply demonstrates. And why, since the person who tells her story knew since adolescence that she was not "meant" to be born, did she suffer a psychotic break only in her late twenties?

I believe we are not enlightened about these and other matters because the author does not consciously know the answers to them, although in her analysis she worked through and mastered her illness. Due to this working through, her disturbance was no longer part of her. Having been exorcised, the "Thing" was no longer the same as it had been when it had dominated and ruined her life; it no longer had power over her; it was no longer the same "Thing." This is why, at the end of a successful psychoanalysis, the former patient often no longer consciously knows many matters which had preoccupied him during his illness and his analysis.

It is also true that this is, after all, a novel, albeit an autobiographical one. The author had to be selective and to present only those of her experiences that suited her artistic purposes, since it would have been impossible anyway to tell all that went on during her seven years of psychoanalysis. However, it is part of successful analysis that the patient frees himself so completely from some aspects of his past and so alters important features of his personality that the shed aspects no longer seem of relevance.

Whether or not this is the case here with such omissions, I am deeply impressed by this novel. It is, in my opinion, as near perfect as a novel can be. I could not help engaging in some clinical speculations in order to comprehend certain of its features further. Perhaps these may be of interest to other readers also.

Having worked with many children whose psychosis was their reaction to the felt death wishes of their mothers (as I described years ago in *The Empty Fortress*), I cannot help wondering: why did the author not become a psychotic child, since she must have felt already in infancy that she was an unwanted child, as her desperate efforts to win the love of her mother clearly indicate? However, her mother's deep and unwavering attachment was to a sister who had died years before the author was born. So the author's dilemma from an early age was that although she felt her mother was capable of the greatest love for and devotion to a daughter, why was this daughter not herself? Yet this child did not become psychotic until she was a grown woman. Why not?

Several possible answers suggest themselves. An important element in them is the mother's deep guilt about having tried to get rid of her pregnancy with this daughter — a guilt that the mother tried to expiate by devoting herself singlemindedly to ministering to poor, sick people. Such positive dealing with one's guilt is not only a redeeming feature, it also alleviates the need to act out the guilt negatively on the child who was its cause and who otherwise remains an ever-present painful reminder of it. So of destructive behavior directed against the child we hear of only isolated incidents.

Probably more important, since she was working out her guilt outside the home, the mother was around but little, and then she was tired and preoccupied with other things — that she found some solace in alcohol may also have helped. What was significant in this context was that, with the mother working outside the home, all of the immediate care of the little girl was entrusted to her nurse, who loved her. Thus the mother's unconscious rejection of her daugher — unconscious because we must assume that, once the girl was born, the death wishes against her were repressed and replaced in the mother's conscious mind by the wish to do right by her child — was compensated by the nurse's and other servants' and retainers' love for her. The free and easy life the girl enjoyed with them and their children during the day-long absences of her mother offered much needed relief.

Her father, too, in his own way was affectionate. Because of the alienation and physical separation of her parents from each other, the little girl had importance to both of them as the continuing link between them. That it was she who brought back from her visits with her father the money the mother needed made the girl feel important and valuable, painful though this type of relation was to her on another level.

Another factor was that the mother's guilt made her wish to have this daughter be a perfect child; only this could prove to her that her efforts to abort her daughter had not ruined her. This gave the child a unique value to her mother, and any childhood illness accentuated the mother's guilt while at the same time permitting her to engage in her main avenue for expiating it: nurturing and ministering to the ill. These were the moments when the daughter was most important to the mother and least ambivalently so; hence the moments of bliss the girl experienced while her mother took care of her when she was sick.

The mother's confession to the girl that she had tried by all possible means to abort her before her birth was also significant since, in the mother's mind, her goal was to protect her daughter. True, this admission occurred only when the girl had reached puberty, and its conscious purpose was to impress her with the dangers involved in becoming sexually active. Terrible as the shock was of being told her mother had wished her not to be born — something she must have felt without knowing since infancy, but never was sure about —it is much better to know such a thing than to suspect it without any chance of certainty.

I have known quite a few children who subconsciously were convinced that they were unwanted and who, correctly, suspected that their mothers had tried to abort them. But in the absence of any statement that this had been so, they could never trust their feelings, if for no other reason that that to do so would be too destructive to their security and self-respect. Thus they were caught up in an agonizing uncertainty about a most important fact of their lives.

This, at least, the woman whose story we followed here was spared. Her mother was not ambivalent about having tried to kill the fetus. This relative honesty explains why her mother's behavior was less destructive to her than has been that of mothers who, caught in severe ambivalence, pretend to their children and thus deny their children's own perceptions.

The following discussion of the debilitating symptom that finally drove the young mother to seek psychoanalytic help is based also on many parallel cases—parallel rather than similar because, while the inner pressures and agonies that lead to symptom formation may be similar, the symptom itself depends to a considerable measure on the age of the individual and the past and present details of that person's life experiences. The psychotic child, like a healthy one, makes the mother's wishes his own by internalizing them and acting them out, utterly destructive as this is for him, and life endangering—as the woman whose story we have been told came very close to bleeding to death. Why should we incorporate into the essence of our being the desire of those who (at least once) wished to destroy us? We do not choose our parents, and often they do not want or choose us either, but the parent-child bond is powerful nonetheless.

The younger we are, the more we respond to what we feel are the most powerful emotions of the person who is most important to us, and it does not matter what the nature of these emotions is. Fortunately, in the lives of many infants, the mother's strongest emotion is love for her baby; the baby responds to this love by building it into his budding personality as self-love, which will give him the strength to surmount many and various difficulties in later life. It is a great tragedy for her child when a mother actively does not desire to bear the child but does —a tragedy the child lives with from the moment it is born, the cause of which is inherent in his being.

It is not only in infancy that we are deeply impressed by those who hold great power over us. In a quite different context, that of the German concentration camps, I described the desperate situation of a person who finds himself in the absolute power of others who hold his life in their hands; I named such conditions "extreme situations." A typical defense of the very weak under such conditions is to identify with the enemy, or aggresor, destructive as such identification is in the long run.

Because of this mother's deep aversion to giving birth to this child from conception onwards, and her guilt about her efforts to abort her, this girl found herself all her life in such an "extreme situation." The psychological mechanisms that induce an infant to identify with and internalize the mother's strongest feelings and those that make the weak in an extreme situation identify with the person who oppresses him, in her case, reinforced each other; their negative force became all pervasive and inescapable until such time when an appropriate life-affirming counterforce, activated by her experience in psychoanalysis, neutralized their effects.

In infancy, when the girl was living under the constant pressure of what went on in her mother's conscious and unconscious mind, she could not help internalizing her mother's death wishes. This was the source of her psychotic break, as she realized during her analysis when she recognized that "my mother had granted me, at my birth, madness and death." As a child, "she had not known how to die in order to please her mother," but as an adult she acted out these internalized death wishes of the mother physically, by feeling that her heart was giving out, that she was bleeding to death, that the "Thing" would destroy her. The woman acted out her mother's feeling that to bear her, the unwanted child, was disgusting, by developing a symptom that made her feel utterly disgusting. Only during her analysis did she slowly realize that all her life she had been existing in an "extreme situation," and why; in a slow and tortuous process, she managed to successfully extricate herself from it.

In analysis she became aware that she had taken into herself her mother's disgust with the fetus that had grown inside of her as a "self-disgust which finally blossomed into madness," a madness in which she became "that hated and pursued fetus." Her way of putting it is the best and most drastic description known to me of this type of madness—the consequence of the internalization of a mother's death wishes by a child whom she had tried to rid herself of. It is the child's identification with both the fetus the mother felt was disgusting and with the mother's destructive wish to get rid of the fetus which explains the details of the daughter's illness.

According to the story, the unwilling mother was 27 years old when she became pregnant with her second daughter; this was the age at which her daughter produced continual menstrual bleeding. Such timing, more than anything else, clinches the argument that the daughter's symptoms were the result of her identification with her mother. (That she had three children, as had her mother, also suggests an identification in this respect.)

As far as this girl's psychosis was concerned, the crucial event in her mother's life—and consequently in her own too—was that, despite all efforts, her mother failed to control her female organs, her own body, by successfully aborting the fetus. The mother felt that her female organs worked against her will and did "their own thing"; in this way they ruined her life, enslaved her.

The daughter had internalized those of her mother's strongest emotions that were concerned with her and combined them with an identification with the mother both on a conscious and unconscious level. She developed a symptom in which her female organs enslaved her and ruined her life by operating against her conscious desires, and they did so at exactly the same age as had her mother's. Only in the daughter's case, she did not stop producing menstrual fluid; on the contrary, it flowed continually. In this way her female organs did what the mother had wished hers would do, since she had wished for some bleeding to indicate the loss of the fetus.

Thus the daughter who had incorporated her mother's

304

strongest emotions acted them out simultaneously on several levels. She felt herself disgusting, as her mother had felt her disgusting when pregnant with her; she nearly destroyed herself as her mother had wanted to see the fetus destroyed; her female organs did not act as she wished them to, as her mother's had not; and these organs simultaneously did what her mother had desired her own to do: they produced menstrual fluid. This woman was forced by her internalizations to act like a puppet whose strings were pulled, against her conscious will, by unconscious processes working deep within her; thus she felt as if she were in the power of an unknowable and terrifying "Thing." It is no wonder that it took seven long years for her to work through these complex and in part contradictory identifications and internalizations and in the process to regain all the energy she had invested in the "Thing," the symptom of this death-wish identification. When she had achieved freedom from this, she felt newborn, because she had finally become mistress of herself.

To round out this discussion, a few remarks about the beginning and the end of the patient's psychoanalytic treatment. One may ask: how come a few words uttered by a psychoanalyst stopped a somatic symptom which had resisted for years all medical treatment by specialists? It does happen. I could refer to many parallel experiences in which a determind disregard for the somatic aspects of a symptom and the assertion that it was of psychological origin by a person the patient accepted as a concerned authority almost at once stopped a life-threatening symptom. The explanation for the cessation of the symptom, however, must be sought in mental processes. Unconsciously the afflicted person has some intimations, however indistinct, of what is causing the symptom, of what it symbolizes, or expresses. Such unconscious feelings are strangely, and strongly, reinforced by the complete failure of prolonged medical treatments of the symptom by various recognized medical specialists, as was the case in the author's story. The patient's experiences of medical failures seem necessary to support his unconscious feeling that the disturbance is of a psychological nature, and to add force to a statement to this effect when it is uttered by the right person at the right time.

Additionally, the psychoanalyst's own deep conviction is necessary for his pscyhological treatment of the disturbance to be effective. Persons who are completely run by their unconscious, as was this woman and as are very disturbed children, respond much more than average people to what they feel are the strong inner convictions of persons of importance to them. The same mechanisms that made the woman in the story respond so powerfully to the strong inner conviction of her mother that she should not have been born made it possible for her to respond positively to the strong inner feeling of her analyst that her illness was of a psychological nature; thus she could respond to psychological treatment. If, on the other hand, a person feels that the therapist has any doubts about whether psychotherapy will cure the symptom or that he wavers in his views about it, then the same readiness to believe the signals coming from the therapist's unconscious will prevent trusting the efficacy of psychoanalytic treatment, and the symptom will continue unabated.

In my experience two more conditions have to be met for the near immediate cessation of such a symptom: one is that the afflicted person needs to, and does, test in some fashion the determination of the therapist not to let himself be threatened or seduced into trying to do something to directly stop the physical symptom, because this would be interpreted as his not really trusting that purely psychological measures will make it disappear; the second condition is that the person seeking help must become convinced that psychoanalytic treatment is strictly his own decision, one not forced on him. From her story, however, the woman whose treatment we followed here did not need exactly these two conditions to have her unconscious trust her therapist about her symptom. This is because she had already made her own decision to stop relying on physical treatment for her symptom before she started analytic therapy. She had done this by refusing to take any longer the medication that was prescribed for her, by arranging for her escape from the hospital in a most determined way, and by following, all on her own, the suggestion to seek help from an analyst.

Such is the importance of parents to their children, particularly the mother, that no psychological freedom is attained until the time one has become able to make one's peace with one's parents. As long as one fails to do so, the negative feelings existing in one's unconsious keep one partially in thrall to the parent's negative feelings towards one. Only when one can finally accept the positive aspects of one's parents and respond positively to these and make peace with them, having resolved one's inner ambivalences about them, is one really free.

But such is the power of a parent over a child, particularly that of a mother who harbored conscious and unconscious death wishes against a child, that the final peace with her can be made only at her death. So powerfully devastating is the impact of parental death wishes that the child of such parents cannot dispel their power entirely until they, and the parents, cease to live.

As this daughter's refusal to have her mother live with her during the mother's terminal illness made clear, the daughter, by means of her analysis, had gained independence from her mother, but only to a degree. Her refusal to let her mother live with her indicated that she feared her mother still had the power to run and ruin her life. That is, she still feared that her mother's unconscious would dominate her unconsicous, as had been the way for so many years before and during her analysis.

She gained final freedom from this inner stranglehold of her mother's hate at the moment when, at her mother's grave, the inner image of the good mother she had desired and loved all along broke through and gained ascendancy over the image of the destructive mother which had ruled her life for so long.

Once the inner freedom to be truly herself was added to the outer freedom of running her own life as she saw fit, which she had gained during her years of analysis, she no longer needed the help of an analyst. Thus at the end of the book, the protagonist does all on her own what a person ought to who has successfully completed her analysis: she stops being the analyst's patient. The analyst who, despite the intimacy of their relationship, has all along been somewhat of a stranger to her, now truly becomes a stranger. And she has become a stranger to her analyst, but not a stranger to psychoanalysis. Psychoanalysis—what Marie Cardinal learned during it and what she became because of it—will remain with her all her life, a fact that this remarkable book, written several years after the completion of her analysis, amply demonstrates.

*Bruno Bettelheim, May 1983*